Lethal Encounters

Captain John Smith, map of Virginia, engraved in 1612. (Smith, Captain John. *The Generall Historie of Virginia, New-England, and the Summer Islands* (1624). William L. Clements Library, University of Michigan. Reprinted with permission.)

Lethal Encounters

Englishmen and Indians in Colonial Virginia

Alfred A. Cave

University of Nebraska Press
Lincoln and London

Lethal Encounters: Englishmen and Indians in Colonial Virginia, by Alfred A. Cave, was originally published in hard cover by Praeger, an imprint of ABC-CLIO, LLC, Santa Barbara, CA. Copyright © 2011 by Alfred A. Cave. Paperback edition by arrangement with ABC-CLIO, LLC, Santa Barbara, CA. All rights reserved.

Manufactured in the United States of America

First Nebraska paperback printing: 2013

Library of Congress Cataloging-in-Publication Data
Cave, Alfred A.
Lethal encounters: Englishmen and Indians in colonial Virginia / Alfred A. Cave.
pages cm
Originally published: Santa Barbara, California: Praeger, c2011.
Includes bibliographical references and index.
ISBN 978-0-8032-4834-2 (pbk.: alk. paper)
1. Indians, Treatment of—Virginia—History—17th century. 2. Indians of North America—Colonization—Virginia—History—17th century. 3. Indians of North America—First contact with Europeans—Virginia. 4. Virginia—Race relations—History—17th century. 5. Racism—Virginia—History—17th century. 6. Genocide—Virginia—History—17th century. 7. British—Virginia—History—17th century. 8. Colonists—Virginia—History—17th century. 9. Virginia—History—Colonial period, ca. 1600-1775. I. Title.
E78.V7C28 2013
305.8009755—dc23   2013022977

To the memory of my mentors

Herschel Mannan

Horace Terrell

Arthur Thompson

Introduction

*I*n an article on "the genocides of indigenous peoples," Elazur Barkan writes that in the United States "the notion of genocide, while warranted as much or more than in . . . other countries, is still confined to radical writers. It is intriguing, indeed, that no mainstream American historians have written about the fate of Native Americans as genocide." The validity of Barkan's observation is immediately apparent to anyone who has read their works. The term "genocide" is rarely encountered in narratives of the American experience, even though the term has been in wide use elsewhere ever since the mid 20th century. That omission is striking, as American folk history has long regarded the story of colonization and Western expansion as a story of racial warfare and extermination. Most often, prior to the mid 20th century, the story was told as a morality play wherein vicious savages sought to halt, through indiscriminate violence, the onward march of civilization and Christianity. Killings of Indians were therefore often necessary for the safety of the civilized. That theme, present in the earliest writings of colonists, figured prominently in the apologias for the American Revolution. The Declaration of Independence spoke of the "the merciless Indian savages, whose known rules of warfare, is an undistinguished destruction of all ages, sexes, and conditions." Among the crimes charged against George III was his alleged use against his dissident colonists of those practitioners of genocide. However, it was not always the Indian in American memory who was the initial perpetrator of mass killing. A quip of uncertain origin that made the rounds of the lecture circuit from the 19th century onward held that when the settlers (most often represented as Pilgrims but sometimes as Scotch-Irish) arrived at these shores, they first fell on their knees, then fell on the Indians. Despite its obvious element of exaggeration, that quip contained historical memories history textbooks seldom, if ever, reflected.[1]

It is now generally agreed that the evidence of brutality in the treatment of native peoples by the colonizers of the New World is extensive and incontrovertible. But were those colonizers guilty of genocide? Historian James Axtell probably speaks for the majority of scholars when he rejects the use of that term in connection with European settlement in the Americas on the grounds that no European colonial regime "ever tried to exterminate all Indians as Indians, as a race." He adds, "you can count on one hand the authorized colonial attempts to annihilate even single tribes." Exterminatory violence, where it occurred, Axtell argues, was aimed at "temporary political or military enemies." In general, Indians "were much too valuable for trade or labor . . . only the rare, certifiable, homicidal maniac sought to commit genocide against the Indians."[2]

The history of the first century of the English colony in Virginia, marked as it was by recurrent episodes of indiscriminate interracial slaughter, would appear to contradict Axtell's assertion. However, historians generally have not used the term "genocide" to characterize that history. One writer has encapsulated their consensus as follows. He grants that "the successful establishment of the first British settlement on the North American mainland was accompanied by a massive destruction of tidewater Virginia's people, the Powhatans. It was destruction on a genocidal scale." However, he argues that it was not actually genocide, as "the English colonists who were invading the Powhatans' country, expropriating their land, reducing them to vassal status, engaging in wars with them, burying their dead, robbing their cornfields, enslaving the survivors, and legislating them into peonage" nonetheless "expressly rejected" the genocide "option" in that they did not seek their complete "physical destruction."[3]

We have here a major problem of definition. The conclusion that driving Indians from their land, waging war upon them, enslaving survivors, and reducing them to a state of peonage did not constitute genocide is rooted in a very narrow conception of genocide that limits use of the term to the systematic and unremitting physical extermination of a people. The original definition of the term, as it was coined by legal scholar Raphael Lemkin in 1944, was broader, as was the enumeration of genocidal acts contained in the 1948 United Nations (UN) Convention on Genocide. The latter held that "genocide means any of the following acts committed with intent to destroy, in whole or in part, a national, ethnical, racial or religious group as such:

a. Killing members of the group
b. Causing severe bodily harm
c. Deliberately inflicting on members of the group conditions of life calculated to bring about its physical destruction in whole or in part
d. Imposing measures intended to prevent births within the group
e. Forcibly transferring children of the group to another group"

That formulation has not won universal acceptance. There have been calls for a more restrictive definition and for one that is more inclusive. Some writers insist that only a state-sponsored effort to effect total physical extermination qualifies as genocide. A few argue that the only example in world history of a true genocide is the Nazi Holocaust. Others argue for the inclusion of cultural genocide in a revised definition that would cover a diverse range of activities destructive of indigenous cultural identities. Although that proposal has won only limited support, many writers on genocide find the exclusion of the slaughter of members of proscribed political and social groups from the UN Convention, exclusions not envisioned by Lemkin but demanded by both the Soviet Union and Great Britain, unacceptable. Two eminent students of genocide, sociologists Frank Chalk and Kurt Jonasshon, accordingly have proposed the following new definition: "Genocide is a form of one-sided mass killing in which a state or other authority intends to destroy a group, as that group and membership in it are defined by the perpetrator." Under that definition, mass killing driven by determination to eliminate a socioeconomic class (as in the Soviet Union and Cambodia, for example), a political faction (mass killing of Communists in Indonesia, to cite only one case), or a group defined by sexual preference (gays in Nazi Germany, for instance)—atrocities not covered by the UN Convention—would be classified as genocide.[4]

Although the Chalk/Jonasshon definition has much to recommend it, its limitation of genocide to official acts is problematic. As students of colonialism everywhere can attest, colonial laws and decrees protecting indigenous peoples were frequently not enforced by local authorities, who were all too often complicit in their violation. The line between officially sanctioned extermination and genocidal private killing is often far from distinct. I believe that genocide should be thought of, not in absolute terms, but as a continuum of discriminatory and violent actions prompted by the belief that the targeted group is unworthy of inclusion in the community and deserves no protection. It is noteworthy that neither Lemkin nor the UN Convention limited genocide to official acts, and both were sensitive to the long-range lethal consequences of measures short of immediate extermination.

A distinction is usually made between genocide and what is now termed "ethnic cleansing." Although ethnic cleansing does not, initially at least, envision the direct killing of its victims, it can be argued that it should be considered a stage in the continuum of genocidal acts, in that it targets all members of the group indiscriminately, results in increased mortality, and is rooted in the belief that certain populations are essentially undesirable because of their inherent group characteristics. It can be argued that by defining genocide as "deliberately inflicting upon members of a group conditions intended to bring about its physical destruction in whole or in part" the 1948 UN Convention on Genocide in effect implicitly included ethnic cleansing. (The term itself was not in use in 1948.) This point is particularly relevant to our examination of colonial Virginia, where, as we shall see, policy pronouncements in the decade after the Opechancanough uprising of 1622 called for killing when possible, but regarded expulsion as an alternative. The English authorities who ordered the destruction of Indian food supplies as a measure to expedite their expulsion were well aware that it would bring about "their physical destruction . . . in part." Although the UN declaration excluded "cultural genocide" (at the insistence of the United States), here, too, it must be recognized that the measures used by dominant powers to eliminate the language, religion, and other cultural attributes of indigenous peoples has usually led to artificially heightened group mortality. Moreover, the attitudes that drive a dominant group to seek to eliminate the culture of the victim group can easily shade over into more directly malign forms of genocide. The Virginia Company's advocacy of the killing of all Indian "priests" is illustrative of that. Here, again, we are dealing with a continuum, not an absolute.

Why does the question of definition matter? If we understand genocide in its most fundamental sense to mean the killing or forced removal of people for reason of their group identity, then it must be recognized that the colonization process was often genocidal. However, definitions can and have been used to obscure rather than clarify. The sharp distinction between the "genocidal consequences" of Virginia's Indian policies and "genocide" itself cited earlier does not help us understand, and indeed serves to obfuscate, the roots of colonialist violence. As A. Dirk Moses has noted, the distinction is essentially rooted in the liberal assumption that true genocide requires the execution of a state policy mandated by a totalitarian ideology. That assumption, Moses points out

> [directs] attention away from the social forces extant in all modernizing and colonizing societies that seek to sequester indigenous land and kill its owners if they are resisted. Implicitly, the liberal position deems the massive deaths on which European and North American societies are based as non-genocidal and therefore less worthy of scholarly attention. They were but the unintended consequences of colonization.

He concludes that "in the end, liberals offer no coherent account of why genocides take place in colonial situations," as they either deny that the mass killings were genocide "or ascribe extermination to contingencies like 'greed.'" An extreme example is found in the argument of Brazil's representative to the UN who, during the deliberations on the genocide convention, argued that despite the mass killing of Indians in the Amazon Basin, no genocide had ever occurred in Brazil, because the killers had not acted to destroy Indians "as an ethnic or cultural group." They killed, he emphasized, "for exclusively economic reasons . . . to take possession of the land of their victims," and thus were presumably innocent of the crime of genocide. Here we have a clever but pernicious conflating of motive and intent. Whatever their motive for killing, the invaders of the Amazon clearly intended to eliminate all Indians. The notion of non-genocidal racial extermination is an absurdity.[5]

Although the exact meaning of the term "genocide" has thus occasioned considerable controversy, most definitions, including the one contained in the 1948 UN Convention on Genocide, have emphasized the importance of intent, "the paramount wish," as Norbert Finzsch puts it, "that the other group should cease to exist." Objects of genocide are regarded as "less than equal, less than civilized, and less than human. These discursive entities coalesce into an image of a 'creature' that is utterly rejected and excluded from humanity." It is at this point that we encounter some very thorny difficulties in the application of the term "genocide" to the interracial violence that plagued early colonial history. The evidence simply does not support the view that the colonial planners intended from the outset to make room for European settlers by exterminating indigenous inhabitants. Their views of Indians were complex and often contradictory, but many hoped that the outcome of European occupation would be their uplift in this life and their salvation in the life to come. The idea that colonization required either the removal or the mass killing of indigenous peoples was not part of the original program of Christian imperialism, but developed later. However, we do find in the writings of the early architects of Britain's North American empire—and this point is often overlooked—numerous expressions of uncertainty, indeed profound anxiety, about the nature and potential of Indians, combined frequently with the conviction that their culture was not only backward and savage, but satanic. The founders hoped for their redemption and transformation, but were by no means entirely confident that it could be effected. In that uncertainty lies the germs of future justifications of expulsion and extermination.[6]

The current study seeks to reexamine the early history of the Virginia colony to understand the failure of early hopes for a harmonious relationship with the indigenous inhabitants of the region, and the descent into racial warfare and episodes of genocide. In this examination, I have been particularly mindful of the theory of colonial genocide developed by Australian scholar Tony Barta, who has argued that we must set aside our preoccupation with original intent. He concedes that European colonizers initially may well have harbored no conscious exterminatory intentions, but argues that by reason of their need to appropriate land and dispossess and dominate indigenous peoples, colonizers were placed in a relationship to indigenous peoples "that implicitly rather than explicitly, in ways that were inevitable rather than intentional," fundamentally constituted "a relationship of genocide." The origins of colonial genocide, therefore, are to be sought, not in statements of intent, but in the patterns of interaction arising out of struggles for control of resources. The argument of "unintended consequences" must not be permitted to obfuscate the actual nature of colonial interactions with indigenous peoples. Barta reminds us that "in real historical relationships . . . unintended consequences are legion, and it is from the consequences, as well as the often muddled consciousness, that we have to deduce the real nature of the relationship." Colonial societies, regardless of professed intent, essentially are "genocidal societies."[7]

Although Barta is correct in speaking of the colonizers "often muddled consciousness," we must not underestimate the role of ideas in prompting and sustaining genocide. Rabbi Abraham Joshua Herschel emphasized that point in his declaration that "Auschwitz was built not with stones, but words." Although ideological justifications of genocide were usually the product, not the cause, of conflicts with indigenous peoples, they were nonetheless instrumental in the sanctioning of continued violence. Rationales for genocide, moreover, were not simply ad hoc inventions. To understand their emergence, we must look closely at the preconceptions the English brought to the New World. The images of Indians as threats to the security and integrity of the civilized, as savages who must be removed or exterminated, that so often became dominant in later stages of colonization, found precedent and warrant in old stories about depraved peoples given to cannibalism, sodomy, witchcraft, and devil worship. In the beginning, those stories were counterbalanced by accounts of "noble savages" living in a state of innocence, and also by a sense of Christian mission to uplift, civilize, and save. In Virginia, as elsewhere, savage stereotypes were not invoked to provide an ideological basis for acts of exterminatory violence until certain inherent conflicts, both economic and cultural, exposed the true nature of the colonialist relationship. However, the "unintended consequences" had deep roots.[8]

In the beginning, the founders of Virginia, and of other colonies, argued that their presence would benefit the region's indigenous peoples. They were soon disillusioned, abandoned their lofty rhetoric, and not infrequently declared Indians savages by nature, incapable of humane and civilized behavior. The encounter of races and cultures on the Chesapeake, as elsewhere, was not uplifting; it is more accurately characterized as lethal. Recurrent racial violence marked the patterns of Indian–white interaction in Virginia throughout the 17th century. Official policy, as it developed throughout the years, came to demand, at a minimum, the subordination, dispossession, relocation, and segregation of the indigenous population, and on several occasions sanctioned unrestricted killing. Was colonial Virginia a genocidal society? I believe that it was. However, to affix the label "genocide," or to withhold it, sheds little light on the real human tragedy. We need, as A. Dirk Moses defines our task, to examine the ways in which "occupation policies that are not initially murderous can radicalize or escalate in an exterminatory direction when they are resisted." It is also important to bear in mind, as Frank Chalk puts it, that although "systemic variables facilitate genocide . . . it is people who kill." Although colonial regimes invariably proved destructive of indigenous cultures, outright wars of physical extermination were by no means inevitable. We are dealing with a dynamic process, with many variables. Each colony's history presents its own unique challenges. No theory, no formula, no definition can answer in advance the questions we must ask of the sources about racial violence in Europe's American colonies. Actual history, in all its messy particulars and often maddening ambiguity, seldom conforms exactly to theoretical models. Virginia founders, as historian Edmund Morgan reminds us, hoped to establish in North America a "biracial society" in which indigenous peoples would be transformed into loyal, God-fearing English subjects. Although we have a number of excellent short-term studies of the failures of Virginia's Indian policies—studies generally focused on a specific decade or so—there is no overall detailed, in-depth account of Indian–white relations in the century that saw a decline in Indian population that exceeded 90 percent. This books seeks to fill that gap and explain the factors—economic, ecological, ideological, and personal—that shaped that outcome decade by decade. The story is not a simple one. Those who hope to find in these pages a simple morality tale about genocide victims and their victimizers will be disappointed. However, I am persuaded that those who accept Moses's challenge to seek to understand how genocide can emerge from colonialist policies that initially had no apparent genocidal intent will find this account instructive.[9]

CHAPTER 1

❦

Prelude: Explorations, Encounters, and Abandoned Colonies

A report of an incident that was said to have occurred on the high seas off the coast of the Azores on September 9, 1583, offers an interesting insight into the mind-set of those Englishmen who, throughout the late 16th century, dreamed of an empire in North America. The chronicler of Humphrey Gilbert's last voyage related that as his small frigate the *Squirrel,* beset by "outrageous Seas," fought a losing battle against the storm, Gilbert was seen sitting on the stern "with a booke in his hande" and heard to cry out: "We are as neere to heaven by sea as by land." Those mythic last words, as David Beers Quinn has pointed out, echoed a phrase in Sir Thomas More's *Utopia.* Gilbert's choice of reading was telling. Recipient through the grace of Queen Elizabeth I of a vast land grant in North America, Gilbert found in More's vision reinforcement of his own imperial dreams. More's fictional ideal commonwealth, contrary to some later misconceptions, was not Native American in origin, nor did his work celebrate the primitive or "natural" peoples of the New World. As More described its origins, Utopia was the work of invaders and colonizers who spoke a language closely related to ancient Greek. He explained that on their arrival in a region called "Abraxia," the newcomers had transformed "a pack of ignorant savages into what is now, perhaps, the most civilized nation in the world."[1]

In their dealings with the Abraxians, the Utopians first offered the option of accepting Utopian rule and embracing the ways of civilized men, which in the improved Utopian version was grounded in an egalitarian communal order that offered security and modest comfort to all citizens, proscribed greed and ambition, valued religious toleration, and exalted learning. Most Abraxians gladly accepted that offer, and surrendered land and sovereignty to the Utopian state. More explained that the process was usually peaceful, as savages and Utopians "gradually and easily merge together and absorb the same way of life, and the same customs, to the advantages of both peoples." However, there was some resistance. Whenever the expansion of Utopian communities required lands occupied by those who rejected the Utopian order, Utopian armies simply took possession by force. More explained Utopia's policy toward indigenous peoples as follows:

> The inhabitants who refuse to live according to their laws, they drive from the territory. . . . If they resist, they wage war against them. They consider it a most just cause of war when a people which does not use the soil but keeps it idle and waste nonetheless forbids the use and possession of it to others who by rule of nature ought to be maintained by it.

One stubbornly independent people, the Zapolitans, described as "fearsome, rough and wild," volunteered as mercenaries in the Utopian armies but refused to accept Utopian rule or conform to Utopian customs. In the Utopian order, there was no place, ultimately, for such recalcitrants. Accordingly, following a policy that one 20th-century scholar declared to be "conscious genocide," Utopian military commanders always placed Zapolitans in the vanguard of their attack forces. "The Utopians," More wrote, "do not care how many Zapolitans they lose, thinking they would be the greatest benefactors to the human race if they could relieve the world of all the dregs of this abominable and impious people." Although internally Utopian society was both tolerant and egalitarian, the Utopians, as More portrayed them, had little regard for those who did not embrace their enlightened ways. To protect Utopia from the savages on the outside, the founders dug a deep channel, transforming the Abraxian peninsula into a fortified island.[2]

Although written long before the establishment of any of England's overseas colonies, *Utopia* contained assumptions and assertions that would come to characterize English imperialist ideology in centuries to come: the right to take land from peoples who presumably failed to use it productively, the mission to civilize such backward folk, the understanding that some would prove to be beyond redemption, the right to wage war against such unregenerate savages, and, if need be, exterminate them should they impede the work of the colonizers, whose mission was the creation of a new society through the transformation or displacement of unenlightened indigenous peoples.

Sir Humphrey Gilbert did not live to enforce that program in North America, but he was a player in an earlier imperial enterprise. As one of the key commanders in the English wars against the Irish, Gilbert had enthusiastically supported Sir Henry Sidney's proposal to anglicize the presumable savage island called Ireland by the expansion of enclaves of English settlement. Sidney, Gilbert, and their supporters envisioned the gradual extension of the blessings of the English common law to the "wylde Irish" beyond the pale, and the ultimate extirpation in Ireland of Gaelic culture, which they regarded as degenerate and barbaric. In justification of their imperial designs, they framed a portrait of the native Irish as a godless and improvident people "little better than Cannibals who do hunt one another." One English report from Ireland in 1572 declared "they blaspheme, they murder, commit whoredom, hold no wedlocke, ravish, steal, murder and commit all abomination without scruple of conscience." Among English claims of Irish depravity were reports of cannibalism. One story related that their old women sometimes ate little children. However, the English claim of the right to occupy Ireland rested most fundamentally on the assertion, unfounded in fact, that the "wylde Irish" made no productive use of the soil, being presumably lawless nomads, and thus violated God's command to cultivate the earth. In the next century, this rationale for the dispossession of indigenous peoples would be invoked many times in defense of England's colonial ventures in the New World.[3]

In his "Discourse on Ireland," a memorandum written in 1572, Gilbert declared that the Irish themselves should rightly appreciate English protection from their presumably fierce and lawless countrymen. However, he lacked More's faith in the civilizing power of good example, and in correspondence with the Queen predicted that Irish resistance would be widespread and would open up great opportunities for extensive reallocations of Irish land to English settlers. Appointed colonel in command of the army occupying Munster Province in September 1569, Gilbert acted on the premise "that no conquered nacion will ever yelde willinglie their obedience for love rather than for feare." His commission authorized him, "for the furtherance of her majesty's service and better understanding of the truth" to "use any kind of punishment" against any whom he "suspected" of being a "malefactor." Disregarding Queen Elizabeth's directives that her Irish subjects be treated leniently, Gilbert in Munster slaughtered indiscriminately, inflicting "fire and sword" on men, women, and children in areas he deemed rebellious. A village did not need to be in open rebellion to suffer such treatment. Gilbert justified the killing of noncombatant Irish on suspicion that they might provide food or other aid to the rebels. Terrorized Irish lords who came to surrender and submit to English rule could approach Gilbert's tent only by walking down a pathway lined on both sides with the decapitated heads of their friends and countrymen. A pamphlet published in celebration of his Munster pacification wrote that it brought "greate terrour to the people when they sawe the heddes of their dedde fathers, brothers, children, kinsfolke and friends Lye on the grounde before their faces, as thei came to speake with the said colonel." The colonel held the Irish in contempt. Even the "greatest noble manne amonst them," Gilbert declared, was no better than a dog.[4]

Although the Queen had never envisioned a policy of "wholesale murder and ethnic displacement," as resistance to English occupation persisted and escalated, "genocidal massacres targeted even larger numbers of Irish." As early as the 1640s, some commanders in Ireland had justified the killing of children "with the metaphor, 'Kill the nits and you will have no lice.'" Throughout the occupation, that murderous premise found expression in action. One chronicler describing military action in Munster in 1580 wrote: "It was not wonderful that they should kill men fit for action, but they killed blind and feeble men, women, boys and girls, sick persons, idiots and old people." As resistance mounted, policy spokesmen were soon penning, not only descriptions, but justifications of the slaughter of the island's indigenous people. The earlier counsels of moderation, for use of "fire and sword" only when absolutely necessary, were replaced by what historian Ben Kiernan has termed "racialist thinking." Edmund Spencer's *A View of the Present State of Ireland* (1596 or 1597) is perhaps the leading example of this transformation. Spencer argued that given the lawlessness and depraved behavior of its people, Ireland could not be governed by the "lawes and ordinances" of England but must be subjected to the "bitterness" of martial law. The Irish must be held down "by the sword."[5]

Were the inhabitants of Humphrey Gilbert's prospective New World domain essentially like the wild Irish, incapable of control through the normal "lawes and ordinances?" The early advocates of an English empire were uncertain, lacking a clear or consistent image of North America's indigenous peoples. Gilbert and other would-be imperialists read extensively in the Spanish accounts of the New World, a number of which had been made available in English at mid century in several English translations. They found in those books a confusing variety of images. Peter Martyr's very popular *Decades of the New World* evoked the myth of a golden age, portraying some of the natives of the West Indies as a gentle folk humane in their reception of strangers, living in "a goulden world, without toyle, lyuing in open gardens, not intrenched with dykes, with hedges, or defended with waules. They deale trewley one with another, without lawes, without bookes, and without judges." They held all things in common. "Myne and Thyne (the seedes of all mysheefe) have no place with them." But not all Indians, Martyr warned, were innocents. Some were cannibals and satanists. The Caribs, for example, sired children by captive women, and ate the boys. Male prisoners they gelded, fattened up, and then devoured. An armchair traveler who never crossed the Atlantic, Martyr described a group of Indian captives on display in Spain as follows: "There is no man able to behold them but he shall feel his bowels grate with a certain horror, nature hath endowed them with so terrible a menacing and cruel aspect." From *Martyr's writings,* some English readers concluded that Christians must undertake to protect the New World's children of nature from their cruel neighbors. His translator Richard Eden also rendered in English portions of Gonzalo Fernández de Oviedo's *Natural History of the Indies.* Oviedo described Indians as devil worshippers and added the suggestion that they were biologically abnormal. Many a Christian, he warned, had broken swords on their heads, with little damage to the Indians. He emphasized also that "the Indians eat human flesh and are sodomites." The publication in 1578 of an English translation of Fránscico López de Gómara's history of the Spanish conquest of Mexico gave further support to the belief that Indians were alien and sinister, as Gómara offered his readers vivid descriptions of Aztec rites of human sacrifice in blood-encrusted temples permeated by a devilish stench. After Aztec priests tore bleeding hearts from the chests of living victims pinioned on sacrificial altars, the bodies, as Gómara related, were skinned and then eaten in cannibal banquets. Three themes dominated the negative characterizations of Indian peoples available to 16th-century English readers: cannibalism, satanism, and sodomy.[6]

English translators also made available some of the writings of Father Bartholomew de las Casas, writings that condemned the savagery of Spanish colonizers and portrayed Indians as innocent victims of their atrocities. They were, de las Casas wrote, a people "very simple, without sutteltie, or craft, without malice, very obedient, and very faithful . . . very humble, very patient, very desirous of peace making and very peaceful, without brawls and struglings, without quarrelles, without strife, without rancour or hatred, by no means desirous of revengement." They had no "desire to have much worldly goodes, & therefore neither are they proud, ambitious or covetous." His accounts of Spanish cruelty to those children of nature were frequently cited by English propagandists. Nonetheless, despite their invocation from time to time of the "Black Legend," 16th-century English portrayals of Native Americans generally do not celebrate "noble savages." Most often, after condemning Spaniards and Papists, they simply restated uncritically the most negative of the Spanish portrayals of the peoples of the Americas. The most popular English treatise on geography, written by George Abbot, Bishop of London, and published in many editions during the late 16th and early 17th centuries, included these statements about Indians: "a people naked and uncivil . . . given to sodomy, incest, and all kinds of adultery," to "adoration of devils," "blind witchcraft," and "intercourse with foul spirits." Sir Walter Raleigh echoed that view of Native Americans when he declared, late in his life, that the peoples of the Americas, North and South, had "been brought by the devil under his fearful servitude." To be sure, not all commentators were quite that harsh. A few who were more sympathetic to Indians lauded their cleverness and ingenuity, and argued that they were like the ancient Britons who had been lifted from barbarism by Roman invaders and Christian missionaries. However, these early proponents of English colonialism also emphasized the need to transform Indians if New World ventures were to succeed.[7]

Reports from early English exploratory probes in North America often portrayed the land as providentially intended for English occupation. Martin Frobisher's three voyages to Newfoundland in 1577 to 1578 were driven by the expectation of gaining access to the wealth of the Orient by locating a Northwest Passage from the Atlantic to the Pacific, a hope that some Englishmen had harbored ever since Sebastian Cabot's 1508 visit to Labrador. A promotional pamphlet written by Sir Humphrey Gilbert to assist in raising funds for Frobisher's venture also suggested that the lands surrounding the passage could be settled with "such needie people of our Countrie, which now trouble the common welt and through want here at home are inforced to commit outrageous offenses, whereby they are dayly consumed with the Gallows." Advocacy of American colonization as a solution to overpopulation on the home island would become a central theme in the later writings of the Hakluyts and other champions of trans-Atlantic ventures. It would permeate 17th-century discussions of the merits of overseas expansion, as well. To cite one example, in 1630, a promoter of New England colonization declared "the Indians are not able to make use of one fourth part of the land . . . great pity it is to see so much good ground for corn and for grass as any under heaven, to be together unoccupied, when so many honest men and their families in old England, do make very hard shrift."[8]

The published accounts of Frobisher's voyages provided the first detailed English descriptions of the Inuit people. They were not encouraging. Dionese Settle's narrative captured the tenor of those reports when he declared the natives "altogether voyde of humanitie." George Best, author of the most comprehensive report, expressed the expectation that from his account readers would learn "howe to proceed and deale with the straunge people, be they neuer so barbarous, cruell, and fierce, eyther by lenite or otherwise." However, he offered little reason for believing that leniency was a viable option. The main message conveyed in all of the Frobisher voyage narratives was that the natives were of "subtile and cruell disposition," and should not be trusted. But perhaps they would be improved by contact with civilized peoples. Best voiced the hope that England's efforts in the New World would lead to "Christs name spred; the Gospell preached, Infidells to be converted to Christianitie, in places where before the name of God hath not once been hearde of."[9]

The actual encounter events described by Frobisher's chroniclers do not offer much real support for their persistent characterizations of the natives as vicious, animal-like savages. Frobisher's men did not understand the natives' language. They could only describe appearances and behavior. Their conclusions about their malign character were generally based on nothing more than interpretations of gestures. It is telling that George Best, the most thorough and detailed of the narrators, lauds Frobisher for perceiving, through study of the facial expressions and the utterances of the natives who came onboard his bark to trade, that they were of a fierce and cruel disposition, not to be trusted despite "any shew of friendship they might make." The Inuit continued to make a "shew of friendship" throughout Frobisher's three visits. They flocked to his bark, scrambled through the riggings, did gymnastics, communicated with the crew through sign language, tried to learn some bits of English, and bartered for trade goods. Nonetheless, Frobisher's chroniclers repeatedly warned that such gestures of good faith and friendship were not to be taken at face value.[10]

English wariness was prompted in part by preconceptions, and in part by the very real difficulty of understanding Inuit intentions. Although eager to trade, they were unpredictable, sometimes fleeing without apparent provocation, sometimes apparently trying to cut off the visitors and seize captives. During the first voyage, there was a particularly disturbing episode at a place later named Hall's Island. Frobisher, through use of sign language, engaged an islander to act as a guide to pilot his bark into an inlet (later named Frobisher Strait) that he believed, erroneously, to be the Northwest Passage. Not long after entering the channel, Frobisher sent five members of his crew in the ship's boat to return the guide to the island. Disobeying Frobisher's order not to go too close to the natives, probably because they wanted to trade, both the men and their boat disappeared. Frobisher's efforts to get them back were thwarted when the natives retreated into the interior, taking the sailors with them. When several kayaks approached his bark, Frobisher was able to take a hostage, a man of "sullen and churlish" countenance, but his efforts to exchange him for his lost men came to nothing. With only 13 men left in his crew, Frobisher was forced to return to England without completing his explorations. His captive took sick and died soon after landing in England.[11]

During the second voyage, landing again on Hall's Island, Frobisher and one of his crew members tried to seize as captives several islanders who had come "skipping, laughing and dancing" to his bark to trade. Frobisher hoped that by taking captives he could force the return of his five lost men, but the Inuit fought back, shooting an arrow into Frobisher's buttock and badly bruising his shipmate. Attempting to land with a larger party, Frobisher was then met by a hail of arrows. He drove off the assailants with gunshots and seized two Inuit women, one of whom they suspected of being "eyther a Deville or a Witche." Examination, however, disclosed that she was not cloven footed. After learning from some Inuit who visited his camp that his lost men were living in a village in the interior, Frobisher sent them a letter, but never received a reply. One chronicler wrote of the fate of the five missing sailors that "considering also their ravennesse and bloudy disposition, in eating anye kinde of rawe flesh or carrion, howsoever stinking, it is to be thought they had slaine and devoured oure men."[12]

The reports of the Newfoundland voyages offer an object lesson on the ease with which preconceptions can distort perceptions. It is now believed that the lost members of the expedition were neither killed nor eaten by the natives. A credible Inuit oral tradition, recorded in 1862, relates that after building a ship from scrap lumber and making their way to the Atlantic, the stranded explorers were lost at sea. The circumstances of their alleged abduction now appear far less certain than they did to Frobisher and his men. The sailors had not fallen into the hands of cannibals. It is not, in fact, clear that they were ever under any restraint. Why did they not return to Frobisher's bark or respond to his letter? Why didn't the natives respond to offers to exchange the captives Frobisher took for his lost men? Were the English sailors really captives? Were they perhaps deserters? Did they receive Frobisher's letter? Did they not reply because they were fearful of his reaction to their earlier defiance of his order not to go to the natives to trade? We will never know. As to the presumed ferocity of the Inuit, the narratives of Frobisher's voyages, although filled with denunciations of the natives' character, offer contradictory accounts of their behavior and no actual evidence of their presumed cannibalism.[13]

After loading aboard ship a large quantity of rock, which they believed to contain precious metals, Frobisher and his men sailed back to England. They took with them two captives, a man and a woman. The English were surprised at the extreme modesty of the captives, who did not conform at all to the usual expectations of savage sexual license. Although forced to share a bunk with the woman, the man would not change his clothes "except he had first caysed the woman to depart out of his Cabin, and they both were most shamefast, least anye of

their privie parts should bee discovered, eyther of themselves, or any other body."
George Best found some other evidence of the Intuits' humanity. They were not
only "sharpe witted" and musically adept, but also "excedding friendly and kinde
harted, one to the other, and mourne greatly the losse or harme of their fellows,
and express their griefe of minde, when they part from an other, with a mourne-
full song, or Dirges." Those observations notwithstanding, the chroniclers of Frobisher's voyages—Best included—seldom deviated from their view that the people
they encountered were essentially vicious, being in their dealings with outsiders
totally "ignorant of what mercy meaneth." The commentators repeatedly stressed
their presumed fierceness and cruelty, and added descriptions of their animal-like
behavior that underscored their alien and sinister character. English readers were
told that sounds the natives uttered on first meeting civilized people in some
cases sounded like the bellowing of bulls and in others resembled the howling of
wolves. Much was made of the refusal of a native woman to accept medical aid for
an injured child. Instead, the mother "by continual licking with hir owne tongue,
not much unlike oure dogges, healed uppe the childes arme." The natives lived
like animals, "in Caves of the Earthe, and hunte for their dinners or praye, even as
the Beare, or other wilde beastes do. They eate rawe fleshe and fishe, and refuse no
meate, howsoever it be stinking. They are desperate in the flighte, sullen of nature,
and ravenous in their manner of feeding." Most crucial were the indications that
the devil ruled the people of the New World. Best reported that the natives "are
greate inchaunters, and use many charmes of Witchcraft . . . they made us by signs
to understand, lying groveling with their faces upon the grounde, and making a
noise downwarde, that they worship the Devill under them."[14]

Frobisher did attempt to plant a colony in Newfoundland, but the venture never
proceeded far enough to necessitate development of a policy for dealing with the
indigenous inhabitants. London assayers had reported, erroneously, that ore samples brought back after the first voyage contained gold. Expecting no cooperation
from the local inhabitants in the mining of that precious metal, Frobisher in his
third expedition transported an English workforce in some 15 ships. They returned
with 11 tons of ore and one native captive. The ore turned out to be worthless.
Although he had earlier claimed the land, which he called "West England," in the
name of the Queen, Frobisher abandoned his plans for a New World colony.

The North American colonial venture planned by Sir Humphrey Gilbert was
far more ambitious than Frobisher's proposed mining outpost. Acting under the
authority of his charter, Gilbert offered vast tracts of North American land to
investors in his venture. The promoters needed to decide how the settlements
they hoped to find would deal with the local inhabitants. Clearly, America could
not immediately be subdued by force. Perhaps alliances could be made with some
of the indigenous peoples. The idea that some Indians needed and would welcome protection from more vicious Indian cannibals, first found in the Spanish
texts, was reinforced by the tales told by David Ingram, a stranded sailor who
claimed to have walked from Florida to Newfoundland in 1568 and 1569. Ingram
eked out a living after his return to England as a tavern entertainer regaling his

audiences with fanciful tales of the strange monsters, devil gods, and cities of gold, silver, and rubies he claimed to have seen on his trek across the American continent. Interviewed by several of the major colonial promoters, the ex-sailor informed them that the natives of Norumbega (located in what is now Maine) had great riches and would be eager to trade, but were much afflicted by raids from cannibals living in the interior. Ingram's report confirmed the hopes of planners who called for a strategy of selective alliances. However, his stories, for the most part, were not true.[15]

The most comprehensive statement of colonial Indian policy to emerge from the planning for Gilbert's venture was prepared by Sir George Peckham, a prominent Catholic nobleman. Peckham advised that when planting colonies in the New World, the English should always seek to win the consent of the natives through peaceful persuasion. Alien peoples, "by constitution of nature," he wrote, "are rendered more tractable and easilier wunne . . . by courtesie and myldnes then by crueltie and roughness." Because the language barrier initially would make communication difficult, the English should convey their intent through "freendly signes and courteous tokens." To help them understand that welcoming the English would "bring them benefite, commoditie, peace, tranquility and safety," the natives should be given, immediately, gifts such as:

> looking glasses, Bells, Beades, Bracelets, Charmes, or Collers of Beagle, Christall, Amber, Jett. . . . For such be the things, though to us of small value, yet accounted by them of high price and estimate: and soonest will induce theyre Barbarous natures to a likeing and a mutuall society with us.[16]

The next stage in the colonization process, as Peckham envisioned it, was the establishment of military alliances with friendly Indians. Those who had welcomed the English should be given to understand that "the Christians from thence forthwith will always be ready with force of Armes to assist and defende them in theyr just quarrels." Such aid, Peckham predicted, would be welcomed with great eagerness. Citing the testimony of David Ingram, he declared that in America,

> the Savages generally, for the most part, are at continuall warres with their next adjoyning neighbors, and especially the Caniballs, being a cruell kinde of people, whose food is mans flesh, and have teeth like dogges, and doe pursue them with ravenous myndes to eate their flesh and devoure them.

By aiding their new friends against cannibals, English colonizers would "mightily stirre and inflame theyr rude myndes gladly to embrace the loving compayne of the Christians, proffering unto them bothe commodities succor and kindness." The natives could also be expected to give to the English all the land they needed for their settlements, "considering the great abundance they have of Lande, and howe small account they make thereof."[17]

What if Indians resisted, either by offering violent opposition to the establishment of trading posts and settlements, or by simply withholding from the English the trade goods and land cessions "for which both painfully and lawfully they have adventured themselves thither?" The Law of Nations, in Peckham's interpretation, declared that no people had the right to remain in isolation. All were obligated to open their domains to traders. He offered no particular arguments in support of that assertion, simply declaring it "a thing so commonly and generally practiced, bothe in our dayes and in tymes past, beyonde the memory of man, both by Christians and Infidels, that in needethe no further proofe." Should the resistance to the English presence in America be violent, "it is allowable by all Lawes, in such distress, to resist violence with violence." It would, however, be prudent for the English "to increase their strength by building of fortes, for avoyding the extremities of injurious dealings." If hostilities continued, the colonizers could launch raids from those strongholds to "pursue theyr enemies and subdue them, take possession of theyr Townes, Cities, or Villages." Next, to protect "such Savages as have been converted" to the true faith from reversion to idolatry and cannibalism, the colonizers should displace native rulers with English governors. Peckham offered extensive citations from the Old and New Testaments and from the Church Fathers in support of the premise that the establishment of protective Christian rule over the unregenerate and the newly converted did not "transgresse the bondes of equitie or civility."[18]

Gilbert also received advice on empire building from the elder Richard Hakluyt, lawyer of the Middle Temple and ardent advocate of overseas ventures. The English, on landing in America, Hakluyt warned, must immediately seek to forge friendships and alliances with the more tractable Indians. They must use those first contacts to gather intelligence, to learn from their new friends "all their wantes, all their stengthes, all their weaknesse, and in whom they are in warre, and with whom confederate in peace and amitie." Should the first Indians they encountered prove hostile, perhaps even cannibalistic, the English, Hakluyt advised, should establish a fortified base at a river estuary and send expeditions into the interior to make alliance with other natives eager to receive aid against their more savage enemies.[19]

Although Sir Humphrey Gilbert visited Newfoundland in 1583, and at St. John's Harbor formally claimed the region for England, his colony was never planted. Some English Catholics interested in establishing an overseas haven invested in Gilbert's venture, but he never received adequate funding. Gilbert was lost at sea on the return voyage. The following year, the Queen granted a new charter to his half brother, Sir Walter Raleigh. To Raleigh and his heirs, as to Gilbert previously, the Sovereign granted the right to discover, occupy, rule, and exploit "remote heathen and barbarous landes Countries and territories not actually possessed of any Christian prince" and not yet occupied "by Christian people." That included the right to seize "all Cittyes Castle townes villages and places in the same" and to expel English or Europeans who intruded without permission. The charter required that Raleigh give the Queen one-fifth of the gold and silver found in his domain. He was also directed to respect the laws of England, the prerogatives of the Church of England, and the rights of all her majesty's English and Irish subjects who might emigrate to Raleigh's colony. However, the charter said nothing at all about the rights of the indigenous inhabitants.[20]

It was left to Raleigh's advisers to address the question of Indian policy. The elder Hakluyt once again offered advice. Writing after the first exploratory voyage to Roanoke had brought to England two young natives of the region, Hakluyt in one of his memoranda was optimistic about the prospects for coexistence, because "the people be well proportioned in their limbs, well favored, gentle, of a mild and tractable disposition, apt to submit themselves to good government and ready to embrace the Christian faith." No cannibalistic and deformed savages here. But in a second memo, intended perhaps only for Raleigh's eyes, Hakluyt warned that the English must nonetheless be prepared for the possibility that the natives might resist efforts to establish "just and lawful traffic" with them. In that event, the colonists must use force. "We will proceed with extremity, conquer, fortify and plant in soils most sweet, most pleasant, most strong, and most fertile, and in the end bring them all in subjugation and civility."[21]

Richard Hakluyt the younger offered a more visionary plan for colonization. He not only spelled out the great economic advantages that he believed England would gain through trade and through the settlement of surplus population in America, but also saw in colonization a way of transforming the country into the predominant world power. Persuaded that the English could make common cause with Indians and fugitive slaves throughout the Americas and thereby end Spanish colonial rule through armed liberation supported by Indian and black warriors, he urged that the indigenous inhabitants everywhere be treated with kindness and generosity, and thereby won over to the cause of an English empire grounded in Protestant Christianity. England thus would come to rule in the Americas. Hakluyt and other proponents of English expansion into the Americas drew heavily on reports, some exaggerated, of Spanish torture and slaughter of the Indians of Latin America. British entry into the continent, they predicted, would be welcomed by natives about to perish under the Spanish yoke. Land controlled by the Papist minions of the antichrist would soon be won for the true faith![22]

Quite apart from that grandiose ideal objective, the planners of the Roanoke venture were well aware of the need for Indian allies. A set of rules for the colonists forbade striking Indians, molesting their women, entering Indian houses without invitation, or forcing them to "labor unwillyngly." Rape was to be punished by death. Other offenses against Indians, including coercion of Indian labor, were to be punished with beating or imprisonment. Those who struck Indians were to suffer 20 blows with a cudgel in the presence of their victims.[23]

Raleigh's first probe, consisting of two ships commanded by Philip Amadas and Arthur Barlowe, sailed from Portsmouth, England, on April 27, 1554, and landed in the Outer Banks of what is now North Carolina, in mid July. The Company, Raleigh was assured, immediately took possession "in the right of the Queenes most excellent Maiestie, as rightfull Queene and Princesse of the same." The report of their survey of the region and their dealings with its inhabitants, prepared by Barlowe and published five years later in Richard Hakluyt's *Principal Navigations* (a massive collection of travel reports), drew an idyllic picture of the region and its people very unlike the accounts of Frobisher's three voyages. The land, Barlowe claimed, was unbelievably bountiful, its "soile . . . the most plentifull, sweete, fruitfull, and wholesome of all the world," covered with "sweete smelling timber trees" far superior to any in England, teeming with fish and game, "the best of the worlde," and yielding three fine crops a year to cultivators. The Indians were no less remarkable, "very handsome and goodly people, and in their behavior as mannerly, and civill, as any of Europe." They revered their leaders, as "no people in the worlde carry more respect to their King, Nobilitie, and Governours, then these do." In their relations with one another,

> we found the people most gentle, loving, and faithful, void of all guile, and trea-son, as such as lived after the manner of the golden age. The earthe bringeth forth all things in aboundance, as in the first creation, without toilie or labour . . . we were entertained with all love, and kindness, and with as much bountie, after their manner, as they could possibly devise.

Describing their first greeting by Granganimeo, the brother of the local "king" (a village chief named Wingina) who was ill, Barlowe related that after summoning the English into his presence, the Indian notable signaled that they should sit on the ground beside him. After they were all seated, Granganimeo "makes all signes of joy, and welcome, striking on his head, and his breast, and afterwards on ours, to shew that we were all one, smiling, and making shewe of the best hee could, of all loue, and familiaritie." During the gift exchange that followed, the other members of the Indian party remained silent, out of respect for the "king's" brother. Several days later, Granganimeo visited the English ship, where he "dranke wine, and ate of our meate, and of our bread, and liked exceedingly thereof." Shortly thereafter, he returned with his wife, an attractive but "very bashfull" woman, and several of his children. In exchange for various trade goods, Granganimeo provided the newcomers with ample quantities of venison, rabbits, and fish. "[T]he best," Barlowe declared, "of the worlde." Barlow had only praise for the Indians' kindness to his men. He concluded an account of a brief moment when the English feared attack from three armed Indians with the declaration that, in reality, "there was no cause of doubt: for a more kinde and loving people, there cannot be found in the world, as farre as we have hitherto had triall." Barlowe's modern editor correctly characterized that passage as "the most precise example in Renaissance English of the myth of the gentle savage."[24]

There were, however, some aspects of Barlowe's brief report that raised questions about his gentle savages. For one thing, they appeared to be worshippers of an "Idoll, which is nothing else, but a mere illusion of the Devill." They engaged in wars "very cruell and bloodie" against their neighbors and were quite capable of treachery. Barlow related an incident during which one local chief invited the members of another band to a feast, then seized all the women and children, and slaughtered the men while they were praying to their "Idoll." The hospitable reception accorded the English, Barlow hinted, was related to the Indians' perception of their prowess, which they believed emanated from some supernatural source. They trembled with fear when the English discharged a firearm, were intrigued by their armor, and tried very hard to persuade the visitors to part with "a sworde." They were able to obtain from the visitors hatchets, axes, and knives, for which Barlowe reported they "offered us a very good exchange" in various animal pelts. When the local chief's brother acquired through trade "a bright tinne dishe" he "made a hole in the brimme thereof, & hung it about his necke, making signes, that it would defende him against his enemies arrows." Clearly, he believed the dish had magical properties. Barlow recorded also the Indians' fascination "at the whiteness of our skinnes," which apparently inspired in them the sense that they were in the presence of the miraculous. The Barlowe account was clearly intended as a promotional document, with its exaggeration of the bounty of the region and its idealized portrait of gentle people living "after the manner of a golden age." However, read carefully, one finds hints of the sinister, and of a lingering anxiety. Barlowe's description of Indian war as "deadlie and terrible" strikes a discordant note in his idyllic portrait of gentle savages. His portrayal of those savages as benevolent is refuted by his own acknowledgment of their violent behavior toward neighboring bands. The Algonquian–speaking peoples of the Outer Banks, we now know, were not unified, but lived in small village-based units seldom exceeding a few hundred residents. Conflicts between villages were often bitter. To village war chiefs, the prospect of supernatural aid in their battles emanating from the miraculous instruments brought into their land by these aliens was a powerful incentive to establish close ties.[25]

Two Indians from the Outer Banks, Manteo and Wanchese, accompanied Amadas and Barlowe on their return voyage to England. They were no doubt interviewed in depth by Thomas Hariot, a young Oxford graduate who would later earn fame as a polymath Renaissance scholar. Hariot, employed initially in Raleigh's household as an instructor of marine navigation, was entrusted with the preparation of a detailed report on the natural and human resources of Raleigh's prospective colony. Having gained a rudimentary command of the Algonquian dialect of the region, Hariot, who may have been with Amadas and Barlowe a year earlier, joined the 1585 expedition commanded by Sir Richard Greenville, a veteran of the Irish campaigns. Greenville departed England on April 27 with around 600 men in seven ships, only four of which actually reached the Outer Banks. A storm off the coast of Portugal sank a pinnace and scattered the other ships. Some, but not all, were reunited in the Spanish Caribbean and engaged in both trade and privateering there. Arriving in North America, Greenville's remaining squadron ran aground on the Carolina banks. Although it easily floated free, a subsequent accident with the flagship *Tiger* destroyed most of the provisions—salt beef and pork, salt cod, dried peas, rice, meal, ship's biscuits—intended to feed the new colony. When

Greenville set sail for home in late August, he left behind as founding colonists on Roanoke Island only one poorly equipped group of about 100 men, although more than 300 of his party were originally earmarked for the task.[26]

The research notes Hariot compiled at Roanoke have been lost, as has the book manuscript he prepared, but we do have a promotional report of the venture that he published in 1588. It provides a remarkably detailed assessment of the plant, animal, and mineral wealth of the area, holding out in particular the prospect of a lucrative trade with the Indians. Thousands of deerskins were to be had annually, Hariot reported, from the "naturall inhabitants . . . for trifles" without appreciably diminishing the area's huge herds. Hariot was concerned to correct the bad impression of Roanoke created by disgruntled members of the previous year's expedition who had not only "spoken ill of their Gouernours, but . . . slandered the countrie itself." He took particular pains to assure his readers that the "naturall inhabitants . . . in respect of troubling our inhabiting and planting, are not to be feared, but . . . shall haue cause both to feare and loue us, that shall inhabite with them." That formula, fear and love, would be invoked repeatedly by English champions of New World ventures in the century to come. As Hariot developed the fear theme, the Indians were highly vulnerable because of the inferiority of their weapons. Without iron, they were completely dependent on wooden bows and arrows, and on crude shields made of bark or sticks. Their towns were small and poorly defended, if at all, by flimsy wooden fences, a point made vivid in the remarkably realistic but captivating paintings and drawings produced by John White, the expedition's artist. Hariot emphasized that in the event of war with neighboring peoples, Indians would find that English aid would be quickly decisive. Their perception of English power would lead them to ally themselves with the colonizers. He also related that whenever the Roanoke settlers had clashed with Indians, the latter found "the turning vp of their heels against vs in running away was their best defense." Lacking understanding of science and technology, they believed the English possessed of supernatural powers. Hariot related that when shown English books, compasses, magnets, telescopes, guns, fireworks, burning glasses that could focus the rays of the sun to start fires, and clocks "that seeme to goe of themselves and manie other thinges wee had," the Indians confessed that they "so farre exceeded their capacities to comprehend the reason and meanes how they should be made and done, that they thought they were rather the works of gods then of men, or at the leastwise they had bin giuen and taught vs of the gods." Despite that lack of comprehension of the nature of English weapons and instruments, Hariot stressed that the Indians nonetheless "seeme very ingenious . . . in those things they doe, they shewe excellence of wit." Through that ingenuity, the Indians of the Carolinas, as described in Hariot's report and as portrayed in White's drawings, had achieved a mode of life that combined a sort of primitive simplicity with great bounty. They were also an attractive people, portrayed in White's drawings and Hariot's word portraits as lean, muscular, and stately. Their dress, and ornaments, although simple, conveyed their individual social rank. They were not by any means simple egalitarian savages, but possessed a well-developed hierarchical system that exalted the local rulers and their families.[27]

In a departure from earlier accounts that described Native American religion as nothing more than the worship of devils, Hariot reported, perhaps erroneously, that despite their polytheism they believed in an ultimate "one onley chiefe and great God which hath beene from all eternity," in personal immortality, and in a last judgment. Given those beliefs, their religion, he concluded, could easily be "reformed." Conversations with them about religion had already brought the Indians "into great doubts of their owne, and no small admiration of ours, with earnest desire in many, to learne more then we had meanes for want of perfect vtterance in their language to expresse." The Roanoke chief Wingina, Hariot reported, joined the English on occasion in psalm singing and prayer, "hoping thereby to bee partaker of the same effectes which wee by that meanes also expected," by which Hariot meant both recovery from illness and bliss in the world to come. Despite his appreciation of Algonquian culture, however, Hariot nonetheless suspected that there were indeed some devil worshippers among them. He believed that they had tried to use witchcraft against the English. Their punishment was immediate and extreme:

> There was no towne where wee had any subtile devise practiced against vs, we leauing it unpunished or not revenged (because we sought by all meanes possible to win them by gentlenesse) but within fewe dayes after our departure from everie such towne, the people began to die very fast, and many in short space; in some townes about twentie, in some fourtie, in some sixtie, & in one six score, which in truth was very manie in terms of their numbers. This happened in no place that wee coulde learne but where we had bene where they had used some practice against us, and after such time; The disease was so strange, that they neither knew what it was, nor how to cure it; the like by report of the oldest men in the country never happened before, time out of minde.

Hariot reported that the terrified Indians conjectured that the English, aided by their God, had the power to "kil and slaie whom wee would without weapons and not come neere them." The English, they thought, probably "did make the people to die . . . by shooting invisible bullets into them" from a great distance. They suspected, moreover, that the newcomers were not really human, noting that "all the space of their sicknesse, there was no man of ours knowne to die, or that was specially sicke: they noted also that we had no women amongst vs, neither did we care for any of theirs." Were they gods? Or were they the beneficiaries of "the speciall worke of God" who extirpated their foes through a horrendous new disease? In a telling commentary, Hariot declared that "we ourselves haue cause in some sorte to think no lesse," noting some of his countrymen found premonitions of divine wrath against Indians opposed to the English presence in a solar eclipse before their landing in America and in a comet that appeared shortly before "the beginning of the said sicknesse." Hariot's attitude toward those omens appears to have been skeptical, but his account anticipates the belief, in the next century to be widely held among the colonizers, that God killed Indians through disease in order to clear the way for English settlement.[28]

Hariot acknowledged, however, that the Greenville expedition had been unable to maintain peace with the local Indians. Interestingly, he did not place the primary blame for conflicts at Roanoke on the natives, but instead charged that "some of our companie towards the ende of the yeere, shewed themselues too fierce, in slaying some of the people, in some towns, upon causes that on our part, might easily enough bene borne withal." Unfortunately, he did not elaborate. However, it is telling that Richard Hakluyt, a few years later after reviewing the documentary evidence available and interviewing some of the colony's survivors, also concluded that Greenville and company had been far too heavy-handed in their dealings with the "naturall inhabitants." Uncharacteristically, Hakluyt, despite his fervid belief in England's New World destiny, declared that the hand of God in this instance had come down hard on the colonizers at Roanoke because of their cruel abuse of the Indians.[29]

Although Hariot, as noted, was cryptic, some information about the 1585 colony's conflicts with Indians are found in the narrative written by Ralph Lane, who served after Greenville's departure as its governor. There were, however, things Lane omitted. From a variety of sources, the main events of this ill-conceived venture can be reconstructed, and they offer much evidence that Hakluyt's condemnation was fully warranted. A close reading of Lane's report supplemented by those other sources, which include Hariot, Hakluyt, and John White, suggests that the violence that marked the Greenville and Lane governorships was not, as Lane would have it, the outgrowth of innate Indian hostility, but rather emanated from cultural misunderstandings and mutual miscalculations exacerbated by English insensitivity and heavy-handedness. Granganimeo, who had assisted the members of the Amadas–Barlowe expedition, immediately befriended the Greenville party and sought their aid in his conflict with a neighboring tribe. The English, however, provided no help, and as winter's scarcity approached, the Indians grew wary and then tired of the non-reciprocating intruders. The Roanoke adventurers were misguided in their belief that, in exchange for a few trade goods, the local Indians would provide them with all their food supply. The sparse Indian population in the area did not have sufficient surpluses to feed 100 nonproductive newcomers. Samuel Eliot Morison, commenting on the behavior and expectations of the early English colonists of Virginia, remarked that

> bounteous initial hospitality always seemed to have convinced Europeans that they could be "freeloaders" indefinitely, that as superior beings they should be supplied with fish, corn, venison, or whatever they wanted. But though they paid with knives, bells, and beads, "consumer demand" was soon satisfied. . . . Why Europeans never seemed willing to fish for themselves is still a mystery, but a fact.

The Roanoke Indians tried to teach the English to build fish weirs. They soon fell into disrepair, as the English insisted that Indians share their food with them. The intruders were not only demanding, but punitive as well. Neither Lane nor Hariot related an incident, which was noted in the journal of the ship Tyger, wherein the English burned an Indian village and then destroyed its crops in response to the failure of a local chief to keep his promise to find and return a silver cup allegedly stolen by a member of his band. As Morrison remarked, "for this and doubtless other unrecorded and rash acts of theirs, the English planters eventually paid dear."[30]

After the death, from a disease probably of English origin, of Grangamineo and of another Indian leader named Ensenore, both good friends of the newcomers, relations deteriorated rapidly. Granganimeo's brother, the local chief Wingina changed his name to Pemisapan (probably a war name and hence a harbinger of hostilities) and sought the aid of neighboring tribes in resisting the intruders, warning, Lane claimed, "that our purpose was fully bent to destroy them." In response, Lane undertook to intimidate and cajole those tribal leaders, disrupting an "assembly" called to form a "confederacie against us." He seized hostages, threatened violence, then tried to negotiate. Tensions mounted throughout spring 1586. Lane reported that Pemisapan alternated between professions of friendship for the English and efforts to starve their colony by refusing to provide food. Hearing from Indian informants that an attack was imminent, Lane decided to strike first. Entering their village under the pretext of a parley, Lane's men assaulted Pemisapan and his people as Lane gave the cry, "Christ our victory!" His narrative described the death of Pemisapan, the Indian leader, shot in the buttocks, who staggered into a thicket where he was overtaken by an Irish soldier, who emerged with Pemisapan's head in his hands. Was Pemisapan actually conspiring to exterminate the fledgling English colony? Some scholars, including David B. Quinn, the leading authority on Roanoke, have expressed doubts, noting that Hariot's account does not support Lane's view of him as an enemy. The evidence available does not permit a definitive resolution of this issue. Richard Hakluyt the younger drew a clear lesson from his study of the Roanoke reports and incorporated into the Jamestown instructions warnings against antagonizing the Indians by excessive demands or unnecessary use of force. In particular, Hakluyt insisted that the colonists must raise their own food and not expect to be fed by the local peoples.[31]

As noted earlier, comparable instructions about the importance of avoiding conflict with the Indians had been an integral part of the instructions given to the Roanoke adventures. What went wrong? Some analysts of the Roanoke failure emphasize the background of the men chosen to plant the colony. Many were veterans of Ireland, accustomed to use of terror at the least sign of resistance. The colonial promoter Walter Raleigh himself, as an infantry captain, had responded to a challenge to English authority in 1580 by the killing of the entire population of the town of Smerwick. As to those who went to Virginia, Karen Kupperman has argued that in choosing colonists, rank and file as well as commanders . . . promoters made it virtually certain that their good intentions would be violated. Sir Richard Greenville and Ralph Lane had served in the bitter and cruel Irish campaigns, and many of the colonists were soldiers. . . . Their Irish experience had convinced them that Hakluyt's "forebearing of revenge" was bad policy.[32]

The ill-considered resort to violence at Roanoke cannot, however, entirely be attributed to memories of Ireland. The instructions of the promoters condoned violence as a response to Indian opposition to the English presence, and indeed even sanctioned its use to force trade. Coercion was, of course, to be a last resort. But how were the colonists to decide when they had reached that extremity? Here, lack of understanding of the Indians and their culture proved crucial. Even Hariot, by his own admission, had only a very shaky command of the Algonquian dialect of the region. Most other members of the expedition could not understand any Algonquian. Nor could they always properly interpret gestures and other body movements, and could too easily misunderstand their meaning. Nor were the common soldier–settlers men of moderate habits. Their commander, Ralph Lane, complained of the difficulty of controlling "wylde men of myne owne nacione" while trying to live "emungst sauuages." It is perhaps telling that Lane also recorded that Pemisapan had warned neighboring tribes that the English planned to kill all Indians. We are left to wonder just what unrecorded acts of violence might have given rise to that idea.[33]

At the very least, the English were exceedingly overbearing in their interactions with the Indians of the Outer Banks. The Roanoke colonists had an exaggerated sense of their own power and of Indian weakness, and hence were both surprised and confused when they encountered resistance to their demands. The belief that the English must always project an image of invincibility to the native peoples, expressed not only in the reports from Roanoke, but also in the later instructions to Jamestown, was rooted also in a profound uncertainty about the character of those peoples. Although the Roanoke adventurers, for a time, may have entertained the illusion that they were in the midst of noble savages still living in a golden age of innocence, they were also haunted by stories of devil-worshipping cannibals dwelling in the American wilderness. With whom were they dealing at Roanoke? It is telling that Barlow spoke of their adoration of an idol fashioned after the devil, and even Hariot believed some of the Indians of the region tried to use witchcraft against the English, and were accordingly decimated by a disease sent to them by God Himself. Uncertain feelings about Indians fostered misunderstandings, misinterpretations of speech and gesture, and excessive reactions to things that, as Hariot noted, "might easily enough bene bourne withal."

The failure to establish amicable and stable relations with the indigenous inhabitants doomed the Greenville/Lane colony. A week after the killing of Pemisapan, the Roanoke colonists spied offshore the ships of Sir Francis Drake's fleet bringing new supplies. Soon thereafter, the fleet was struck by a hurricane, which sank four ships, including the one intended for Lane's use. Hariot was convinced that the storm came upon the English in punishment for their mistreatment of the Indians. Most of the colonists were immediately evacuated. Those left behind subsequently disappeared. They may have joined Manteo's tribe nearby, which was headed by his mother. However, it is also possible that they may have perished at the hands of less friendly Indians.

A second colony was founded in 1587. Originally intended to be planted at Chesapeake Bay and called the City of Raleigh, this colony's founders were unceremoniously deposited at the old site at Roanoke, as the crew of the ship that had carried them across the Atlantic was eager to go privateering. Under the governorship of John White (who may or may not have been the same adventurer who painted the peoples of Roanoke), the colonists numbered 115 and, unlike the earlier venture, included 17 women (two of whom were pregnant) and nine children. The colony was assisted in its relations with the local Indians by Manteo, who, unlike Wanchese, remained pro-English. (After converting to Christianity, he was named by the English "Lord of Roanoke.") After a month, the colonists persuaded Governor White to return to England to seek supplies. He did so, and in response to his appeal, preparations were made to send a fleet of eight ships to Virginia to provision the colony. Those plans, however, were disrupted by the outbreak of war with Spain and by the Spanish Armada crisis. When White finally returned in August 1590, he found no trace of the colony at Roanoke, other than a word carved on a tree—Croatoan—which led him to believe that the settlers may have moved to that island. Once again, storms disrupted efforts to help the colony. White was forced to sail back to England without making any further effort to find the "Lost Colony."[34]

What happened to the Roanoke settlers and to Virginia Dare, the first English girl born in North America? There have been many romantic stories of both their survival and their demise. One holds that the colonists did move north to the Chesapeake Bay, where they settled among the Chesapeake tribe, but were wiped out by the Powhatan Indians around the time of the founding of Jamestown. Captain John Smith, some years after the event, claimed Powhatan confessed to him in December 1608 that he had slaughtered the Roanoke survivors the year before and had some of their "utensils" to prove it, including a musket barrel. Smith was not always completely truthful in his historical recollections, but it does appear that some of the English at Jamestown and their supporters in London from 1608 onward did believe Powhatan had exterminated all of the Roanoke remnant. However, rumors that their descendents are to be found in various Indian communities remain part of the folklore of Virginia.[35]

The Jamestown settlement was not the only New World venture established by the privately sponsored Virginia Company in 1607, some 30 years after the abandonment of the Lost Colony. In June of that year, two ships under the command of George Popham and Raleigh Gilbert carried around 100 English colonists to Maine's Sabino peninsula, where they established a colony that came to be known as "Sagadahoc" after a local river. (The river is now called the "Kennebec.") From the well-fortified, palisaded village they built there, the settlers hoped to engage in a lucrative trade with the Abenaki Indians and mount a search for the Northwest Passage to Asia. The colony did not flourish, and was abandoned after less than a year of occupancy. The reasons for its abandonment given in the official record included severe weather (Maine's winter cold was unexpected), a fire that destroyed much of the settlement, a crisis of leadership after George Popham's death and Raleigh Gilbert's recall to England on family business, the absence of either gold or silver in the region, and the failure to establish a trading relationship with the local Indians. Later reports, in French sources and Puritan folklore, of an Indian massacre at Sagadahoc were fanciful. Withdrawal, not massacre, was the Indian strategy for dealing with these unwanted intruders. The documentary evidence left by the Sagadahoc adventurers is incomplete, but it does clearly indicate that the locals shunned the colonists, who were consequently unable to maintain an economically viable settlement.[36]

To understand that failure, we must examine the assumptions of the colony's founders. The chief promoter of the Sagadahoc project was Sir Fernándino Gorges. Gorges had little knowledge of Indians and even less sympathy for them. They were, he declared in a letter to Sir Robert Cecil dated August 7, 1607, a "people daungerouse to bee dealt with." But he took great comfort in the belief that a demonstration of English power and superiority would bring the natives to "fear and love" the newcomers. He was particularly confident that through the good offices of Skidwarres and Tahenedo, two kidnapped Abenaki then residing in England, his venture in Maine would succeed. Gorges declared their kidnapping part of a divine plan for "giving life to all our plantations" in America. When Popham and Gilbert set sail for Maine, Skidwarres and Tahenedo accompanied their party. These two Indians, Gorges believed, would persuade their countrymen, not only to welcome the English and trade with them, but also to lead them to gold, silver, and the Northwest Passage. None of that happened. The two captives, upon landing on their home soil, at first pretended to collaborate, but soon deserted. Thereafter, the people from their villages avoided contact with the English. Efforts mounted by the English commanders to open up trade with other villages proved generally fruitless. Although the Abenaki were familiar with European trade goods, having dealt previously with the Basque and the French, they were disinterested in the English offerings. They may have been aware of earlier kidnappings carried out by English ships visiting their coast. Whatever their reasons, they were not interested in becoming trading partners, let alone agents of English exploration and expansion. Gorges never understood the reasons for the failure to establish profitable trade at Sagadahoc, but his comments on that failure shed much light on English attitudes toward the peoples of America at the dawn of the 17th century. Wedded to the formula of "fear and love," he faulted the Sagadahoc pioneers for their inappropriate "familiaritie" with the "savages." They had failed to inspire fear, seemingly forgetting that a "discrete" show of force would work wonders, as Indians, Gorges affirmed, although treacherous, were "a people tractable."[37]

In summary, contemporary accounts of early English–Indian interactions in the 16th century are riddled with both misconceptions and misperceptions.

We find in the early accounts a pervasive belief in the existence of two kinds of savages: simple, gentle folk who would welcome the protection and guidance of Christians, and ferocious, bestial cannibals who had to be fought. In their dealings with actual Indians, the English in 16th-century North America were often, indeed usually, quite confused regarding just which type they had encountered. Frobisher and company were convinced that the Inuit were cannibals and devil worshippers, even though there was no evidence of the former, and only misinterpretation of gestures and speech to support the latter. The participants in Roanoke explorations and settlement described the peoples of the Outer Banks in more positive terms, even sometimes even suggesting that they were children of nature who recalled stories of a golden age. However, they also reported the presence of witchcraft and satanism. As we have noted, the most astute of the English visitors, Thomas Hariot differed from his colleagues in his refusal to characterize Indian religion as satanic, arguing that the Indians for the most part worshipped the creator, not the devil. However, his chilling conclusion that the diseases that decimated Indian villages after their first contact with the English were acts of God punishing Indian witches reveals the depth of English confusion about the peoples they met on the Atlantic shores of North America. That confusion, and the mistrust it engendered, made it difficult, sometimes impossible, for the English to understand Indian motives and actions. Believing that "good Indians" would immediately "love and fear" them, the leaders of the 16th-century exploratory probes were all too quick to attribute the worst of intentions to those gestures and actions that did not meet their expectations. We now understand that the peoples of North America, were neither simple children of nature nor diabolical savages. When the English failed to see them simply as human beings driven by the same wants and needs as other humans, as they so often did, they took the first steps on the road to their demonization.

CHAPTER 2

~

"Our Mortall Enemies": Early Encounters at Jamestown

In 1607, some 30 years after the demise of the Roanoke venture, the Virginia Company, a private undertaking chartered by King James I, established two English outposts in North America. One, planted on the coast of Maine, as we have noted, was abandoned within a year. The second, at Jamestown in Virginia, ill conceived and poorly managed, nearly ended in disaster, but survived to become the first of a series of successful British colonial ventures in the New World. Those who planned the Jamestown venture expected it to generate profit for the investors by exploiting the mineral wealth believed to be abundant in the interior, as well as by the cultivation and export of crops not suited to England's soil. They also hoped that its settlers would locate the Northwest Passage and thereby provide a quick route to the Orient for English traders. Some also thought Virginia might become a lucrative base for privateers, should the precarious peace with Spain break down. They understood that, initially at least, success of their plans required the cooperation of the region's indigenous peoples, but they were uncertain about the prospects for long-term productive relationships. The instructions given the first colonists by the Virginia Company were not reassuring.

Among the authors of those instructions was Richard Hakluyt the younger, by then an elderly clergyman who had devoted his life to the promotion of overseas trade and expansion. Nineteenth-century historian J. A. Fronde declared Hakluyt's massive collections of traveler's reports of the non-European world "the prose epic of the English nation," containing as they did a bold vision of a future empire. Hakluyt, who never visited the Americas, drew upon those reports in framing instructions to the prospective colonists on their dealings with Virginia's Indians. Those instructions insisted that the natives not be abused, but stressed no less emphatically that they were also not to be trusted. The colonists were warned that as soon as their intention to remain in Virginia was understood by the Indians, they would be in danger. "You Cannot Carry Your Selves so towards them but they will Grow Discontented with Your habitation and be ready to Guide and assist any Nation that Shall Come to invade You." Reminding the adventurers that Spaniards commanded by Pedro Menéndez de Avilés had wiped out a French settlement in Florida some years earlier with Indian help, the instructions advised them to establish a fortification on a major river, taking care not to allow "any of the natural people of the Country to inhabit between You and the Seacoast." Their site should be surrounded by open ground, and not located in "a low and moist place" (instructions Jamestown's founders disregarded to their great loss). They must never allow those "Country people" to handle their weapons. When they fired those weapons in the presence of Indians they were to use only their best marksmen, "for if they See Your Learners miss what they aim at they will think the Weapons not so terrible" and would be emboldened to attack. They should give the Indians the impression that they were supernatural beings.

> Above all things do not advertise the killing of any of your men that the Country people may know it if they Perceive they are but Common men and that with the Loss of many of theirs they may Deminish any part of Yours they will make many Adventures upon you . . . you shall Do well also not to Let them See or know of Your Sick men if you have any which may also encourage them to many Enterprizes.

The colonists should immediately open trade relations with the local people, because they would need to look to them for at least part of their food supply during the first year. To facilitate that trade, the Company provided a store of glass beads, square pieces of copper, and other items that earlier reports had suggested were greatly coveted by Indians, but the colonists' instructions warned against long-term dependency. They were to seek to attain self-sufficiency by planting their own crops as quickly as possible.[1]

What role were "the Country people" to play in the colony after it was established? The king who issued the charter saw the venture as destined to draw the natives to "true service and knowledge of God and the obedience of us" and to that end prescribed "severe pains and punishments" for any settler who abused his prospective new subjects. Others echoed the king's noble sentiment. Robert Johnson, in a Virginia Company promotional tract, promised that the Indians would not be conquered in the Spanish manner "by stormes of raging cruelties [as West India was converted] with rapiers point and musket shot, murdering so many millions of naked Indians, as their stories do relate, but by faire and loving meanes suited to our English natures." He declared the undertaking a vital part of the divine plan of redemption. "God," Johnson wrote, "hath reserved in this last age of the world, an infinite number of those lost and scattered sheep, to be won and recovered by our means."[2]

Although the records from the earliest years of the Virginia colony are sparse, the evidence we have suggests that its leaders, from the outset, were skeptical about that possibility and that they were not reassured by their first contacts. There is a strikingly ambivalent assessment of the character of the indigenous inhabitants written by Gabriel Archer, a participant and chronicler of Bartholomew Gosnold's 1602 voyage to New England. Archer, who later served as secretary to the colony, prepared in spring 1607 a report that he titled "The Description of the Now Discovered River and Country of Virginia, with the Likelihood of Ensuing Riches by England's Aid and Industry." He described Virginia's natives as "a very witty and ingenious people," who learned very quickly to communicate with the English "in our language." However, Archer was wary, believing that, despite appearances, "they are naturally given to treachery." He acknowledged that during their first trip into the interior, the English were greeted warmly by "a most kind and loving people," but those people also stole from them and expressed resentment when asked to return the property they had purloined. Their disrespect for property, Archer suggested, was indicative of deeper character flaws. Perhaps they might be transformed by conversion to Christianity. He was struck that "when they saw us at prayer they observed us with great silence and respect, especially those to whom I had imparted the meaning of our reverence." His report ended with the hope that God "will make us authors of his holy will in converting them to our true Christian faith." But on balance, Archer was dubious. His fear that the "kind and loving" people the Indians first appeared to be were really treacherous amoral savages was shared by most, perhaps all, of Archer's colleagues. As we shall see, as conflicts between Indians and English in Virginia broke out over access to resources, the adjective "treacherous" came to displace other descriptions of Indian character.[3]

A narrative account of early encounters with the Indians, written a year or two after the first landing of the company in Virginia probably by George Percy, brother of the Duke of Northumberland and on two occasions acting governor during the colony's early years, sheds further light on the mind-set of the founders. Percy's first reference to the inhabitants of the New World comes in his description of a landfall at Dominica in the Caribbean made en route to Virginia and reflects the prejudices he and others brought to their venture. The indigenous people, he related, "go all naked, without covering . . . they are continually in wars, and will eat their enemies when they kill them, or any stranger if they take them . . . they worship the devil for their God, and have no other belief." But that description was based on supposition, not experience. The actual behavior of the Indians Percy and his compatriots encountered on Dominica did not conform to those preconceptions or support allegations of cannibalism. They proved to be friendly, and were indeed eager to trade with the English sailors, flocking to their ships in canoes bearing native fruits, vegetables, and tobacco, as well as cloth taken from Spanish shipwrecks. Landing soon thereafter on Nevis to seek provisions, the English, as Percy related, mounted a strict watch, as they feared "the treachery of the Indians, which is an ordinary use amongst them." Once again, however, expectations of savage behavior were not confirmed by events. Percy conceded that during their week ashore, the men were not actually "molested by any." Instead, the Indians ran away when they sighted the newcomers. Percy thus found the natives of the Caribbean either eager to trade or exceedingly shy. In his experience they were not aggressive, but that did not alter his preconceptions about their treachery or about their involvement in devil worship and cannibalism.[4]

The first landing on the Virginia shore finally confirmed Percy's expectations. On their first night, he recounted that as they were returning to their ships, "there came the Savages creeping upon all four, from the hills like bears, with their bows in their mouths." They "charged us very desperately," wounding Archer and one of the sailors. "After they had spent their arrows, and felt the sharpness of our shot, they retired into the Woods with a great noise, and so left us." The next day, marching some eight miles inland, the English saw no Indians, but did come "to a place where they had made a great fire, and had been newly a-roasting Oysters: when they perceived our coming, they fled away to the mountains, and left many of the Oysters in the fire: we eat some of the Oysters, which were very large and delicate in taste."[5]

Percy's report of the first exploratory probe upriver, carried out in the shallop built soon after their landing, gives further testimony to the power of preconceptions about savagery. At first the Indians remained hidden, then the English met five men walking along the riverbank. Visiting their village, Percy related that "we were entertained by them very kindly," but he remained suspicious and apprehensive. Their Indian hosts, in the midst of some sort of ceremony when they arrived, "made a doleful noise, laying their faces to the ground, scratching the earth with their nails." That, Percy believed, was surely a sign of "Idolatry," an impression reinforced later at a welcoming feast, where the Indians "shouting, howling, and stamping against the ground, with many antic tricks and faces" made "noise like so many wolves or devils." After that display, the party proceeded farther upriver to another village, where again "they entertained us with much welcome; an old Savage made a long Oration, making a foul noise uttering his speech with vehement action, but we knew little what they meant."[6]

While there, the English were accosted by a *werowance* (chief) from a nearby village who, Percy believed, wanted the English to associate only with him; however, it is not clear just what he was saying. We now know that men from a European ship a year or so earlier had killed his predecessor and abducted some of his countrymen. Was the chief trying to ascertain if these newcomers were the malefactors? Perhaps. Whatever case, the next day, with their muskets at the ready, the English visited his village and presented their host with "trifles which pleased him." Archer related that as they landed, the *werowance* "came down to the water side with all his train, as goodly men as any I have seen of Savages or Christians." They put on an impressive show. The chief led the procession, playing a flute, wearing a crown of red-dyed deer hair and copper plate topped by two feathers "in fashion of a pair of horns." His face was painted blue, his body was covered with crimson paint and sprinkled with "silver Ore." Pearls and bird claws fashioned of copper or gold adorned his ears. He wore around his neck a chain of beads. Percy was struck by his stately demeanor, worthy of "a Prince of civil government." At the chief's village, surrounded by "the goodliest corn fields that ever was seen in any country," Percy related that "he entertained us in good Humanity."[7]

Sailing farther upriver, the party was confronted by Indians standing on the shore who threatened them with arrows and with swords—like weapons crafted of stone and pieces of iron that Percy believed could cut a man in half. Their leader ordered the newcomers to leave at once and only with some difficulty could he be persuaded to allow them to land. Despite that initial expression of hostility, the Indians did not attack. The English did not linger, but quickly returned downriver and rejoined the other members of the company. Percy's brief account of their exploration contained no indication that they had encountered any serious hostility. The Indian villages they visited were generally hospitable, but the English remained on edge, expecting the worst.[8]

After looking over several other possible sites, the colonizers began construction of a fort, originally called James Fort in honor of the monarch, on an uninhabited island on the James River, some 40 miles from its mouth, in territory belonging to the Paspahegh people. Of their selection of a site, one writer notes that the settlers

at the time . . . took no notice of the mosquito-infested swamp nearby. The James River, from which they would often have to get their water, was deceptively fresh at that time of year; it would turn brackish in the summer and stay that way. Jamestown Island was an excellent choice for a temporary visit, but a poor one for a long-term settlement. Archaeology shows that over the centuries the Indians merely camped there occasionally; they knew what they were doing.[9]

The Jamestown men soon found themselves in a very confusing relationship with Wowinchopunck, the local *werowance* of the Paspahegh. Percy related that on their first night there, around midnight, several Indians in a canoe approached the river shore near their camp, but fled after the lookouts gave the alarm. Soon thereafter two high-ranking Indians, both wearing "crowns of colored hair upon their heads," called to announce that the *werowance* himself would be calling shortly and "would be merry with us with a fat deer." When the chief arrived, he was accompanied by around 100 warriors. As Percy related, he "made great signs to us to lay our arms away, but we would not trust him so far." Percy suspected the Indians "thought at that time to execute their villany." Thwarted by their vigilance, the chief's next gambit, Percy believed, was to make "signs that he would give us as much land as we would desire to take." Given the mutual lack of understanding of the languages each spoke, it is unlikely Percy really knew just what the chief intended. Efforts to communicate were soon disrupted by an altercation over a hatchet allegedly stolen by an Indian. An English settler struck the supposed thief and in turn was threatened by one of his companions who "came fiercely at our man with a wooden sword, thinking to beat out his brains." The English brandished their weapons and "the werowance went suddenly away with all his company in great anger." A few days later, the *werowance* "sent forty of his men with a Deer, to our quarter." Percy was not impressed by that show of friendship, declaring "they came more in villany than in any love they bare us." The Indians asked to stay overnight, "but we would not suffer them for fear of their treachery." A few days thereafter, the Indians delivered another deer to the men constructing the settlement they called James Fort. However, the English remained on edge, because the meaning of the words and gestures of the visitors were not always clear. Sometimes they seemed friendly and loving, but at other times their feelings were very hard to read.[10]

To reassure the local people of the Englishmen's peaceful intentions, the colony's president, Edward Maria Wingfield decided to leave James Fort unfortified for a time. Only a flimsy enclosure of brush was put up around the encampment, and the guns unloaded from the ships were left in their packing cases. Wingfield's order was controversial, challenged by several other leaders who opposed that very risky show of good intentions. They were right. On May 27, around 200 Paspahegh warriors assaulted Jamestown. They were driven away by cannon fire from the ships in the harbor only after their arrows had killed a boy and wounded 11 of the men, one fatally. John Smith related that without the ship's cannon, all the English would have "been slaine." The settlers immediately set to work to build a proper fortification. The structures they finally erected were substantial. The enclosure was triangular in shape. Two sides were some 300 feet long; the other, 420 feet. There were three blockhouses equipped with cannons, and, within the walls were several buildings, two of which were 170 feet in length.[11]

Although intimidated by the artillery and by the muskets that were now broken out of their cases and made available to the defenders, the Paspahegh in the days that followed continued to mount small-scale raids. During the first raid, the only casualty was an English dog, but during the second, a man "straggling without the forte" was hit by six arrows and died in agony a week later. Later, several others, including one hapless fellow who, as Archer recalled, left the fort "to do a naturall necessity" were also shot by Indians hiding in the tall grass. The colonists understood their vulnerability and their need for good relations with the "Country people." The Indians in the region greatly outnumbered them. When an Indian from a town upriver who had earlier served Christopher Newport as a guide into the interior appeared with a companion at the fort's gate and suggested that they could mediate, they welcomed the offer. However, although their good offices may have helped, they did not end hostilities. Although the attacks were less frequent during the summer months, they persisted. An unstable mixture of friendship and enmity, and of dependency and distrust soon came to characterize early Indian–white relations in Virginia. It would persist for many years to come.[12]

It may be that the initial decision to attack the fledgling English settlement was not made by the Paspahegh chief. During an exploratory probe into the interior, conducted from May 21 to May 27, and still underway at the time of the first attack, Christopher Newport and his company had learned that most, although not all, of the local Indian bands paid tribute to a paramount chief, called in the local dialect the *Mamanatowick*. His name was Wahunsenacawh, but he was generally referred to by the English as "Powhatan," after the name of his home village. The term "Powhatans" would be used to designate all the tribes subject to him, although the territory within Powhatan's domain was called "Tsenacomoco" in the local dialect. Newport and company believed that they had met and negotiated with Powhatan during their trip upriver, and that he had expressed interest in friendly relations. In fact, the man with whom they had dealt was a local *werowance* and a son of the paramount chief. It would be some seven months before any Englishman would gain access to Wahunsenacawh himself. Those who did so were deeply impressed. Powhatan was probably between 60 and 70 years old in 1607. Captain John Smith's first impression was of a man of "grave and Majesticall countenance," adding that it "drave me into admiration to see such a state in a naked Salvage." Later, he described the principle chief as "a tall, well-proportioned man, with a sour look, his head somewhat gray, his beard so thin that it seems none at all his age near 60, very able and hardy body to endure any labor." Virginia settler William Strachey, several years later, described him as an old man "well beaten with many cold and stormye winters" who was still physically imposing, "of a tall stature, and cleane lymbes." His was "a daring spirit, vigilant, ambitious, subtile to enlarge his dominions."[13]

Powhatan was the head of a tributary network of some 30 discrete tribal groups in the northern Virginia tidewater region, including some 200 villages, most of them conquered and subjugated during his reign, which began around 1572. From his mother (the Virginia Algonquians were matrilineal), "Powhatan had inherited six chiefdoms: Pamunkey, Yougthanund, and Mattaponi in the York River drainage and Powhatan (the town), Arrohatexk, and Appamattuck in the James River basin near the fall line." By the beginning of the 17th century, he had added to his dominions, by war and diplomacy, most of the tribes of tidewater Virginia from the Potomac River to the James. His methods could be quite ruthless. It was said that when the *werowance* of Kecoughton passed away, Powhatan mounted an attack before the new chief could get his bearings, killed that hapless leader along with a number of his warriors, deported the survivors, and resettled the village with his own people. His struggle for dominance had not ended at the time Jamestown was founded. Powhatan attacked the Chesapeakes just before the English arrival, and the Piankatanks the following year. One major group in his immediate area remained independent. The Chickahominys of the upper James River were ruled, not by a *werowance* tributary to Powhatan, but by a council of elders and priests. They occasionally joined Powhatan's war parties (for a price paid in copper) and might participate in communal hunts, but they were not part of his domain, and sometimes opposed him. They would, however, be incorporated by Powhatan's brother and successor Opechancanough.[14]

The non-Algonquian–speaking tribes to the North, South, and West of Powhatan's domain were generally hostile. Long-standing enmities marked relations with the Sioux–speaking Monacans and Manahoacs of the Western piedmont. The tribes comprising the Monacans were seated along the James River near the fall line. The 12 or so tribes of the Manahoac were found at the headwaters of the Rappahannock. Villages in both areas regularly launched fall raids against the Powhatans. Relations with the tribes to the South, although sometimes troubled, were less turbulent, but raiding parties from a more distant Northwestern location also periodically struck tidewater Virginia. These people were called the "Massawomecks." Although little is known about them, some evidence suggests they were Iroquoian, possibly Seneca. Also from the North, and probably also Iroquoian, were the Bocootawanaukes or Poughtanocks, who reputedly were very fierce cannibals. (Iroquoians, on occasion, did engage in the ritual cannibalizing of enemy war prisoners whom they had tortured to death.) In 1606, according to John Smith's testimony, the Bocootawanaukes attacked Powhatan's tributaries the Patawomecks, killing about 100 men. This was but one of several Iroquoian raids, which along with continuing Monacan hostilities no doubt played a role in the drive to consolidate Powhatan's "empire," which in its policy toward these raiders was defensive. Powhatan and his people made no effort to extend their control beyond the tidewater.[15]

Smith believed that Powhatan wielded absolute power over his subjects. "His will," he wrote in 1612,

> is law and must be obeyed: not only as a king but as halfe a God they esteem him. . . . What he commandeth they dare not disobey in the least thing. It is strange to see with what great feare and adoration all these people doe obey this Powhatan, For at his feet they present whatsoever he commandeth, and at the least frowne of his browe, their greatest spirits will tremble with feare, and no marvel, for he is very terrible and tyrannous in punishing such as offend him.

Strachey concurred: "Powhatan doth at his pleasure, despoyle them both of their lyves and goodes, without yielding them any reason, or alledging or proving just cause against them." The lesser *werowances* whom Powhatan appointed also, according to Smith, wielded the same tyrannical authority, "and have the power of life and death at their command."[16]

Modern scholars agree that Smith and Strachey exaggerated. Seventeenth-century Algonquian leaders elsewhere in Eastern North America did not possess anything close to the arbitrary and absolute power Smith attributes to Powhatan, although it should be noted that some of the peoples of the Southeastern gulf region did endow their rulers with divine attributes. Their influence may have prompted Powhatan's people to grant their paramount chief greater power and influence than was typical of other Algonquian peoples. In their efforts to understand Powhatan's role, the English sometimes termed him a "king" or "emperor." His title in his own language, as noted earlier, was *mamanatowick,* a word derived from the root *Manitou,* meaning, roughly, supernatural or spiritual power. He is best described in English as a "principle" or "paramount chief," if one includes in that concept a sacerdotal role. Anthropologist Helen Rountree, the leading authority on the Powhatans, has summarized current understandings of Wahunsenacawh's office. She finds that he clearly played a central ceremonial and religious role in the life of his people, and served as a powerful political unifier. However, his authority over his subjects was limited. He could not always command the obedience of the lesser chiefs, having "only partial control over the distant parts of his 'domain' and relatively little power over even the loyalists close to home." He was unable to prevent conflicts between rival chiefs in his Confederation. Indeed, in the incidents observed by the English, he did not intervene at all. Nor did his authority extend to disputes between tribal members, who were expected to exact their own private vengeance for injuries and murder. However, those who openly defied chiefs and priests were, on occasion, put to death by Powhatan. English observations of those executions led to an exaggerated view of the paramount chief's power. That misunderstanding led the English to suspect Powhatan of treachery when lesser chiefs failed to honor the guarantees and promises he had given them.[17]

As noted earlier, Powhatan was the head of a tributary network of some 30 discrete tribal units in the Virginia tidewater. Their total population is believed to have been around 15,000. Strachey claimed that they paid tribute to Powhatan amounting to some 80 percent of their food supply and trade goods. Included in that tribute, according to Smith, were "skinnes, beades, copper, pearle, deares, turkies, wild beasts, and corn." The 80-percent estimate is doubtlessly an exaggeration. It is likely that tribute to Powhatan consisted primarily of nonperishable, non-foodstuff items like copper and pearls. Although some scholars believe that he was the head of an elaborate intertribal redistributive network, the evidence is inconclusive. Powhatan probably was not in control of basic food distribution, but he and the *werowances* did possess many goods of an exotic nature obtained largely through trade, goods believed to be of great supernatural potency. John Smith made note of a large structure, some 50 or 60 yards in length, in which Powhatan housed a "Treasure, as skinnes, copper, pearle and beades, which he storeth up against the time of his death and burial." That depository was presided over by priests and guarded at each corner by "Images as Sentinels, one of a Dragon, another a Beare, the 3(rd) like a Leopard and the fourth a giantlike man, all made evill forwadwardly, according to the best workmanship." After death, the *mamanatowick's* remains, mummified and bedecked with necklaces of copper and pearl, would be placed with great pomp in a temple.[18]

Despite those signs of high status and power, Powhatan did not lead the life of luxurious leisure contemporary Europeans associated with monarchy. Smith, as we have noted, was struck by Powhatan's physical strength, by his ability, despite his advanced age, to endure any labor. The evidence indicates that Powhatan, when not exercising the ritual and administrative tasks of his office, did work as a hunter along with his "subjects." The Powhatan economy did not generate substantial surpluses. It is estimated that about half the total caloric intake came from horticultural products—corn, beans, squash, primarily—cultivated by the women. In the absence of domesticated animals, hunting and fishing remained essential sources of protein.[19]

Powhatan's military command was not absolute, as several reports indicated that he had to offer incentives, in the form of special gifts, to induce some of his *werowances* to send men to join his various war parties. His control over the half dozen tribes he inherited was tighter than his authority over the larger number he had incorporated later. As Rountree has noted, "the groups on the periphery of the empire retained considerable autonomy, despite Powhatan's confident statements to the English." In 1612, while the Powhatans were at war with the English, the Patawomecks entered into a trade agreement with Jamestown that furnished the colony with badly needed foodstuffs. The Patawomecks, who lived on the South bank of the river later named after them, were ostensibly part of Powhatan's empire. The various members of the Powhatan Confederacy often made their own decisions about relations with the English. This was particularly true of those who lived at some distance from the paramount chief. His control over the Eastern Shore and South bank of the Potomac was particularly tenuous. The Patawomecks, like the Chickahominys, provided aid to the English at Jamestown in their struggles against Powhatan.[20]

The English who landed on the James River shore in 1607 were not the first Europeans to encounter Powhatan's people. As we have noted, Captain John Smith and others came to believe that Powhatan had exterminated the Roanoke survivors several years earlier. The evidence on that matter, as noted earlier, is inconclusive. However, there was another, better documented encounter early in the paramount chief's career that may have influenced his response to the English presence. Indians had killed some Spanish Jesuit missionaries on the York River some three decades before the English landing at Jamestown, and had suffered in consequence a brutal Spanish reprisal. We must digress to tell the story of the ill-fated Jesuit mission. Accompanied by a local Indian they called Don Luis de Valasco, the Jesuits in 1570 established a small outpost in a region the local inhabitants called "Ajacan." Their Indian guide, formerly the chief of a village farther upriver, had been taken to Spain in 1561 on a Spanish ship that had conducted an exploratory probe of the Chesapeake Bay region. Don Luis's exact identity is not clear. One tradition suggests that he was Powhatan's brother Opechancanough, but that is highly unlikely, because Opechancanough did not appear to have the knowledge of European culture that Don Luis would have gained. The sources do agree that Don Luis was a member of a local ruling family and suggest that he personally had claim on a chiefdomship.[21]

In Spain, Don Luis embraced the Catholic faith, met King Philip II, won that monarch's favor, and finally persuaded his hosts to send him back to Virginia. After a sojourn of several years in Mexico, where he fell ill and nearly died, Don Luis set sail for North America under the sponsorship of Pedro de Menéndez de Avilés, an ardent expansionist who hoped to follow his recent extermination of a French Protestant colony in Florida with the establishment of a chain of Spanish outposts extending up the Atlantic coast. Don Luis, Menéndez believed, would be ideally suited to assist in the conversion of the local inhabitants to the true faith. However, in 1566, the ship Menéndez dispatched to the Chesapeake with Don Luis and several missionaries aboard failed to find the bay and, after wandering along the coast in stormy weather, made its way back to Spain. It was not until 1570 that Don Luis, then based in Cuba, was able to join a small group of Jesuits intent upon the conversion of the Indians of his homeland.

Don Luis and the Spanish missionaries found, as one Jesuit report related, a land that had been afflicted

> with six years of famine and death. . . . Since many have died and many also have moved to other regions to ease their hunger, there remain but few of the tribe, whose leaders say that they wish to die where their fathers have died, although they have no maize and have not found wild fruit.

For a few days, Don Luis assisted the Jesuits in their uncertain efforts to establish productive relations with the starving inhabitants, hoping to provide them with seed and teach them new methods of farming. However, Don Luis, although badly needed as an interpreter, abruptly abandoned the missionaries and rejoined his relatives in a village ruled by his uncle some 30 or 40 miles away.[22]

Some months later, the Jesuits, wondering why he had not returned, were scandalized to learn that once established there, their convert "allowed himself free reign in his sins, marrying many women in a pagan way." Jesuit efforts to persuade Don Luis to return to the mission, acknowledge his sins, obey the Fathers, and assist them again in their struggle for survival backfired. Angry, no doubt humiliated by the reprimand, their Indian convert first killed their emissaries, then led a war party that wiped out all the Spaniards with the exception of Alonso, a young boy. The Jesuits who reviewed the account of the massacre later provided by Alonso declared Don Luis "a second Judas." During the following year, Menéndez sailed to Ajacan, slaughtered a number of Indians, rescued the captive boy who was living in a nearby village as the adopted son of a local chief, demanded that Don Luis be surrendered to the Spanish, and, when refused, hanged eight or nine hostages from his ship's rigging. At one point, the Spanish ship approached the river's bank, as if to parlay, then opened fire killing a number of Indians who had flocked to the shore. A Jesuit account of the revenging of the missionaries declared with much satisfaction that Menéndez's actions had left "the country very frightened."[23]

Why were the Jesuit missionaries killed? The accounts of their "martyrdom," based on Alonso's recollections and written by other members of the order, stressed Don Luis's sinfulness and suggested that he acted under the inspiration of the devil himself. Upon his return to his uncle's village, Don Luis, declared one Jesuit narrator, "indulged in vices and sins publicly without fear of God or man." The sole example of his sinfulness provided in this explanation was "the marrying of many women in a pagan way." The Jesuit Father sent to persuade Don Luis to repent and abandon "his sinful life" found that neither reason "nor any other method" of persuasion "had any effect." Because members of Algonquian ruling families were not only allowed, but expected, to take multiple wives, the Jesuit demand was not only insulting in its imputation of sin, but also degrading. To submit would be to lose status. Most later historians agreed with the Jesuits that conflict over Don Luis's marital status triggered the massacre of the missionaries. However, there may have been other points of conflict as well, including the Jesuit failure to reciprocate properly for gifts of food in a time of terrible scarcity and resentment over their providing a nearby village hostile to Don Luis with iron hatchets. On one point we are clear: This encounter with the Spanish left a lingering distrust, if not fear, of Europeans among the Indians of the region. It may also have given impetus to the movement of political consolidation led by Powhatan from the 1680s onward.[24]

There were other, less clearly documented encounters with Europeans prior to 1607 that had ended badly. English records relate that a ship captained by Bartholomew Gilbert driven off course by a storm in July 1603, entered an unidentified bay that may have been the Chesapeake. Indians attacked and killed five members of its landing party, including the captain. Powhatan's people told the story of another European ship of uncertain nationality that visited Powhatan himself around the same time, but despite a friendly reception, proceeded to murder the *werowance* of Rappahannock and kidnap several of his people. Some believe the ship in question was captained by Samuel Mace, an associate of Gilbert's, and that the abducted Indians may have been the ones "who are documented in 1603 as giving a canoe-handling demonstration on the Thames River."[25]

How did Powhatan react in 1607 to word that the English had returned? We do not really know. It is possible, but by no means certain, that the warriors who attacked the colonists at their first landing and later as they built Jamestown were acting under the paramount chief's direct orders. Writing in 1612, William Strachey, who served for a time as secretary to the Jamestown colony, suggested that Powhatan had been frightened by a shaman's prophecy that warned that "from the Chesapeake bay a nation should arise which should dissolve and give end to his empire." Strachey believed that, in response to that warning, Powhatan, during the year previous to the Jamestown landing, had attacked and exterminated the Chesapeake tribe. Did Powhatan now fear that the English in fact might be the people of whom the prophet warned? Strachey thought so, but the evidence raises doubts. After the initial skirmishes, Powhatan vacillated. We don't know why. Perhaps he was reassured by reports of the weaknesses of the Jamestown settlers, and thus discounted them as a serious threat. One historian writes that as they watched through spring and summer 1607, the Powhatans

remained most perplexed by the baffling behavior of the white aliens. Because the strangers did not hunt, fish, or clear fields as was expected of Indian men, arrived without women from an unknown world, and died in droves on an abandoned peninsula of "waste ground" while harvesting common timber, the Powhatans could only conclude that the English were an odd, inferior race from a desolate homeland, most similar to the primitive, non-farming Monacan "barbarians"—except for their awesome ships and sophisticated weapons.[26]

However, those weapons were pretty frightening. After weighing reports from the abortive assault on Jamestown, Powhatan, on June 25, sent a messenger who, as one settler recorded, declared that "he desired greatly our friendshipp," and offered assurances the *werowances* who had previously attacked the fort would now live in peace with the newcomers. They were henceforth obligated to let the English "sowe and reape in peace." If they failed to do so, he promised to join with the English and "make warrs upon them."[27]

That bold declaration notwithstanding, the peace Powhatan proclaimed, in reality was nothing more than a very uneasy truce. Indian attacks were much less frequent in the succeeding months, but they never entirely ceased. Some no doubt occurred without Powhatan's knowledge. However, the paramount chief and his people never trusted these strange newcomers. Strachey related that the Powhatans were soon troubled by a new prophecy that foretold that they would fight three battles against invaders, win the first two, but then "fall into their subjection, and under their conquest." In consequence, "suspicions have bred strange feares amongst them," as the Indians reacted with terror to "the noyse of our drums, of our shrill trumpets and great ordinance." Their leader came to be obsessed by the suspicion that the English at Jamestown intended to mount a surprise attack and take "awaye his land from him." Strachey believed that Powhatan's fear was constantly "inflamed by his furious and bloudy priests," the same malevolent prophets who, he believed, had inspired his extermination of the Roanoke survivors some years earlier. Although Powhatan blamed the sporadic but continuing Indian attacks on Jamestown settlers as the actions of unruly individuals or disobedient lesser *werowances,* he was, Strachey believed, only waiting for the right moment to unleash an exterminatory war. Strachey's account is, of course, biased, but it tells us much about the mutual suspicion and lingering fear that characterized English–Powhatan relations during the early years of the Virginia colony. The principle chief's edginess, however, cannot be explained away as the work of Powhatan's "furious and bloudy priests." Conflicts over access to food resources and the English attempt to expand and build new settlements, as we shall see, gave substance to Powhatan's anxieties in the years immediately after the founding of James Fort. There is another point that must be made. Strachey did not recognize that, because Powhatan—during the early years of contact—enjoyed a manpower advantage of at least 30 to 1 and possessed food resources the Jamestown colonists lacked, he could have easily wiped out the colony had he resolved to do so. His responses to the English presence, in fact, were both complex and contradictory.[28]

Despite Powhatan's initial declaration of friendship, Jamestown suffered an alarming increase in mortality in summer 1607. Built on swampy ground, the fort lacked a supply of clean water, so many sickened and died from drinking from a river "full of slime and filth." Modern analysis of the records indicates a massive outbreak of typhus, complicated by beriberi. The infected were greatly weakened by malnutrition. Under the incompetent leadership of the hapless Wingfield, the colony, ridden with factionalism and burdened with gentlemen adventurers who did not care to labor, could not feed itself, but waited passively for supplies from England or hoped for help from the Indians who, given the drought, were simply not able to provide the quantities of food required. Before the summer ended, half the colonists were dead. Although occasional Indian raiding parties continued to strike and kill, they accounted for only a very few of the total deaths at Jamestown. "For the most part," Percy wrote of his compatriots, "they died of mere famine." Some limited trade with the local Indians, exchanging hatchets and trinkets for food, helped but fell far short of Jamestown's needs. Only divine providence, Percy believed, saved the colony from total extermination at the hands of the "savages."

> If it had not pleased God to have put a terrour in the savages hearts, we had all perished by these wild and cruel Pagans, being in that weak estate as we were; our men night and day groaning in every corner of the Fort most pitiful to heare, if there were any conscience in men, it would make their harts to bleed to heare the pitiful murmurings & out-cries of our sick men without reliefe every night and day for the space of sixe weekes, some departing out of the World, many times three or four a night, in the mourning trailed out of their Cabines like Dogges to be buried; in this sort did I see the mortalitie of divers of our people.[29]

Powhatan's people were suffering from a drought that had lasted some seven years and deprived them of much of their accustomed food surpluses. They did not have the means to supply all of Jamestown's requirements. Nonetheless, when a stunted late-summer crop finally came in, Powhatan ordered his *werowances* to send food to the English. In Percy's recollection:

> It pleased God, after a while, to send those people who were our mortall enemies to releeve us with victuals, as Bread, Corne, Fish, and Flesh in great plenty, which was the setting up of our feeble men, otherwise wee had all perished. Also we were frequented by divers Kings in the Countrie, bringing us store of provisions to our great comfort.[30]

Although Percy and other English commentators, including John Smith, were convinced that God had softened Powhatan's savage heart, there are other more mundane explanations of his actions, specifically his desire to acquire English trade goods and his determination to strengthen and secure his own position by incorporating the English as subjects and allies. In Virginian Algonquian society, copper, which the English could offer in trade, was the paramount symbol of wealth and power believed to be of supernatural origin, so exchanges of corn for that metal they regarded as very favorable transactions. The Powhatans, in common with other Native American peoples, believed that shiny English metal and glass objects possessed magical properties. One scholar has argued very plausibly that it was the Powhatans' interest in acquiring from the English "such media of power" that saved the colony in its first years. The harder metals, iron and steel, and implements made from them, were also highly desirable. The Powhatan Indians were a Stone Age people living in a region where even stone was scarce and bone often utilized. Their interest in the acquisition of steel weapons and of guns was intense. Powhatan was fascinated by artillery and at one point asked the English to send him cannons. English weaponry, he believed, might well guarantee his political supremacy. A chronicler of Christopher Newport's 1607 expedition into the interior related that, on first hearing the discharge of a cannon, the Indians were terrified, stopping up their ears and even leaping into the water from aboard Newport's shallop. However, when he told the local *werowance* that the English would assist him in his wars by using "this thunder . . . to Terrify and kill his Adversaries," he "rejoiced." That promise, the narrator noted, "bred a better affection in him toward us." The Jamestown men sought to cultivate the favor of their neighbors with such promises. Newport, on one occasion, even claimed that a cross the English erected in their territory symbolized their alliance with a local tribe.[31]

Powhatan hoped for an English alliance, but he wanted that alliance on his own terms. He regarded trade exchanges with the newcomers as something more than "ritual expressions of professed friendship" between independent peoples. They were rather "a conscious effort to incorporate the strangers, or *tassantasses,* into the native system of exchange and tribute." The English were expected to become Powhatan's subjects and fight on their behalf. The Jamestown settlers, as we shall see, had a different idea about the relationship, and intended to incorporate the Powhatans into their own polity. A key to understanding the recurrent violence that plagued early English–Powhatan relations lies in their mutual failure to achieve an objective from which neither deviated: the incorporation of the other. There were, as we shall see, a number of reasons for that failure, including mutual misperceptions and suspicions, errors of leadership on both sides, and, ultimately, a radical incompatibility of economic systems as well as religious beliefs and practices.[32]

Captain John Smith, the flamboyant, controversial, self-made leader who would shortly be entrusted with the conduct of relations with the Powhatans, provided (after his return to England) a succinct statement of his understanding of Indian character that tells us much about English attitudes. Despite personality differences—some being bolder and more aggressive than others—all Indians, the Captain asserted, were "savages" and "inconstant in everie thing but what feare constraineth them to keepe." Although they were highly intelligent ("quicke of apprehension"), they were by nature not trustworthy, but rather "craftie." Above all, Indians were vengeful, "soone moved to anger and so malitious, that they seldom forget an injury." Such people could not be trusted nor dealt with in terms of honor or even self-interest. The Indians, Smith believed, could be managed only through intimidation. Any other policy, in his view, would lead to disaster.[33]

In none of the Jamestown narratives do we find any dissent from Smith's view of Indian character, even though some argued on practical grounds that his treatment of the Indians was too harsh. It was generally agreed that all "savages" were essentially malevolent. The older, hopeful belief in Indian goodness cannot be found in the reports from Jamestown after the initial conflicts with local tribes. Some commentators, like Smith, spoke highly of the natives' intelligence, resourcefulness, and courage, but never of their moral integrity. As we have seen, Powhatan's generosity in saving the colony from starvation was attributed, not to his benevolence or, even more realistically, to his self-interest, but to divine intervention, God having held in check, for a time, his naturally cruel nature. That cruelty, moreover, reflected something truly sinister: an alliance with the devil himself. The Jamestown colonists commonly believed that the Powhatans, when not so restrained by the Almighty, sacrificed prisoners to the devil, and did so in a singularly sadistic manner. Percy, to cite just one of several examples, related that Captain John Ratcliffe, seized during an abortive trade mission, was stripped naked, tied to a tree, skinned alive by women wielding mussel shells, and forced to watch his own dismembered flesh burn in a nearby fire.[34]

In no area of Powhatan culture were English perceptions more distorted than in their perceptions of Indian religion. The most comprehensive accounts of the customs and mores of the coastal Virginia Algonquian were written by Captain John Smith and by William Strachey, who drew heavily on Smith but added some observations of his own. Both agreed that the Powhatans were satanists who did not worship a benevolent creator god or affirm in their devotions the principles of love and charity. Instead, Smith explained that they bestowed "their kinde of divine worship" on "all things that were able to do them hurt beyond their prevention," examples being fire, water, lightning, thunder, and even English guns and horses. "But," Smith continued, "their chiefe God they worship is the Divill, they call him *Oke* and serve him more of feare then love." Strachey added that the Powhatans did not bother to worship the creator god Ahone, because he was by nature benevolent and not to be feared.[35]

Smith (and others) believed that they had found definitive proof of their devil worship in a ceremony they called "the Black Boys." His evidence came from an eyewitness description of what appeared to be a human sacrifice provided by William White, a settler who had taken temporary refuge in the nearby Indian village of Quiyoughcohannock to escape the famine at Jamestown. As Smith recorded the story White told when he returned to Jamestown, the local *werowance* staged a great ceremony wherein the town's people, painted, some "blacke like Divells, with hornes and loose haire, some of divers colours," were marshaled into two opposing columns that danced in a quarter mile circle for two days, emitting a "hellish noise" when the columns converged. As the dance proceeded, 14 or 15 young boys between the ages of 10 to 15 years painted white were confined under guard at "the roote of a tree." At the end the dance, "priests" came to claim the boys. The women of the village then wept and cried out "very passionately," and brought "Mosses, skinnes, Mats, and dry wood as things fitting the childrens Funerall." The boys were beaten by their guards, then carried away "into a Valley where the King [*werowance*] sate." Although kept at a distance, White saw men with cudgels dancing around the prostrate children, as others brought piles of wood to the *werowance* who stood before an altar. They then made a "great fire" of the wood—a fire, White was convinced, that was used "to sacrifice their children to the Divell [whom they call Kewase]." Barred from the ceremonial ground, White did not see the end of the ceremony, but the continuing lamentations of the women persuaded him that the children had been immolated.[36]

John Smith retold White's story many times, adding in one version an account of a conversation with the *werowance* who presided over this ceremony who presumably explained that only some of the boys had been killed, not by cremation, but by having their blood drained by Oke. The survivors were made "their Priests and conjurers." Why was the killing of children necessary? The *werowance* allegedly explained if they "should omit it, their Oke or Divell, and their other Quiyoungcosughes, or gods, would let them have no Deere, Turkies, Corne, or Fish, and would make a great slaughter among them."[37]

The story of the Black Boys is found in several other early reports from Jamestown. It served very well to emphasize and dramatize the dominant and malevolent image of the indigenous peoples, which served to rationalize violence against them. However, the story was not true. To his embarrassment, Samuel Purchas, who printed the original White account as retold by Smith in his great collection of reports from overseas, later learned that several of the children for whom the women reportedly mourned were later seen alive. He accordingly removed the reference to human sacrifice from the 1625 edition of his travel compendium and blamed the Virginia Indians for deceiving their English visitors. Their "false reports . . . delude our Men, and say they were sacrificed when they were not . . . the mourning of the women is not for their children's death, but because they are for divers months detained from them." White, it is now clear, had witnessed a puberty ceremony, not a human sacrifice. Purchas's claim that Smith was misled by the Indians into believing the boys were actually killed is, of course, improbable. It is far more likely that they tried to explain that they had killed none of the boys. The ones whose blood was drained by Oke were considered dead, not because they had been slain literally, but because they had been called to become his "priests" and were thus removed from the mundane. As Williamson notes, among the Powhatans,

a shaman's life was the inverse of the ordinary man's. He lived in the wilderness; pursued no productive economic activities, remained unmarried and apparently childless, wore his clothing inside out; painted himself black instead of red or white; shaved his head but sometimes wore a beard; and had as his dwelling a sepulcher in which the figure of Oke, lord of the underworld, was also kept.

They were then "to be classified with the dead rather than the living."[38]

The Black Boy ritual, called the *huskanaw* by the Powhatans, for all participants was an exceedingly demanding process of initiation into manhood that lasted several months. From conversations with Indian participants, the English were given to understand that in addition to physical trials, including beatings, the initiates were also subjected to drugs derived from various roots that produced mental derangement. It may well be that some of the boys did not survive, but this was not a human sacrifice ritual dedicated to the devil. As Helen Rountree notes, essentially the Black Boys were "ceremonially 'killed,'" then "reborn as [real] men." "Rebirth," she adds, "is often a leitmotif of male puberty rites, but rarely is it acted out with such long-term violence. But the Powhatan *huskanaw* combined two functions common to male puberty rituals in other parts of the world: hazing to gain the victims' loyalty, and a shared secret to set them off from others." The ceremony reflected the needs and values of a militant chiefdom-level society frequently at war with its neighbors. It was intended to give birth for future priests and future *werowances* to the new governing elite. The word *huskanaw* meant "he has a new body."[39]

For the English, belief that human sacrifice was occurring among the Powhatans was far too useful to be set aside. The story persisted, enjoying wide circulation for many decades after the exposure of its errors. Robert Beverley repeated Smith's account in *The History and Present State of Virginia,* published in 1705, and although noting that some had doubted its accuracy, he argued that there were eyewitnesses. Whatever the case with the Black Boys, Beverley followed earlier English writers in stressing that Indian worship was satanic. "They use many Divinations and Inchantments, and frequently offer Burnt sacrifice to the Evil Spirit."[40]

The English characterization of Ahone as an equivalent of the creator god and of Oke as the devil was as misconceived as the White/Smith tale about child sacrifice. Algonquian deities were not thought of in dualistic terms, and their creator gods, unlike the Christian creator, were neither omnipotent nor omnipresent. They were, in fact, generally unconcerned with human affairs. Williamson suggests that the term "Oke" probably did not only designate a particular deity, but may also have been equivalent to the terms used to designate spirit power, having roughly the same meaning as *manitos* used by other Algonquian speakers, and as the Sioux *waken* and the Iroquois *orenda.* This may well be, but quite apart from the question of what Powhatans meant when they spoke of Oke, it is now well established that Native Americans generally believed the world to be permeated by a power or presence conceived of as the force that gave potency not only to human beings, but most specifically to various other-than-human beings (gods, spirits, demons) and to some animals. It was not a supernatural transmission from some anthropomorphic deity or devil, but was inherent in the world itself. It might well be embodied in some apparently inanimate material object. There is no reason to believe that the Powhatans conceived of reality in any other terms. Although the Jamestown records give no indication that the early English settlers understood the underlying premises of Native American spirituality, Beverley, a century later, noted that the Virginia Indians believed all their "idols" partook "of the same nature." The "wonderful power . . . with which the universe is believed to be charged," noted Ruth Benedict, was seen as morally neutral, and could be used for good or ill. Its attainment, for the benefit of both individuals and the community, was the central purpose of Native American religious practice and ritual. The men the English called "priests and conjurors" and equated with witches were, in fact, dedicated to securing and manipulating spirit power for the common good. However, the English in Virginia did not understand that fundamental fact about Powhatan culture.[41]

William Strachey believed that Indian religious leaders were so evil that both the protection of the English and the well-being of the Powhatans required their extermination. He based his call for their mass killing in part on the Black Boys story. "These monsters doe offer up unto the devil their own children and being hardened against all compassion, naturall and divine, enforce their own mothers to deliver them to the execution with their own hands." Their priests, if not eliminated, would see "to the destruction and extirpation of all straungers, knowing or acknowledging the true god." He alleged that it was at their insistence that Powhatan had massacred the Roanoke survivors. In seeking means to secure the safety of Jamestown, Strachey found guidance and inspiration in the biblical example of Jehu, King of Israel, who pleased God when he "assembled all of the priests of Baal, and slew them, to the last man, in their own temple." Strachey's proposal was not original. In instructions to the Virginia colonists in 1610, the Company declared that Indian "priests" were hopelessly bonded to the devil and would therefore continue to "poison and infect" all around them. There could never be "civil peace" until the English removed them. If necessary, they should be killed.[42]

Several London–based divines in the pay of the Virginia Company were even more extreme. Their sermons, often delivered in the great open-air space called "St. Paul's Cross" (by the cathedral) sometimes contained justifications of practices that would later be termed "genocide" and "ethnic cleansing," all grounded in assumptions about the debased nature of Indians and their culture. In *A Good Speed to Virginia* (1609), the Reverend Robert Gray expatiated on Joshua 17:14, wherein God assures the Israelites that they will drive the Canaanites out of the Promised Land. Virginia, Gray proclaimed, is England's Canaan. Although it was true that God "had given the earth to the children of men," the Indians had no right to share in that inheritance, by reason of "their godless ignorance and blasphemous idolatry." They were not truly human, but partook of "the nature of beasts." In fact, they were "worse than those beasts which are of most wild and savage nature." Like the Canaanites, they were to be driven out of the land by God's people. The Reverend William Symonds, in a sermon published the same year, also invoked the Canaan analogy and declared that those Indians who resisted the English presence should be dealt with as the Israelites of Old dealt with the Canaanites. Convinced that Indian blood was tainted, Symonds declared it essential that the English in Virginia not intermarry with "savages."[43]

Gray and Symonds were extreme in their very negative assessments of Indian potential and their justification of genocide. Other English divines—Daniel Price, Richard Crakanthorpe, George Benson, Robert Tynley, and Richard Eburne—held the founding of Virginia a part of the divine plan for the conversion of her benighted people, who were to be raised to "civility, and brought to Christ," not exterminated. All agreed, however, on the essentially satanic nature of Indian religion and on the deep-seated flaws in the Indian character. It is telling that when Robert Johnson, speaking for the Council for Virginia in 1612, urged the colonists to follow a policy of "peace and gentleness," he added that through "patience and humility" they would be able "to manage their crooked nature to your form of civility." Clearly, Johnson, who never crossed the Atlantic, agreed with those who emphasized the need to transform the Indians' "crooked nature." The colonists themselves were far less sanguine than Johnson about the transformative power of "peace and gentleness."[44]

The image of Indians as satanists was sustained not only by persistent stories about the killing of the Black Boys, but also by distorted and often grotesque descriptions of Native American religious rites. The Reverend Alexander Whitaker, writing from Virginia in 1613, declared "their Priests . . . are no other than such as our English witches are," and added a description of what was probably a curing rite wherein the "witch," through bodily contortions, presumably gave evidence of being "possessed of some evil spirit." John Smith, describing a similar scene in an earlier report, wrote "a more uglier thing cannot be described . . . to cure the sick a man with a Rattle and extreme howling, shouting, singing, and such violent gestures, and Anticke actions over the patient will suck out blood and flegme from the patient out of their unable stomacke, and any diseased place, as no labor will more tire them." In proof of the essentially satanic nature of the being they worshipped, Smith, when describing their "temples," wrote of idols, fashioned "with such deformity as may well suit with such a god." Within their temples were found the mummified bodies of dead *werowances* as well as an image of the devil god Oke adorned with strings of pearls, as well as effigies of wolves, ravens, foxes, and other wild animals stuffed with straw with beads in their eye sockets. The overall effect was truly sinister.[45]

Strachey prefaced his account of the religion of the Powhatans with the assertion that Indians were the descents of Ham, the son of Noah exiled and cursed by God for viewing his father's drunken nakedness. In consequence of that curse, they had become "so grosse and barbarous" that it was hard to see any difference "between them and brute beasts." Indeed, their worship consisted of adoration of "brute beasts, naie, things more vile," as the Indians had now lost "the inbredded notions of nature itself." They had fallen into "bloody ceremonies." In their temples, pagan priests, "painted as ugly as they can devise," communed with Satan himself. Out of doors, on higher ground, their conjurors, standing on rocks or sometimes deep within "thick and solitary woodes," invoked demons "with most impetuous clamours and howlings, and with such paynes and strained accions," making the countryside resound with their violent invocations, after which they collapsed "in a sweat."[46]

English observers of Powhatan "priests and conjurors" agreed that they wielded great power, not only in advising on policy matters, but also often in dictating their course. Strachey declared that they "do at all tymes . . . absolutely govern and direct the werowances." Smith also saw their role as more than advisory, declaring that, in policy disputes, "chiefly the priests determine their resolution." The Powhatan Confederacy, as one recent historian demonstrates, was a "dyarchy" with "dual rule by a religious authority and a secular power." Although the local *werowances* were subordinate to the local religious leaders, Powhatan himself was a sacerdotal figure, "accorded semi-divine status among his people . . . the priestly king of his polity." English reports from Jamestown, after one discounts their obsession with satanism, shed much light on the functions of "priests and conjurors." Some performed priestly functions in the sense that they invoked power external to themselves through the performance of ceremonies that, through ritual, guaranteed the continuation of communal life. Those rituals often included sacrifices intended to reenact the creator's killing of the primal deer and its regeneration, an act that "brought about both fecundity and social order" by the miraculous birth of hosts of deer from the hairs of the victim, thereby "producing life from death." Other sacrifices served "to avert or dispel divine anger and to offer thanksgiving." Powhatan religious life also depended upon the shaman, whose power was personal and individual. Among shamanic functions were the healing of the sick, the control of weather, the summoning of game, the empowerment of warriors, and the foretelling of the future. Belief in their potency endowed the shamans with exceptional influence in the Powhatan polity.[47]

The indigenous society the Jamestown planters encountered was an evolving and expansionist principal chiefdomship grounded in a value system in which courage and success in battle were the hallmarks of manhood. Prisoners of war, including Englishmen on occasion, were commonly tortured to death by flaying and dismemberment. They were expected to endure that torment stoically, indeed defiantly. The failure of English captives to observe that protocol, their propensity to cry out and scream under torture, earned them the contempt of the Powhatans. Strachey related that after several English captives pled for their lives and died badly, the Powhatans began singing a scornful song about cowardice whenever they encountered colonists. The Powhatan rites of torture were interpreted by the English as human sacrifices dedicated to the devil, but the Powhatans, like Indians elsewhere, placed limits on violence. They generally did not kill noncombatants. (Strachey's claim that Powhatan exterminated all of the Chesapeake is questionable.) Captive women and children were not tortured, but were commonly adopted into the tribe often after a period of enslavement. Enemy leaders, unlike other warriors, were usually spared. However, such restrictions on killing would soon be eroded, on both sides of the cultural divide, as English relations with the Powhatans deteriorated during the early years of colonization.[48]

CHAPTER 3

~

"To Subdue the Wilde Salvages":
Captain John Smith and the Powhatans

After an initial period of uncertainty and blundering, Indian relations at James-town were entrusted to Captain John Smith. His voluminous writings constitute our most important single source on those early interactions. To place Smith's actions and explanations in proper context, we must digress and consider some of the salient aspects of his personal history. In his autobiography, published in 1630, Smith wrote that the lessons he had learned as a young man in "the Warres in Europe, Asia and Affrica taught me how to subdue the wilde Salvages in Virginia, and New England, in America." Like many other statements in Smith's voluminous writings, that claim is problematic. He did not, in fact, subdue "the wilde Salvages." His dealings with the Powhatans and other Indian peoples did not lead to their acknowledgement of English supremacy or even to stable, productive relationships. Nor were they characterized by quite the same uncomplicated confrontational bra-vado we find in Smith's descriptions of his career as a soldier. However, we do find in his earlier life keys to his dealings with the Powhatans, as his larger than life persona left its stamp, sometimes for better, sometimes for worst, on the colony's interracial encounters.[1]

John Smith was born around 1580, at Willoughby in Lincolnshire. His father was a prosperous farmer. Smith's middling social status—he was not considered a "gentlemen," despite his father's extensive land holdings—would prove an obsta-cle to his ambition. A short, redheaded, and pugnacious boy, Smith, as he related, set his mind "upon brave adventures" and, while still a grammar school student, planned "secretly to get to sea." It is possible that he may have tried to run away. In any case, he was apprenticed at age 15 to a prominent import/export merchant at King's Lynn in nearby Norfolk. His father died a year later, and Smith, frus-trated by his master's refusal to send him abroad, left his apprenticeship before its expiration, obtained some funds from his grudging guardians, crossed the channel, and enlisted with the army of English Protestants fighting in France and in the low countries. After three or four years of undistinguished soldiering, he returned to his home village in England and obtained from the Lord of Willoughby, Peregrine Bertie, an appointment to serve as companion to the Lord's two young sons, who were about to set out on a tour of the continent. After a short stint in France with the Bertie brothers, he was released from their employment and journeyed to Scotland, where he tried unsuccessfully to gain a place at the court of King James VI. Scotland offered no opportunities for a young man of Smith's modest means and limited connections. Now 19 years old, he returned home, where, as he recalled, he found a remote wood-lined pasture and, by a brook, built "a Pavillon of boughs." There, aided by an admiring boy who served as his "page," Smith read *Machiavills Art of Warre* and *Marcus Aurelis,* dreamed again of "brave adventures," and engaged in military exercises. His friends, disturbed by his seclusion, persuaded the Earl of Lincoln's riding master, to call on him. His visitor was Theodore Paleologue, a descendent of the Byzantine emperors deposed by the Turks. Smith accompanied Paleologue to Tattersal castle, where he received training in horsemanship and listened to stories about the struggle to save Europe from the Muslim invaders.[2]

In 1600, Smith returned to the continent, intending to "trie his fortune against the Turks." As he reflected on his earlier military service in the low countries, he was "both lamenting and repenting to have seen so many Christians slaughter one another." En route to the holy war he was now eager to fight, he was robbed and stranded by French traveling companions, but, he claimed, was soon rescued by several well-bred ladies, the first in a string of noble women presumably captivated by the dashing young Englishman. Determined to make his way to Hungary, Smith boarded a ship at Marseilles bound for Italy. Beset by a storm in the Mediterranean, Smith's Catholic shipmates, as he told the story, decided that their lives were in jeopardy because there was a heretic in their midst and threw Smith overboard. To add insult to that injury, they loudly cursed all Englishmen as members of a race of pirates and reviled Queen Elizabeth. Smith swam to a nearby uninhabited island and hailed a passing ship. Taken aboard, he was given fresh clothes and some provisions by a kindly French passenger. After delivering cargo to several North African ports, the ship sailed on to the Adriatic, where it was fired upon by a Venetian vessel. In the battle that ensued, the Venetians lost, and Smith shared in the prize money. He made his way to Rome, watched Pope Clement VIII say mass at St. John Lateran, then went on to Austria, where he enlisted in a regiment commanded by the Protestant Count of Modrusch.[3]

In the war against the Turks, Smith proved to be an innovative and resourceful tactician. Drawing on his reading, he taught the Austrians to use torches to signal on the battlefield, thus improving the coordination of the Austrian forces. He devised a way to mislead the enemy by burning fuses up and down the line to give a false impression that a large force had assembled at places where, in fact, there were few Austrians. Those tactics were of great use in breaking the Turkish siege of lower Limbach. Smith also excelled at siege tactics, fabricating "fiery dragons" composed of gun powder, brimstone, camphor, turpentine, and linseed oil surrounded by chunks of musket ball, packed into pots and hurled by sling into the midst of the enemy. Smith's incendiaries were instrumental in retaking Alba Regalis, the ancient Hungarian capital at Stuhlwissenburg, a fortified city that had long been occupied by the Turks and was considered impregnable. In his autobiography, Smith, writing of his use of those "fiery dragons" at Alba Regalis, recalled that it was "a fearful sight to see the short flaming course of their flight in the aire, but presently after their fall, the lamentable noise of the miserable slaughtered Turkes was most wonderfull to heare." In recognition of his skill, Smith was soon promoted to captain and given his own command.[4]

Captain Smith's coat of arms, earned in Transylvania, displayed three severed Turkish heads. One represented the head of the Turkish commander Turbashaw, who had challenged the Christians besieging his headquarters to send a champion to meet him in man-to-man combat. Such a contest, the Turk claimed, would delight the ladies in his entourage who were bored by the slow course of the siege. Smith, selected by lot, impaled the Turk on the first thrust of their joist, then severed his head. The second head on Smith's emblem represented Grualgo, who tried to avenge Turbashaw on the field of honor and was shot and decapitated by Smith, who soon thereafter issued a challenge to the Turks to send out another contender. A man named Bonny Mulgrow accepted. As the Turks cheered their champion, Mulgrow gained the advantage, knocking the battle-ax from Smith's hands and nearly "dehorsing" him. Smith turned the tables on the Turk, however, driving his sword into a gap in his armor. "Although he alighted from his horse, he stood not long ere hee lost his head, as the rest had done." Smith claimed that after the beheading of Mulgrow, he was escorted to the commanding general's headquarters by an honor guard of 6,000. Three horsemen carried the severed heads on lances, trophies of war to be presented to the general. A renewed offensive against the Turks in Transylvania led to the fall of the town Turbashaw had tried to defend. For his part in the victory, Zsigmond, Prince of Transylvania, awarded Smith his coat of arms and a lifetime pension worth 300 ducats.[5]

His triumph was short-lived. A Turkish counteroffensive left 30,000 of Smith's comrades in arms dead. He was wounded, captured, and, "like a beast in the market place," sold into slavery. Chained by the neck to other enslaved prisoners of war, Smith was marched some 500 miles to Constantinople, where he was assigned to the service of Charatza Tragabigzanda, the mistress of his owner, the Bashaw Bogall. Then, as so often occurred in Smith's account of his adventurers, he charmed a lady, in this case Charatza herself. Enchanted by Smith's stories, angered by the Bashaw's false claim to have personally captured Smith in battle, the lady placed the Englishman in the care of her brother in Tartary with instructions that he be treated kindly and instructed in the Turkish language in preparation, Smith believed, for his ultimate emancipation. However, the brother disregarded her wishes and, instead, abused Smith, striping him naked, shaving his head, encasing his neck in an iron ring, feeding him on foul scraps of food, and putting him to hard labor. When the brother, however, alone in a field where his English slave was threshing grain, began to "beat, spurne and revile him," Smith killed his tormenter with a blow of his thresher, stole his clothing and horse, and set off "he knew not whither." He followed signs that by the emblem of the cross pointed to Russia and, after a desperate 16-day trek, found himself at a Russian outpost on the River Don. The Russians severed the iron ring from his neck. Once again a gracious lady, in this case named Callamata, "largely supplied all his wants." After a short sojourn in Russia, Smith made his way back to England (by way of central Europe, France, Spain, and North Africa), stopping briefly in Transylvania to obtain a parchment containing his coat of arms (which bestowed upon him the status of a gentleman) and to exchange his lifetime pension for $1,500 ducats.[6]

It is not clear to what extent we can believe Smith's account of all his fabulous adventures in Europe and Turkey. We have only his word for most of it. Some errors of fact—for example, the date of his parent's deaths—have been uncovered, but the claim, advanced by Hungarian historian Lewis L. Kropf in 1890, that Smith never set foot in Eastern Europe or the Levant has been proved false by analysis of historical details and geographical references in Smith's writings and by exposure of Kropf's misreading of sources. There may, however, be certain exaggerations or even fabrications in Smith's accounts of his adventures, accounts that were always driven by an intense self-promotion. Whatever the case, his autobiographical writings tell us much about Smith's character, his view of the world, and his sense of himself. He was a man of rash self-confidence, not given to doubt or self-analysis. He was a believer in bold self-exertion. He was bright, resourceful, and always interested in exotic and alien peoples, as the descriptions of his travels in the East attest. Those qualities were assets in his dealings with Virginia's indigenous peoples, even though his accomplishments in Indian diplomacy have often been exaggerated.[7]

Smith's activities immediately after his return to England cannot be traced. One story, told by Jamestown's first president, no admirer of the brash captain, held that he first went to Ireland, but failed to find a place there and ended up "begging like a rogue, without a license." That claim cannot be confirmed in any of Smith's writings, or in any other source. If he spent any time there, his sojourn was brief. He was soon on the lookout for overseas opportunities, and in 1605 considered taking part in an expedition to Guiana. He later expressed regret that he was not "a party to it," but offered no explanation. Not long after the Guiana voyagers departed, acquaintance with the adventurer Bartholomew Gosnold, veteran of two exploratory voyages to New England, opened up another opportunity. Smith joined the expedition, commanded by the one-armed privateer Christopher Newport, with Gosnold second in command, that would found Jamestown in Virginia.[8]

Smith's relationship with his shipmates on the cross-Atlantic voyage was troubled. He soon clashed with the high-born Edward Maria Wingfield, a portly, self-satisfied 56-year-old former soldier who had fought in Ireland and the low countries and who, alone of the voyagers, was a patentee of the Virginia Company.

Wingfield, acutely conscious of his own status, regarded Smith as an insubordinate social inferior, a brash troublemaker who threatened his own authority. His dislike and distrust was shared by some other members of the Company who, among other things, were angered when Smith vehemently supported his friend the controversial Protestant chaplain Robert Hunt, who had been accused of being some sort of religious schismatic. Smith's enemies allegedly charged him with trying to foment a mutiny. He related that he was "restrained as a prisoner, upon the scandalous suggestion of some of the chiefe (envying his repute), who feigned that he intended to usurp the government, murder the Council, and make himself king." Smith biographer Philip L. Barbour comments: "It is impossible to know whether anyone actually accused Smith of such preposterous notions or plans, for the percentage of pure rhetoric in Elizabethan verbal pageantry is not always simple to calculate."[9]

Whatever the circumstances, Newport responded to the complaints of Wingfield and others by imprisoning Smith below deck on the *Susan Constant*, but released him during landfall on the island of Nevis in the Caribbean. Smith soon fell into an altercation with other members of the expedition. The events that then transpired are puzzling. Smith was apparently condemned to death. His enemies ordered the construction of a pair of gallows, but, as Smith later wrote, "Captain Smith, for whom they were intended, could not be persuaded to use them." We do not know why the execution was canceled. It is most likely that Captain Newport, well aware, as others may not have been, of the esteem in which Smith was held by some of the London associates, found it expedient to overrule Wingfield and his friends. He may also have believed that the charges were without foundation. It is telling that, after Wingfield fell from favor at Jamestown, Smith won a libel suit against him, a suit that charged Wingfield had falsely accused Smith of having concealed his knowledge that some others were plotting a mutiny. In any case, instead of dying on the gallows on Nevis, Smith was imprisoned once again and remained in restraint at the time of the landing in Virginia. The voyage had taken four months. Smith was imprisoned below deck throughout most of the voyage.[10]

During the crossing, the identity of the colony's seven-member governing Council was kept secret, so as to not impinge upon Newport's command authority. Upon landing in Virginia, the instructions were unsealed. Wingfield's name was on the list, to no one's surprise, and he was promptly elected president. However, the alleged traitor John Smith was also named a member of the governing Council, an honor not extended to several men of greater social prominence. The planners of the Virginia venture obviously valued Smith's expertise as soldier, but the other Council members, yielding to pressure from Wingfield, initially refused to admit Smith into their deliberations. He was, however, released from confinement, and in late May accompanied Newport's party on an expedition into the interior. As we have noted, it was during that exploratory probe that the English first learned of Powhatan. Smith later recorded that although some of the Indian villages they visited appeared friendly, others he described as "churlish."

His suspicions of Indian hostility were confirmed when Newport's party returned to discover that Jamestown had been attacked.[11]

On June 6, the Council, urged by chaplain Hunt and by Bartholomew Gosnold, revoked its prior action and seated Smith as a member of the governing Council. The Council and the fledgling colony were soon engulfed in bickering and dissension originating in personality conflicts exacerbated by the hardships of the summer's famine. The well-fed Wingfield was removed as president, charged with hoarding food and other acts of malfeasance, and imprisoned aboard ship. He was succeeded by John Ratcliffe, a man of questionable background whose real name appears to have been Sicklemore. A faction soon formed to agitate against Ratcliffe, who was suspected of being a spy and possibly a Papist. Ratcliffe, catching wind of a plot to restore Wingfield, fell into an altercation with the blacksmith James Read, whom he had tried and condemned to death for mutiny. As Read was led to the gallows, the condemned man begged for an audience with Ratcliffe, and when that was granted, claimed that George Kendall, another man of questionable background, was the ringleader of the Wingfield restoration movement. Ratcliffe pardoned Read, imprisoned Kendall with Wingfield, then had him tried for mutiny and shot. Kendall's revelation of Ratcliffe's real name did not save him, but contributed to the atmosphere of distrust that infected Jamestown. In the midst of this intrigue and turmoil, Smith, quietly allied to the anti-Ratcliffe faction, gained appointment as colony's cape merchant. He was now in charge of trade relations with the Indians. The turmoil within the Council continued. Finally, on September 10, 1608, Captain John Smith was elected its president.[12]

Smith's first trading venture at the village of Kecoughton, downriver from Jamestown, illustrated his particular mix of firmness, conciliation, accommodation, and selective terrorism in dealing with the native peoples. As his vessel approached the shore, the Indians, as Smith later related, "at first . . . scorned him as a famished man, and would in derision offer him a handful of Corne, a peece of bread, for their swords and muskets, and such like proportions also for their apparel." Although he conceded that his next move was "contrary to his Commission," which forbade attacks on Indians, Smith's response to the insult was to "let Fly his muskets," as he ran the boat aground. The Indians fled into the woods. Smith and his men then marched toward their village, passing along the way "greate heaps of corn." Smith, determined to establish friendly trade relations at Kecoughton despite that bad beginning, but at the same time very aware of the imminent danger of an Indian attack, maintained discipline and, with some difficulty, kept his hungry men from seizing the Indian corn then and there. The "assault" he expected soon materialized. Making "a most hydeous noyse, Sixtie of seventie of them, some blacke, some red, some white, some party-coloured, came in a square order," singing and dancing out of the woods. They carried before them an "Idoll made of skinnes, stuffed with mosses, all painted and hung with chaines and copper." Armed with clubs, shields, bows, and arrows, they charged the English party, which responded "with their muskets loaden with Pistoll shot." The attackers fled, and "downe fell their Idoll sprawling upon the ground." Soon thereafter, an Indian priest came out of the woods, offering peace and asking for the idol's return. Smith agreed, but stipulated that he be supplied with food in exchange for "Beads, Copper, and Hatchets." The Kecoughtons loaded Smith's boat with grain, venison, turkeys, and wild fowl, and celebrated their newly forged friendship in "singing and dauncing." On his way back upriver, Smith also bought grain at another village. The grain he brought home, combined with a sudden influx of migratory water birds delivered Jamestown, for a time, from the specter of starvation. Reflecting on this expedition many years later, Smith declared:

> That God unboundlesse by his power
> Made them thus kind, would us devour.[13]

God's intervention in filling the savage Indians' hearts with kindness was not, however, sufficient to secure good results in some of Smith's subsequent trading ventures. Soon after the Kecoughton expedition, Smith called at the village of Quiyoucannock. He found it largely deserted. The few remaining women refused to trade with him. Proceeding to Paspahegh, Smith encountered villagers accustomed to receiving very generous terms from desperate visitors from Jamestown. They demanded that Smith surrender his company's guns and swords in exchange for a little food. When he refused, the Indians tried to seize them. Facing a potentially deadly confrontation, Smith prudently withdrew. He was able to trade with a few of the villagers who followed his course downriver, but finally obtained only a measly dozen bushels or so of corn.

In early November 1607, Smith made his way to the Chickahominys, a people who had had no previous dealings with Jamestown. He received a warm welcome and soon, in exchange for glass beads and other objects exotic to the Chickahominys, received more corn than he could carry on his barge. His hosts were intrigued by English guns and asked that as Smith began his return trip downriver that he fire them. The unaccustomed sound, reverberating loudly on the river, astounded the Indians. Smith was convinced that he had found, not only a good trading partner, but a staunch ally, as well. He returned to the Chickahominys several times before the end of the year. Some of his later forays to other tribes were not, initially at least, as auspicious. To cite one example of several difficult encounters, during an expedition in 1608 to explore Chesapeake Bay in search of gold and the Northwest Passage, his party was attacked by the Rappahannocks. He fought back and, in a most fortuitous gesture, spared the life of a wounded tribesman whom his Indian guide was about to kill. The captive, named Amoroleck, was treated with kindness and given gifts. Through an interpreter, Smith told his attackers that he had spared Amoroleck and would return him in exchange for their friendship. The Rappahannocks agreed, and the English and their new friends sang, danced, and feasted together. That episode illustrated the combination of violence and moderation that characterized Smith's dealings with "savages."

His critics at Jamestown faulted him for his frequent resort to force, which they argued violated the instructions they had received from London. Their charge was correct. Smith did not follow the company's orders not to coerce the Indians. He dealt harshly with those who stole from the English. One, who had picked up two swords while visiting Jamestown, he placed in shackles within the fort; others he threatened with hanging. On one occasion he opened fire within the stockade on some Indian visitors he suspected of thievery, driving them away "with five or six shots." On another, he responded to the theft of a pistol by a Chickahominy by seizing one of his friends and confining him in a smoky dungeon, where the other Indians at the fort believed he had suffocated, then promised to restore him to life as soon as the gun was returned. When the gun was given back, the man, presumably resurrected by Smith's magic, was let loose. Smith had earlier threatened to hang the hostage if the Chickahominys did not produce the pistol. One neighboring *werowance* was so intimidated by reports of Smith's reprisals and his supernatural power that "he sent us a Hatchet which they had stolen from us" earlier during a visit to their village. In that instance, Smith, who believed in combining severity and generosity, responded by sending the messenger who returned the hatchet home with gifts.[14]

Basically distrustful of all Indians, Smith never let down his guard, as an episode in summer 1608 illustrated. An Indian from Paspahegh, the village that had mounted an attack on Jamestown soon after its founding the year before, brought the English "a glistening mineral stone," suggesting by signs that many more were to be found in the interior. Smith, accompanied by a dozen or so men, determined to bring back more samples, employed the Indian as a guide. However, when their guide seemed unsure of the way, Smith became suspicious, fearing that he intended either to rob them or to lead them into an ambush. Unable to understand just what the Indian was saying, Smith concluded that he was "scoffing and abusing us," and accordingly "gave him twentie lashes with a rope." In a show of bravado, as he recalled, he then gave the man "his bowes and arrows, bidding him shoote if he durst, and so let him go." Calculated coercion remained the cornerstone of Smith's Indian policy. To cite another example, in late 1608, wihen the Nansemonds, whose village was situated at the mouth of the James River some 30 miles from Jamestown reneged on an earlier promise to trade with Smith, pleading scarcity, he ordered his company to open fire and shoot into the air. The frightened Nansemonds ran into the woods, but as Smith began to burn their village, they sent emissaries to beg him to stop, promising that they would supply grain. Once again, he returned to Jamestown with food. Later that winter, the Indians at the village of Kiskiac, who in their "insolencie" at first declined to provide Smith's party with food, were persuaded, as Smith recalled, "to give us what wee wanted."[15]

How successful was Smith in dealing with the people he termed "salvages?" His admirers point out that, although he did provoke some reprisals, fewer whites died at the hands of Indians than before or immediately after his management of trade relations. His departure from the colony, as we shall see, was followed by an escalation of violent encounters termed by some writers "the First Powhatan War." Whether Smith could have prevented that war is questionable, as his own relations with Powhatan were troubled from the outset. His conduct, it can be argued, set the stage for a guerrilla war that in fact was already underway before the end of his presidency. To understand its origins, we must examine closely Smith's dealings with the paramount chief.

Smith's first meeting with Powhatan occurred in December 1607. He related the story of that encounter in a letter to London, published without his permission or editing in a truncated version the following year. After journeying by barge with nine companions up the Chickahominy River in search of its source and of the Pacific Ocean, Smith came to narrows that could not be traversed in his bulky vessel. He therefore engaged two Indians guides, left his main party, and, accompanied by "Master Robbinson and Thomas Embry," proceeded upriver by canoe. After landing to prepare dinner, Smith left his two countrymen, with instructions to fire their musket "at the first sight of any Indian," and walked away from the camp "to see the nature of the soile." He took one of the Indian guides with him. About a quarter of an hour later, Smith heard "a loud cry and the hollowing of Indians." Assuming that he had been betrayed by the Indian guides, he seized the one with him and threatened to shoot him with his pistol. But the Indian, Smith related, seemingly unaware of the plot, "advised me to fly." As they talked, Smith was "struck with an arrow on the right thigh, but without harme." Spotting two Indians nearby drawing their bows, the captain fired at them several times, but soon was overwhelmed by some 200 warriors.[16]

He was now in the hands of a party led by Opechancanough, brother of Powhatan and "king of Pamaunck." Smith tried to negotiate terms of withdrawal, but was informed that his men were dead and he, a prisoner. Although he expected to die, and at one point was tied to a tree in apparent preparation for execution, his captors spared Smith's life, in keeping with their custom of not killing commanders. He was led into the presence of Opechancanough, whom he had met some months earlier during Newport's first venture into the interior. Smith, perhaps recalling Hariot's account of the Roanoke Indians' fascination with English technology, sought to impress Opechancanough by showing him a compass with a moving dial. He followed that demonstration with "a discourse of the roundness of the earth, the course of the sunne, moone, stares, planets." Given Smith's rudimentary command of the Powhatan's Algonquian language and the improbability that Opechancanough knew much English, we don't know quite what to make of Smith's story of his science lecture. Smith, however, believed Opechancanough was deeply impressed. The chief, Smith related, delivered "kinde speeches" and fed Smith bread, but then he took him to the body of John Robbinson "with 20 or 30 arrowes in it. Embry I saw not." (He was also probably killed.) Although Smith was unaware of it at that time, another Englishman, George Cassen, left downriver at the barge had also been lost. Cassen was seized when he wandered into the woods and was put to death by torture, tied to a tree and flayed alive with shells. The others in Cassen's party probably made it back to Jamestown.[17]

Smith wrote that during his captivity, he was in constant fear for his life, paraded through several villages, at each place given "more venison than ten men could devour." Having little if any understanding of the Powhatans' customs, he feared he was being fattened up for a cannibal feast. His anxieties were heightened at one village where, at 10 in the morning, seven visitors to "the house where I lay" began "to sing around the fire," shaking rattles and spreading a circle of grain upon the floor. As the day progressed, dancers appeared clad "in the little skinnes of Weasels and other vermin . . . painted as ugly as the devil." Their "howling," Smith recorded, continued until nightfall. He was told that the ceremony was intended to determine "where to hunt the next day." Smith was not reassured, believing "they intended to have sacrificed me to the Quiyoughquosicke, which is a superior power they worship: a more uglier thing cannot be described." Although Smith provided a more thorough description of the ceremony in one of his later books, we cannot determine exactly what really transpired. There is no reason to believe, however, that he was actually being prepared for a human sacrifice. The great quantities of food with which he was presented were a mark of honor, of recognition of high status. Although the Algonquians did use shamanic divination to locate game, the ritual Smith describes does not resemble what is now known of those rituals. One authority has concluded that the circles drawn on the floor before Smith indicate that "the Powhatans were redefining the world to include the English colony." Given their paramount chief's later interactions with Smith and other Jamestown leaders, this is quite plausible.[18]

Throughout his forced journey through Powhatan's domain, Smith tried hard to win Opechancanough over, and was encouraged by the fact that his captor "tooke great delight" in the things Smith told him about the English navy and about the English God. Smith was not entirely reassured, however, and resorted to some cautious intimidation, suggesting that he should be allowed to send a letter to Jamestown, assuring his countrymen that he was being well treated, "lest they should revenge my death." He emphasized the threat by speaking of the English fort's "ordinance and the mines in the fields." He was allowed to send the letter. Learning that the *werowance* of Paspahegh had sought support for another assault on Jamestown, Smith warned his compatriots that an Indian attack was imminent. The next day, an Indian, whose son Smith had shot, tried to kill him. Smith was rescued by his guard and then sent to another village. After visiting several additional "kingdoms," Smith was finally taken to Werowocomoco, seat of Powhatan.[19]

Ushered into the presence of "their Emperour," Smith found him "proudly lying upon a Bedstead a foote high upon tenne or twelve Mattes, richly hung with manie Chaynes of great Pearles about his necke." He wore an impressive raccoon skin robe, and "at his heade sat a woman, and at his feet another." A fire burned in the middle of the audience chamber, and on either side sat "his chiefe men," accompanied by their women who wore large chains of white beads over their shoulders, with "their heades painted in redde." Powhatan's countenance, Smith related, was "grave and Majesticall," hardly what one would expect "in a naked Salvage."[20]

Once again, the captive was offered great quantities of food. Powhatan welcomed him "with goode words," expressing pleasure at the report he had received from Opechancanough, promising friendship and assuring Smith he would be set free in four days. The principal chief then asked a pointed question: Why had the English come into his territory? Smith lied, claiming that their vessels had been in a fight with the Spanish, had nearly been overpowered, were forced to retreat, and finally had been driven into Chesapeake Bay by a storm. They were now waiting for the return of "Captaine Newport my father," who would "come to conduct us away." Powhatan was skeptical. Why, then, he asked, had they sailed upriver? Smith told another lie. Captain Newport, he said, "had a childe slaine," by Powhatan's enemies the Monacans and intended to take revenge. Powhatan replied by describing some of the fierce people who lived beyond the falls, some of whom were cannibals. He also told stories of a saltwater sea to the West, of great cities, and of peoples who sailed in ships like those of the English. Powhatan, if Smith understood him correctly, claimed those "great and spacious Dominions" were "his Territories." The game of mutual deception and manipulation was well underway. Smith warned Powhatan of "the innumerable multitude of ships" commanded by the English King and of "the terrible manner of fighting" used by Captain Newport. Powhatan countered by asking that Smith and his people abandon Jamestown and come to live in a place in the interior he called Capahowosick, "upon his River." There the English were to make hatchets and copper ornaments for Powhatan and would receive, in return, protection and ample food.[21]

In the 1608 account, Smith related that after he agreed to Powhatan's proposition, he was treated by the principal chief "with all the kindness he could devise," and escorted back to Jamestown as promised. He told essentially the same story in 1612, but in his *Generall Historie of Virginia, New-England, and the Summer Isles,* published in 1624, Smith added some crucial, and controversial, details. He now claimed that he had been sentenced to death by Powhatan, but rescued by the great chief's favorite daughter, the Princess Pocahontas. As he told story in his 1624 version, "after a long consultation," Powhatan's men brought two great stones and placed them before Powhatan. Then, "as many as could layd hands on him [Smith], and thereon laid his head, and being ready with their clubs, to beate out his brains, Pocahontas, the Kings dearest daughter, when no entreaty could prevaile, got his head in her armes, and laid her own upon his to save him from death." Powhatan then relented, agreed to Pocahontas' plea, and declared that the Englishman was to "make him hatchets, and her bells, beads, and copper." However, Smith soon had to endure yet another frightening encounter as, two days later, "Powhatan, having disguised himselfe in the most fearefullest manner that he could, caused Captaine Smith to be brought forth to a great house in the woods, and there upon a mat by the fire to be left alone." From "behinde a mat that divided the house" came "the most dolefullest noyse he ever heard." Then, after a time, "Powhatan more like a devil than a man" appeared, accompanied by "two hundred more as blacke as himselfe." The principle chief assured Smith that they were now "friends, and presently he should goe to James Towne, to send him two great gunnes, and a gryndestone, for which he would give him the Country of Capahowosick, and for ever esteeme him as his sonne Nantaquod."[22]

Smith's failure to mention his rescue by Pocahontas until many years had passed (and the other principles had died), combined with his penchant for claiming that he was often rescued from dire straits by high-born women, has led a number of scholars, beginning with Henry Adams in 1867, to charge Smith with lying. However, the absence of this episode from the 1608 and 1612 accounts does not necessarily prove that it did not happen, as Smith's earlier reports omitted many details and appear to have been edited in order not to detract too severely from the attractiveness of the Virginia venture to investors. Moreover, as Smith hoped to emphasize his own capacity to control the "salvages," admission that he had been rescued from death by an Indian child hardly helped his personal cause. He had reasons not to be too forthcoming about what happened during his first visit to Powhatan's court. In 1612, Smith not only made no mention of being rescued from execution by Pocahontas, but claimed his demeanor at Powhatan's court inspired such awe "that those Salvages admired him as a demi-God."[23]

Most scholars, although by no means all, now accept Smith's 1624 account of his rescue, albeit with some qualifications. There is, in fact, no contemporary testimony to impugn it. It is worth noting that Samuel Purchas, who continued Hakluyt's work as the master complier of reports from the New World, believed that Pocahontas had indeed saved Smith's life. Purchas was acquainted with several Powhatan Indian visitors to England as well as a number of men who had been in Virginia with Smith. Some were enemies of Smith, eager to discredit him. None challenged his story of his rescue, a story Smith apparently first told in a letter to Queen Anne in 1616.[24]

However, if some sort of execution ceremony was indeed staged by Powhatan and interrupted by his daughter, Smith misunderstood its nature and purpose. It is unlikely that there was ever any intent to kill Smith by knocking his brains out. Smith testified that he was feasted for many days prior to the ceremony, and that afterward Powhatan offered him a village and called him his son. Those events, when assessed in the light of ethnographic data about Algonquian adoption customs, suggest that Smith probably underwent a ceremony in which he died ritualistically and was reborn as a Powhatan. Pocahontas's role in that ceremony was not the role Smith attributed to her. Her intervention did not save his life, but rather symbolized his incorporation into the tribe and family of Powhatan. That interpretation is supported by the evidence we have of Powhatan's interest in bringing the English into his own polity. I agree with those who are convinced that some sort of ceremony was indeed performed to symbolize Smith's adoption. Although some of the details may well have been exaggerated or even fabricated, Smith's testimony about Powhatan's determination to make him a "son," a subject, and a village ruler is credible. It is telling that Pocahontas herself, meeting Smith in England some years later, reminded him, as Smith recorded, that "you did promise Powhatan what was yours should be his, and he the like to you, you called him father being in his land a stranger, and by the same reason so must I to you." To Smith's reply that such a thing could not be, as he was a commoner and she a king's daughter, Pocahontas replied that she would call him father, as he should properly call her "child." What are we to make of that exchange? Anthropologist Frederic Gleach suggests that "after almost ten years, Pocahontas recalled the terms of this arrangement that Smith never understood. Through this ritual process, he and the English colony had become fellow countrymen of the Powhatans, with all due responsibilities."[25]

Smith did not fulfill the commitments Powhatan believed he had agreed to undertake at Werowocomoco. Smith related that Pocahontas, during their 1616 encounter, reproached him for his bad faith. He recorded that she did not seem "well contented" and at first would not speak, then reminded him, as noted earlier, of the promises he had made to her father. Smith may not have been aware of the full nature of his new relationship to the Powhatans as they understood it, but his writings leave no doubt that his promise to send two cannons and a grindstone to Powhatan was one he had no intention of keeping, as he noted with some satisfaction that the two Indians sent to transport those acquisitions back to Werowocomoco couldn't carry or drag them. (The cannons each weighed between 3,000 pounds and 4,500 pounds!) The English offered no help in transporting the weapons, but did offer a demonstration of their power. The shot demolished a nearby tree heavy with icicles, showering the area with flying branches and shards of ice. Smith noted with pleasure that "the poor salvages ran away half dead with fear." Smith called them back and sent them on their way with some "toyes" for Powhatan and his family. Although Smith reported that they were satisfied with those offerings, the paramount chief most certainly was not.[26]

When Powhatan asked at their next meeting why Smith had not given his messengers smaller, more portable guns, he had no reply. Even more significant in undermining Powhatan's trust was Smith's failure to comply with the request that he arrange to move the settlement to Capahowosick where the English would live under his close supervision, with Smith as his adopted son serving as the village chief. Powhatan was determined from his first meeting with Smith to contain and control the English. However, Smith and his colleagues had no intention of taking up residence in one of Powhatan's villages. When the English failed to move as directed, Powhatan grudgingly tolerated their presence at Jamestown. He was angered, however, by Smith's explorations outside the Jamestown area. Smith spent most of summer 1608 visiting numerous Indians tribes throughout the region, some of them subject to Powhatan, some semi-autonomous, and some actually hostile to the paramount chief. Smith encountered considerable resistance on the lower Potomac River, and concluded that Powhatan had ordered those peoples not to receive him. Farther upriver, however, the villagers were far more hospitable, perhaps because of rivalries with Powhatan. For his part, the paramount chief found Smith's independent diplomacy very offensive. When, on his return from the Chesapeake Bay region Smith entered into a formal alliance with the Piankatanks, who promised to supply Jamestown with corn, Powhatan retaliated by driving Smith's new trading partners off their land and resettling it with people totally loyal to him. Powhatan's reaction to English efforts to expand their colony was no less extreme. When Smith, in early 1609, tried to establish a new settlement upriver, at the falls of the James, Powhatan sent raiding parties to kill settlers found outside Jamestown's limits.[27]

However, those events were in the future. In the months immediately after Smith's return to Jamestown, relations with Powhatan appeared to be good, as the principal chief sent ample food to Jamestown. Without that aid, he later declared, the colony would "have starved with hunger." In his 1624 history, Smith attributed Powhatan's generosity to "the love of Pocahontas," a love that was "the strange means" God used to save the colony. As Smith did not mention in his earlier accounts the role presumably played by that 11-year-old girl in averting starvation at Jamestown, we have reason to be somewhat skeptical. In any case, although Smith may or may not have believed that it was his special relationship to the Indian princess that had saved Jamestown, Powhatan had his own reasons for keeping the English alive. He still hoped to use them to his advantage.[28]

Smith's enemies at Jamestown were not happy about his reappearance after the first visit to Powhatan. They had hoped to abandon the colony and sail back to England. Smith, at gunpoint, now forced them to stay. Led by Council president John Ratcliffe and sometime-lawyer Gabriel Archer, they retaliated by charging Smith with murder through command malfeasance in the deaths of Robinson and Embry, citing a very obscure and tortured reading of Leviticus's injunction "an eye for an eye, a tooth for a tooth." Smith was sentenced to death. He claimed, in 1624, that he refuted their reading of the law by argument that "layd them by the heels" and then sent some of his accusers in chains back to England. There is no confirming evidence for this. Edward Maria Wingfield, also imprisoned by the Archer/Ratcliffe faction, related that, after Smith's trial, he was scheduled for hanging "the same or the next day," but "it pleased God to send Captain Newport unto us on the same evening." Newport's arrival, Wingfield wrote, saved Smith's life and probably his own.[29]

Although Captain Smith once again owed Newport his life, their relations from this point onward were strained. Newport, who had delivered to London tons of "ore" that turned out to contain nothing of value, was under orders to find real gold in Virginia to repay the investors. The search for precious metals was thus Newport's highest priority. Smith, by contrast, was more concerned with order, discipline, and self-sufficiency, without which, he argued, the English could not survive in Virginia. Smith later wrote that although the settlement was in dire straits, short of provisions and shelter, under Newport "there was no talke, no hope, no worke, but dig gold, wash gold, refine golde, load gold, such a bruit of gold, that one made fellow desired to be buried in the sands least they should by there art, make gold of his bones." Smith protested that the colonists "to fraught such a drunken ship with so much guilded durt" neglected essential work and thereby threatened the colony's survival. For all that effort, no gold was found in Virginia.[30]

Newport brought in his supply ship 80 new settlers. Another 40 were in a vessel commanded by Captain Francis Nelson that had been separated from Newport shortly before reaching North America and the whereabouts of which were unknown when Newport made landfall at Jamestown on January 2. Newport immediately ordered the newcomers to build shelters for themselves, but a fire broke out on January 7 that destroyed everything at Jamestown except for three very small huts. Newcomers and old hands alike were now bereft of clothing, supplies, and shelter. (Also lost in the conflagration was Reverend Hunt's meager book collection, the only one at Jamestown.) Efforts at reconstruction were hindered by extreme cold, hunger, and new outbreaks of sickness. Only deliveries of food from the Powhatans kept the colonists alive. Half the meat (venison and raccoon) and bread, the Indians explained, was intended for Smith's father, Captain Newport. Fascinated by the stories Smith told of his time at Powhatan's court, Newport determined to visit the great Indian "emperor."[31]

Smith's accounts of that visit reveal considerable anxiety and distrust on the part of both Englishmen and Powhatans. In late February, Newport, accompanied by Smith and a company from Jamestown, sailed upriver to Werowocomoco, Powhatan's seat. During the voyage, Newport, as Smith recalled, was seized by "many doubts and suspicions of trecheries." He remained on the pinnace while Smith took a party of 20 men ashore "to encounter the worst that could happen." To guarantee the safety of his party, he seized several Indians who had come out to escort them to Powhatan, making them go first across several creek bridges while he held "some of the chiefe as hostages." (Among those hostages was a son of Powhatan's.) The bridge was so unstable, however, that Smith and several members of his party allowed the Indians to convey them to the shore by canoe. Once landed, Smith related, "we made a guard for the rest until all were passed." Approaching Werowocomoco, Smith's company was led into the town by "two or three hundred Salvages." He was relieved to find them "kindly" in manner.[32]

Brought into the presence of Powhatan, Smith was once again impressed by his majestic appearance, "sitting upon his bed of mats, his pillow of leather imbrodered (after their rude manner with pearle and white Beads), his attire a faire robe of skinnes as large as an Irish mantel." The principle chief was surrounded by his "Concubines," handsome women painted red and adorned with great strands of white beads, and by "his chiefest men. . . . fortie platters of fine bread" were lined up "on each side of the doore." Smith presented Powhatan with a suit of red clothes, a fancy hat and a white greyhound. After lengthy orations of welcome, Powhatan, if Smith whose command of Algonquian was still limited understood him correctly, declared that anyone who "would presume to doe us any wrong or discourtesie should suffer death," and once again proclaimed Smith one of his *werowances*. Powhatan did, however, ask a pointed question about Smith's failure to keep the agreement to send him cannons, and received, as we noted earlier, an answer he apparently deemed less than satisfactory. However, Powhatan, stressing again adoption and incorporation, proclaimed the two peoples one; after that declaration, the English and Indians at court engaged in feasting, singing, dancing, and "such like mirth." Unable to return to his ship and to Newport because the tide was out, "we quartered that night," Smith recalled, "with Powhatan." Despite the many professions of friendship and unity, however, Smith firmly declined

Powhatan's request that the English lay down their weapons. It was, explained to told his host, "a ceremony our enemies desired, but never our friends."[33]

Newport came ashore the next day, marching in a small procession led by a trumpeter. Just before his arrival, Powhatan and Smith had strolled along the river-front, as the paramount chief had shown the English captain his fleet of canoes, and boasted about the "Countries" that paid him tribute in "Beads, Copper or Skins." Meeting Powhatan, Newport presented him with 13-year-old Thomas Savage, whom he described falsely as his son. Savage would serve as a hostage and, after learning the Powhatan language, as an interpreter. About a week later, Powhatan reciprocated, presenting Newport with a young man named Namontack, whom Smith described as "one of a shrewd, subtill capacitie." Savage became fluent in the Powhatan Algonquian dialect and soon earned Powhatan's trust and affection. Returning to Jamestown in 1609, Savage also befriended the *werowance* of Acco-mac, who gave him a substantial grant of land on the Eastern Shore, upon which he settled. Savage remained in the colony until his death in 1635. Namontack was less fortunate. Misrepresented to the English as Powhatan's son (they were, in fact, not related), Namontack visited England twice with Newport and received a warm reception. However, on his final voyage home in 1609, he was shipwrecked on Bermuda with Sir Thomas Gates and his party. Unlike Gates, he never reached Virginia, but was killed by a fellow Indian voyager, Machumps, a son-in-law of Powhatan. The paramount chief was never told of Namontack's death.[34]

Returning to the story of Newport's first visit to Powhatan, the latter remained very uncomfortable with having arms-bearing strangers in his village. He therefore raised the issue again. To Smith's dismay, Newport agreed to Powhatan's request that the English disarm. Newport and his party remained several days with Pow-hatan, exchanging information (and misinformation) and engaging in trade. Smith warned Newport to be careful, that Powhatan's "intent was only to cheat us," but Newport was mostly concerned with creating a good impression. So, when the principle chief suggested that it was beneath their dignity as rulers to haggle over price, and asked him to "lay me downe all your commodities together; what I like I will take, and in recompense give you what I thinke fitting their value," Newport agreed. The result, Smith complained, was disastrous. Powhatan gave very little in return for the trade goods Newport laid before him. (It would have been cheaper, Smith declared hyperbolically, to buy corn in Spain.) To try to salvage the situ-ation, Smith persuaded Powhatan that some blue beads he had were very rare, worn only by royalty, and got a good price for those items. Smith's account of this episode betrays his lack of understanding of the relationship of the two people. The charge that Powhatan cheated Newport in trade assumes that this particu-lar exchange was a commercial transaction to be judged in terms of profit and loss. Newport was more sensitive than Smith to its symbolic implications, which related to protocol, status, and reciprocity. The very ample food deliveries from Powhatan that Smith recorded before and after Newport's visit indicates that the English were not victimized by Powhatan's alleged rapacity. However, control of white settlers and sailors engaged in Indian trade was a major headache for Smith.

In particular, the sailors who had brought Newport back to Virginia were engaging in transactions that depressed the price of English goods even before Newport met Powhatan. Soon, Smith complained, provisions that once had been available for an ounce "could not be had for a pound of Copper." He unfairly blamed Newport's desire to appear great in the eyes of the Indians for that unfortunate situation, which he believed placed the colony at a very serious disadvantage.[35]

Overall, Newport's meeting with the Indian "emperor" had yielded mixed results. Smith believed that a short side visit to the village of Powhatan's powerful brother Opechancanough had gone well, as the *werowance* and "his wife, women, and children came to meete me with a naturall kind of affection, hee seemed rejoiced to see me." Later events would suggest Smith had been misled by appearances. Powhatan, for his part, seemed uninterested in proposals for joint military action against his enemies the Monocans, suggesting that although his people might do some spying and perhaps send 100 hunters under Opechancanough to draw them out into an ambush, the English should do all the fighting. They were to kill all the men but spare the women and children, who, the paramount chief insisted, were to be turned over to him. Despite Smith's interventions, economic relations between the two peoples remained problematic. A letter from a Jamestown settler dated March 28, 1608, indicates that the Powhatans were trying to teach the English to fish and plant corn. Their pupils, as we shall see, never quite mastered the use of fish weirs, nor did they commit sufficient effort in 1608 and 1609 to the cultivation of their fields. If the Powhatans hoped to relieve the pressure on their own food supplies by helping the English achieve self-sufficiency, their efforts were in vain.[36]

Smith believed Newport's priorities were misplaced. The captain was concerned with the immediate security and well-being of Jamestown, and adapted measures to the circumstances on the ground. As we have noted in our earlier discussion of his rather aggressive Indian policy, this often meant departing from the literal instructions of the Virginia Company. Newport regarded it as his responsibility to carry out those instructions of to the letter. In a letter delivered by Newport, the Company ordered the Council president at Jamestown (the post to which Smith had recently been elected) to defer to Newport's orders. One of Newport's most urgent tasks, as noted, was to find gold. Another was to locate a passage to the Pacific. He was also to locate survivors of Raleigh's Lost Colony. Above all, he was to cement friendly relations with Powhatan and his people. Newport agreed with the London critics who faulted Smith for his "crueltie" in dealing with Indians. To improve relations, the Company had mandated a coronation ceremony that would both exalt Powhatan and make him a subject of James I. To that end, Newport brought from England a crown, a bedstead and mattress, a china basin, clothing (including a bright-scarlet coat symbolic of his new status), and various other "costly novelties." It was expected that Powhatan would be impressed, indeed awed, by those trappings of English power. Smith remarked sarcastically that Powhatan would rather have a lump of copper. The Company clearly did not understand cultural realities or the real nature of power relationships in Virginia.[37]

Smith, since his election as president in September, had worked hard to rebuild Jamestown and place it on a firm military footing. Refusing to defer to the pretensions of the "gentlemen," Smith insisted all the colonists help in the hard physical work of building a new settlement, and also demanded that they all participate in military exercises. His regular Saturday drills, outside the fort near the West wall on a field that came to be called "Smithfield," were carefully watched by Powhatan's people. He recalled that "sometimes more then a hundred Salvages would stand in an amazement to behold" English target practice. Smith believed that keeping them in that state of amazement was absolutely essential to the colony's survival. He regarded the proposed crowning of Powhatan as yet another indication that Newport and the London partners did not understand the situation in Virginia. Crowning Powhatan, in his judgment, would not make him subordinate to the King of England, as Powhatan would give the ritual a very different interpretation. And so it turned out. "This stately kind of soliciting," Smith complained, "made him so much overvalue himselfe, that he respected us as much as nothing at all." Newport originally intended to journey to Werowocomoco with a full force of 120 men to carry out the coronation. Smith objected that such an expedition would strip Jamestown of men badly needed for the task of rebuilding and drain scarce food supplies. He volunteered to go to Powhatan and invite him to come to Jamestown for the ceremony.[38]

Newport accepted that proposal and Smith, along with four companions, made the 12-mile journey to Powhatan's capital, where they found that the paramount chief was not in residence. While they were awaiting his return, camped outside the village, Smith and his men, as he recalled, heard "such a hydeous noise and shrieking" that they supposed "Powhatan with all his power was come to surprise them." Fearing for their lives, the Englishmen grabbed their weapons and seized a couple of elderly Indian men as hostages. But soon Pocahontas appeared and joined other villagers, who had arrived at the scene, in assuring Smith that there was nothing to fear. Then, as Smith recounted, "thirtie young women came naked out of the woods, onely covered behind and before with a few greene leaves, their bodies all painted, some of one colour, some of another, but all differing. All the dancers wore deer horns and carried various weapons: bows, arrows, swords, clubs, and sticks. Despite reassurances of friendly intention, Smith found the display sinister. "These fiends with most hellish shoutes and cryes, rushing from among the trees, cast themselves in a ring about the fire, singing and dauncing with most excellent ill variety, oft falling into their infernal passions." After about an hour, the dance ended and the women conducted their guests to lodgings. Smith complained that "he was no sooner within the house, but all these Nymphes more tormented him then ever, with crowding, pressing, and hanging about him, most tediously crying, Love you not me? Love you not me?" Smith, disturbed both by hellish images conjured up by the dance and by the sexual solicitations of the hospitable Indian women, found in that welcoming ceremony reinforcement of his anxiety and distrust.[39]

The next day, he met with Powhatan. That "subtile Savage" responded to his invitation to journey to Jamestown to receive presents from the King of England by declaring he would not "bite at such a bait." The king's representative, Captain Newport, should come to him. "I also am a King, and this is my land; eight days will I stay to receive him." Powhatan also rejected the notion that if he traveled to Jamestown he and Newport could plan for joint military action against their presumed common enemy the Monacans, stating bluntly "I can revenge my owne injuries." Informed of Powhatan's response, Newport made the trip to Werowocomoco. Smith's account of the coronation emphasized Powhatan's presumed confusion, explaining that the Indian would not kneel to be crowned, because he did not know "the majesty nor meaning of a Crowne, nor bending of the knee." The English found it necessary finally to lean "hard on his shoulders" to make Powhatan stoop little before three of them clapped the crown on his head. The English then saluted the Indian king with gunfire, at the sound of which Powhatan jumped up "in horrible fear." Calmed and reassured he then gave "his old shooes and his mantell to Captain Newport" in acknowledgement of the various gifts Newport had brought to him. After the ceremony, the two leaders discussed a proposed English expedition into the interior, but Powhatan offered no assistance other than to suggest that Namontack, who earlier had accompanied Newport to England, might now go along as a guide. Newport's hope of enlisting Powhatan's aid in locating gold, the Pacific Ocean, or Roanoke survivors came to nothing. As to Smith's assertion that Powhatan did not understand what was going on during his coronation, he may be correct regarding the details, but his account makes it clear that the paramount chief had no intention of allowing himself to be subordinated to the English. He was not about to become a subject of James I.[40]

Despite Powhatan's refusal to assist, Newport soon embarked on exploration of the interior, taking with him 120 of the most able men at Jamestown. Smith was left behind. He worked hard to whip into shape the 80 or so who also remained, most of them, Smith claimed, idlers and fops both unaccustomed and disinclined to physical labor. His efforts led to some good results in the rebuilding of Jamestown, but Newport's expedition accomplished nothing. He found no precious metals, learned nothing about the fate of the Roanoke colonists nor the route to the South Sea, and greatly antagonized the Indians whose food reserves he tried unsuccessfully to seize. When Newport sailed back to England a second time in December 1608, he carried with him, in addition to a load of lumber cut under Smith's supervision, a sealed letter from Smith highly critical not only of his conduct (Smith recommended Newport's dismissal from the Company's service), but also of the Company itself, which had failed to provide either adequate provisions or appropriate manpower for the colony. Virginia, he warned, badly needed skilled men willing to work hard. Smith declared that 30 "Carpenters, husbandmen, gardeners, fishermen, blacksmiths, masons and diggers up of trees" would be worth more than "a thousand of such as we have." Firm and productive trade relations with the "inconstant Salvages" were also essential. Newport's blundering,

Smith charged, had so inflated the price Indians expected to receive for foodstuffs that adequate provisions could not be obtained. Newport's own visit to Powhatan for the coronation had yielded only a measly 21 or 22 bushels of corn, 14 by purchase, the remainder a gift. As a result, half the colonists, Smith reported, were now famished and sick.[41]

Smith's complaint notwithstanding, inflation was not the most serious problem in the Indian trade. Powhatan now seemed unwilling to provide food at any cost. Smith attributed the failure to obtain more corn at Werowocomoco to Newport's ineptness, but it soon appeared that the Indian villages were reluctant to sell any food at all, or in some cases even allow the English to enter their territory. After Newport's departure, Smith, as we noted earlier, forced the Nansemonds to trade by threatening to burn their village. Ominously, the Nansemonds claimed that Powhatan himself had forbade them to sell anything to the English, or to enter their territory. The Chickahominys, who were not Powhatan's subjects, had also provided food only after Smith threatened to put them to the sword. They protested, however, that they really were facing serious shortages, because the crops had been poor. Expeditions to other Indian communities proved mostly fruitless. "All the people," Smith recalled, "were fled." Smith was able to engage in some trade with "the people at Appamatuck," but they had very little to offer. Because Newport had carried away much of their sparse food supply to feed his crew on the return voyage, the English at Jamestown were soon facing starvation. Smith tried to get support from the Council at Jamestown for an attack on Powhatan, but failed. (Given Powhatan's great numerical advantage, it was probably fortunate for the English in Virginia that his proposal was rejected.) He then heard from the paramount chief himself, a messenger related, that Powhatan now offered to "load his Ship with Corne if he would but send him men to build him a house," and also provide a grindstone, 50 swords, some muskets, a cock and a hen, and "much copper and beads."[42]

Smith was suspicious, but being also desperate, he dispatched five workmen (three German immigrants and two Englishmen) to build Powhatan's "castle." Then, on December 29, he set out himself for Werowocomoco in the settlement's pinnace, accompanied by 46 volunteers and two barges. Stopping at the village of Warraskoyack, they were urged by their hosts to abandon the expedition. The local chief, as Smith recalled, warned that Powhatan might seem "to use you kindly, but trust him not, and be sure he have no opportunitie to seize on your Armes, for he hath sent for you onley to cut your throats." Given the food shortage at Jamestown, the captain had little choice but to proceed, but, as ever, remained on guard against Indian "treachery." Delayed in their trip upriver for about two weeks by a fierce winter storm, Smith and party stayed at several villages where, Smith recalled, "they repressed the insolency of the salvages." It is not clear just what he meant by that claim, perhaps that he forced them to accommodate his party. We need to bear in mind, however, that Smith was hardly in a position in January 1609 to subdue all the "salvages" he visited. Despite his superior weaponry, he was badly outnumbered and very vulnerable. Throughout his writings,

Smith labored hard to create the myth of Captain Smith the indomitable Indian vanquisher. He may well have believed in his own remarkable capacity to inspire the fear and love that had long been central to the English formula for dealing with the indigenous peoples of the New World. We may wonder, however, whether the Indians he visited were as intimidated as he imagined.[43]

Smith and company arrived at Powhatan's capital on January 12, but had to break the ice in the river to make their way to a landing. To Smith's alarm and embarrassment, his barge became mired by the outgoing tide, so he and his men had to wade through icy mud. Indians led them to shelter so they could dry out, and Powhatan sent them ample quantities of venison, turkey, and bread. The next day, on their way to call on the principle chief, they were led by a row of long-haired scalps. The victims, historian Helen Rountree tells us, were Piankatanks, "punished for their overfriendliness to the aliens not long before." By that display, Powhatan sought to teach the English "their place in his world." His opening remarks to John Smith were not encouraging. He demanded to know how long they intended to stay, denied that he had sent for them, and claimed he and his people had little corn. He did suggest that he would sell 40 baskets of grain for 40 swords. He added that there could be no trade at all if he were not given both guns and swords, and explained that he was no longer interested in exchanging corn for copper, because he could eat the corn but not the copper. (We have here a sign that food was, indeed, in short supply, for copper had earlier been in great demand.) Smith replied by charging Powhatan with bad faith in not keeping his promise to "supply my wants," conceded that he himself had failed to deliver the cannons previously promised, but explained that he could not spare any swords or guns. He complained that by forbidding his people to trade with the English, Powhatan was trying to starve them out as punishment for not meeting his "strange demands."[44]

Smith appealed to Powhatan to restore their friendship. His account of Powhatan's reply was written 15 years after the event. It is telling, but not entirely credible. As the captain recalled, although Powhatan promised that he would provide some supplies, he admonished Smith that his tactics had created ill will. "Many doe informe me your coming hither is not for trade, but to invade my people, and possesse my country." His people "dare not come to bring you corne, seeing you armed with your men." The English, should leave their weapons behind, "for here they are needlesse, we being all friends, and forever Powhatans." Once again, the paramount chief informed Smith that he was part of his tribe, and should act accordingly. He reprimanded Smith for his coercion of the Nansemonds, who were so traumatized by his food raid that they believed "you are come to destroy my Country." Smith should realize that if he continued to try take by force what he "may quickly have by love," Powhatan would hide all the food, "flee to the woods," and let the intruders starve. He professed, however, to prefer friendly relations, and urged Smith to abandon his coercive tactics.[45]

In his accounts of this encounter, Smith placed in Powhatan's mouth at this point a very eloquent oration on the horrors of war wherein he expressed among other things a great personal fear of Captain Smith and a clear understanding of the horrible consequences of incurring his wrath:

> Thinke you I am so simple, not to know it is better to eate good meate, lye well, and sleepe quietly with my women and children, laugh and be merry with you, have copper, hatchets, or what I want being your friend: then be forced to flie from all, lie cold in the woods, feede upon Acorns, rootes and such trash, and be so hunted by you, that I can neither rest, eate, nor sleepe; but my tyred men must watch, and if a twig but breake, every one cryeth there commeth Captaine Smith: then I must fly, I know not whether, and thus with miserable fear, end my miserable life.

He then promised to supply food to Jamestown every year to keep the peace. That speech, so often quoted, is perhaps the least believable of the utterances Smith attributed to Powhatan. The power advantage in 1609 rested with the Powhatans, not with Jamestown. Smith's effort to embellish his own larger than life image is particularly striking in this speech. His account of Powhatan's abject submission to trade demands out of fear of being pursued and punished by Smith is simply not consistent with his overall account of the paramount chief's behavior. There are parts of Smith's reconstruction of this conversation with Powhatan— specifically, his expression of anger and dismay at Smith's coercive tactics and his insistence that the captain behave as a subject and son—which are more credible. Smith, however, did not give those issues the emphasis we suspect they deserved, raising a question about how clearly he really understood what Powhatan was saying.[46]

Whatever the case, Smith, as he recalled, responded to the threat of "your flying into the woods," with bluster. He assured Powhatan that the English would not starve, as they had means "beyond your knowledge." He added a thinly veiled threat. If the English had wanted to destroy his people, they had the means to do so, and also much provocation, but had restrained themselves "for your sake only." He declared that although he was Powhatan's friend, "I live not here as your subject," but owed loyalty only to God and the King of England. He would, however, call Powhatan "Father" and love him accordingly. Powhatan then, after contrasting Newport's generosity with Smith's unkindness, asked that, to secure the peace, Smith and his men not come into his presence carrying swords and pistols. After all, Newport had disarmed. Convinced that Powhatan intended "to cut his throat," the captain played for time, promising to lay down arms "tomorrow."[47]

Powhatan was soon alarmed by the landing of more armed Englishmen, as Smith ordered some of the men remaining on the pinnace and barges ashore. The paramount chief first tried to slip away (to mount an attack, Smith believed), then, when the captain, brandishing a pistol and swords mustered 18 of his men, sent Smith "a great bracelet and a chain of pearle," delivered by an elderly notable who delivered an oration wherein he repeated the request that that the English lay down their weapons. That evening, Smith claimed in his 1624 history, "the eternal all-seeing God . . . by a strange meanes" saved him and his company from slaughter. Pocahontas, Powhatan's "dearest jewel and daughter," moved by love of the English came in the "darke night . . . through the irksome woods" to warn that her father intended to attack and kill them at supper. Thus warned, they remained vigilant, and no such attack occurred. After loading their vessels with the corn Powhatan supplied, Smith and company sailed back to Jamestown, leaving behind two German workmen to finish Powhatan's house, and an Englishman to shoot water fowl for him. Were Smith and his company really in danger at Werowocomoco? Did Pocahontas betray her father's plan to kill Smith? Or is this just Smith's myth making? Because we have only his account, we cannot corroborate his story. However, this much is clear: The visit revealed Smith's failure to establish a stable, productive relationship with the Powhatans. The tensions apparent during this visit would soon grow more acute. As Smith continues his narrative of events, he continued to stress the need for further intimidation of the Indians, and his genius in dealing with them.[48]

Smith assured his readers that he tried hard to keep English weapons out of Powhatan's hands; but, he related, the two German artisans and some of the others he had left at Werowocomoco defected and, according to Smith, plotted with Powhatan the destruction of Jamestown. Under the paramount chief's orders, the Germans led a party of Powhatans to Jamestown. Arriving before Smith's return, they claimed Captain Smith had asked that he be sent swords, muskets, and pikes, along with some other supplies. Peter Winne, in charge during Smith's absence, was taken in, and turned over weapons, tools, and clothing. Several of the men at Jamestown, hungry and fearing for their lives should Powhatan attack, also defected, stealing more weapons to add to the growing Powhatan arsenal. Two Englishmen from Smith's party who had remained with Powhatan tried slip away to warn the fort, but were apprehended. Curiously, Powhatan did not punish them. Was this perhaps because of Powhatan's fear of the great captain? Smith's most prominent modern biographer suggests that it was. However, perhaps he was simply biding his time. As Smith repeatedly noted, he was a "subtil salvage."[49]

Smith and his company, still upriver, were unaware of the defections or of Powhatan's acquisition of English weapons. Having been assured by the paramount chief that they could now obtain what they needed through peaceful trade, they went to the seat of Powhatan's brother, Opechancanough, on the Pamunkey River, where they expected to receive ample provisions. The *werowance's* village, however, was deserted, except for "a lame fellow and a boy." When Opechancanough and his entourage finally did appear, they were fully armed with bows and arrows, but carried little worth trading for. Smith immediately reprimanded the *werowance* for his "deceit," claiming that contrary to his previous professions he had now "invited mee to starve with hunger." Opechancanough replied with a promise to do better. When Smith, accompanied by 15 of his men, went to the *werowance's* house the next day, they found "foure or five men newly arrived, each with a great basket." Opechancanough, Smith related, "with a strained cheerfulnesse held us with a discourse what paines he had taken to keep his promise."[50]

Smith remained wary. His suspicions were confirmed when one of his men shouted that hundreds of warriors had surrounded the meeting place. The captain charged Opechancanough with treachery, then, as he later remembered, suggested that to avoid excessive bloodshed they settle matters in man-to-man combat. The *werowance* denied the accusation, ignored the challenge, and tried to placate Smith by claiming there was "a great present" for him just outside the door. But, Smith related, "the bait was guarded with at least two hundred men, and thirty each under a great tree," all of them ready to shoot their arrows. Smith would not bite, but instead, "in such a rage," grabbed Opechancanough by "his long locke" and thrust a loaded pistol into his ribs. Opechancanough, "trembling . . . near dead with feare amongst all his people" surrendered his weapons to Smith and ordered his men to do the same. If we may believe Smith's account (and some skepticism is in order), it was an incredible feat of daring and courage, as he had only 15 men with him and Opechancanough was guarded by "fortie or fiftie of his chiefe men" within the house (probably a large assembly hall) and 700 or so outside. (Smith's numbers were exaggerated. It is now believed the total Pamunkey population was around 300 in total.) Thoroughly intimidated by the indomitable captain, the Indians now loaded his boats with foodstuffs. Smith ended his narrative of this incident with a chilling account of his departing speech—an account that tells us much about his mind-set. Smith, in effect, threatened Opechancanough's people with what we would now call "genocide." He promised to hunt down and kill every member of the tribe if "you shoot but one Arrow to shed one drop of bloud of any of my men, or steale the least of these Beads or Copper." His campaign of extermination would continue "so long as I can heare where to finde one of your nation." Moreover, should they now fail to fill his ship the provisions he required, "I meane to load her with your dead carcasses." Compliance, however, would bring peace, "for I am not come to hurt any of you." Smith intended his account of his intimidation of Opechancanough and his people to provide evidence of his masterful handling of "salvages." There are probably elements of exaggeration in the story Smith told of his escape from Opechancanough's clutches, but there is little reason to doubt that Powhatan's brother had indeed been humiliated in some manner by Smith in front of his "chief men." If Smith's accusations that the chief was planning his murder was untrue, it must have left Opechancanough deeply embittered. If Smith really threatened to fill his ship with the carcasses of dead Indians should they not turn over their food, the captain added to the chief's humiliation, for a *werowance* was supposed to be able to protect his people. Smith did not have to wait long for Opechancanough to seek revenge. He related that when he called at nearby Potauncac a few days later, the local *werowance*, with Opechancanough's connivance, tried to poison him at the welcoming banquet. After a violent bout of nausea, Smith recovered, with his belief in Indian treachery once again confirmed.[51]

It is worth noting that Smith threatened to punish not only resistance to his food demands, but even incidents of petty theft with a campaign of total extermination against the innocent as well as the guilty. Smith never acknowledged in any of his accounts the possibility that his exactions created hardship, perhaps even severe hunger, in the villages he coerced. Instead, their reluctance to load his ships with food is always attributed to some form of treachery emanating from their essentially depraved savage nature. He asserted, therefore, the right to respond with mass killing. Smith, unlike some of his successors, did not actually carry out that policy, but carefully restricted the scope of his reprisals. However, he provided a rationale for later atrocities. You will recall that during the previous century, advocates of the empire had argued that no people had the right to exclude traders from their territory, and could justly be coerced into commerce. Smith carried that further, pressing trade demands on Indians irrespective of the effect his exactions would have on their communities. The leading modern authority on the Powhatan Indians writes that

> Tsenacomoco's people were not accustomed to making the land produce as much as possible and then trading for life's other necessities, real or imagined. They therefore had limited corn to spare, even in bountiful years. They were certainly not prepared to begin supporting—temporarily, much less for the long term—a horde of intrusive "visitors" who were unable or unwilling to feed themselves.

Virginia experienced a long period of drought, beginning in 1606 or earlier, which did not end until 1612. Smith's food demands came at a very bad time, and his accusations of bad faith whenever those demands were not met promptly were not only insensitive and unfair, but deeply offensive.[52]

After the incident with Opechancanough, Powhatan (as Smith told the story) in connivance with some white deserters, enlisted Wowinchopunck, the *werowance* of Paspahegh, in a plot to take Smith prisoner. The captain, however, captured Wowinchopunck instead, and demanded the surrender of the renegade Germans who had been aiding Powhatan. The Germans, however, remained at large, the *werowance* escaped from Jamestown, and the clumsy efforts of a force led by Peter Winne failed to apprehend him. Smith then mounted a punitive raid up the Chickahominy River, burning houses, killing some villagers, and destroying fish weirs. After receiving a weak promise to provide the English with food when the crops ripened, he withdrew, having accomplished very little. Back at Jamestown, rats devoured the settlement's grain supply, the colonists lived for a time on game, but worried about the coming of winter. Those worries, as we shall see, were well founded. Many of the provisions sent from England would be lost at sea in a hurricane that summer, and the Indians would remain recalcitrant.[53]

In spring 1609, after Newport's departure, Smith had undertaken his own extensive exploration of the region—an exploration that took him into Chesapeake Bay and up the Potomac River. En route, he sometimes met with a friendly reception from the Indians, but also had several skirmishes. On one occasion, his party was threatened by warriors acting, Smith believed, on orders from Powhatan. His voyage up the Potomac led to some contacts with local *werowances* that helped set the stage for their later betrayal of Powhatan and Pocahontas. Smith, continuing the search for gold, found no evidence of any precious metals, but was gratified by Indian reports that suggested the "South Sea" was not far from Chesapeake Bay. He returned to Jamestown on July 21. The following fall, Smith was badly injured by the explosion of a "powder-bag, which tore the flesh from his body and thighes, nine or ten inches square in a most pittifull manner," probably damaging his genitals. He returned to England in October.[54]

At the time of his departure, relations with Powhatan and his people had reached a new low. The paramount chief abandoned Werowocomoco shortly after Smith's last visit, and relocated in a remote region hard for the English to reach, and supplied no more food to Jamestown. His new capital at Orapax was in upland country near the mouth of the Chickahominy River, accessible by canoe but not by English shallops and barges. Powhatan remained there several years, then moved to Matchut on the upper Pamunkey River near Opechancanough's seat at Youghtanund. However, although he would no longer trade with the English, Powhatan did not disengage. Using classic tactics of guerrilla warfare, his warriors roamed the woods and struck down whites who ventured outside the confines of Jamestown. Smith, unable to recognize, or reluctant to admit, that he had mismanaged negotiations with Powhatan, blamed the problem on the Indians' presumed natural treachery and malice, and in part on the foreign defectors (Germans and Poles) who, he charged, had turned the paramount chief against the English and urged him to withdraw into the interior. It is indicative of Smith's failure to face facts that, in his two histories of Virginia (published in 1612 and 1624), he titled his discussion of relations with the Powhatans during his final year "How the Salvages Became Subject to the English." Therein, he boasted about the effectiveness of his punishments of Indians imprisoned at Jamestown, being particularly proud of his seizure and incarceration of the *werowance* at nearby Paspahegh who had sheltered the renegade Germans (even though the *werowance* promptly escaped). He also offered, in demonstration of his particular prowess in the subjugation of Indians, a story about an incident in which a group of warriors supposedly threw down their weapons in panic and begged for peace as soon as they realized that they were facing the fearful Captain Smith, not Peter Winne, who had commanded an earlier incursion into their territory.[55]

Throughout, Smith would have us believe that his very presence often pacified Indians, and that his resolute action did the job when that was not enough. However, the facts, as we can dig them out of his accounts, and from other sources, suggest that was far from the truth. Near the end of his administration, Smith tried to relieve the food crisis at Jamestown by establishing new settlements. None of those ventures succeeded, undercut, Smith argued, by the ineptness of his subordinate commanders. At Nansemond (later called "Martin's Hundred"), as Smith's rival and antagonist George Percy related, the local *werowance* did not respond to an offer to buy land. (It appears that the English asked for an area used for religious observances and burials—in effect, sacred ground not open to strangers.) Convinced that he had probably killed the English envoys sent to his village, Percy and company simply seized what they wanted. "We beat the savages out of the island, burned their houses, ransacked their temples, took down the corpse of their dead king from off their tombs, and carried away their pearls, copper, and bracelets." Indian counterattacks, however, soon forced the evacuation of the would-be colonists. Smith recorded that the Indians carried off "a thousand bushels of Corne," and killed numerous settlers. In fact, half of the 100 who tried to occupy Nansemond died at the hands of the Indians. The Nansemonds were not only angered by English encroachment on their land, they were also deeply offended by the newcomers' desecration of their holy places.[56]

A larger undertaking upriver at the falls under the command of Francis West was also mismanaged. Smith believed the site West picked for his fort was not defensible. To provide a better one, he persuaded Tanx-Powhatan, a son of the paramount chief, to sell an Indian village, complete with a log palisade, a number of houses, and a 200-acre cornfield, paying for it with copper and with a pledge of military assistance against the Monacans. After exacting from the *werowance* what he believed was a promise to pay tribute to King James and turn over to English justice all Indians accused of stealing, the captain renamed the village, originally called "Powhatan" and reputed to be the paramount chief's birthplace, "Nonsuch," after one of the late Queen Elizabeth's palaces. We are not certain just how Tanx-Powhatan and his people really felt about all that. One historian suggests, plausibly, that they were probably scornful of "the puffed up little creature [who] bragged that his forces would protect the town against the Monacans. All this from a set of aliens who were known to be on the verge of starvation!" We do know that West and his men refused to occupy that village. Instead, they built their own fort at the site closer to the falls they had picked out earlier, successfully resisting Smith's efforts to relocate them. Their undertaking ended in disaster. Smith charged that West's men were a "disorderly company" that not only defied his authority, but also abused the Indians, "stealing their corne, robbing their gardens, beating them, breaking their houses and keeping some prisoners." The Indians struck back and "slew many, and so afrighted the rest" of the English settlers that the Indian prisoners they held were able to escape. Smith claimed that his personal reappearance at the settlement at one point so cowed the Indians that they pled for peace. That peace, however, was very short-lived. Before the end of fall 1609, 50 of the 120 Englishmen at the falls had died during Indian raids. The survivors returned to Jamestown. Historian J. Frederick Fausz writes that "Smith's presumption in sending rude and raucous colonists to eat up the provisions of alienated local tribes was the final provocation that precipitated England's first Indian war." But Smith's interactions with Powhatan were provocative from the outset. Smith did not understand, let alone honor, the protocols that governed relations with the *mamanatowick* in Powhatan's world. Through his "rejection of . . . [Powhatan's] basic assumptions of subordination and asymmetrical exchange in prestige goods" Smith essentially declared war. Powhatan expected Smith, as one of his *werowances,* to show appropriate deference, supply willingly and generously exotic goods, confirming and enhancing the paramount chief's power, and receive in reciprocation both goods and status. The English captain's sharp dealings, manipulative dishonesty, and presumptuous coercion profoundly offended the Powhatans' sensibilities.[57]

Smith's boast that he could manage "salvages" notwithstanding, guerilla warfare between Indians and English was well under way in Virginia before the end of Smith's presidency, provoked both by his coercion and humiliation of Powhatan, Opechancanough, and other *werowances*, and by his inability to control "rude and raucous colonists." It soon intensified. George Percy, who succeeded Smith as president, reported that shortly after the captain's departure, some 17 men he had sent to Port Comfort "to build a fort there" violated their orders and went to a nearby village to trade. They were later "found slain, with their mouths stopped full of bread, being done as it seemeth in contempt and scorn that others might expect the like when they should come to seek for bread and relief amongst them." Percy, a homely, quiet man not well regarded by his fellows, was not equal to the challenge. The brother of the Earl of Northumberland, he was determined to maintain proper, civilized decorum in what he called "this savage kingdom." As one historian notes, "in the midst of muck and mire, the extreme heat and cold, he insisted on wearing the finest clothes: a stiff-colored taffeta suit, accessories by a hat with a silk and gold band, shoes laced with ribbons, a pair of kid gloves and a garter." Percy himself took pride, as he reported, in keeping "continual and daily table for gentlemen of fashion." However, the return of the survivors of West's ill-fated venture at the falls forced him to cut the ration to "half a can of meal for a man a day." Even with that austerity, he calculated that the food supply would be exhausted in 12 weeks.[58]

In November, Powhatan sent two of his children and three white youths to Jamestown with a gift of venison and a promise to sell the colony grain. However, when Percy dispatched John Ratcliffe to his village to trade, Powhatan first cheated him, using false-bottom baskets that contained very little corn, then, when Ratcliffe protested, had him seized and "bound unto a tree naked with a fire before, and by women his flesh was scraped from his bones with mussel shells and, before his face, thrown into the fire." Of the party that accompanied Ratcliffe, by one estimate two-thirds, or some 33 men, were also killed, some when they entered Indian houses expecting food or entertainment, others shot with arrows as they tried to carry the baskets of corn to their ships. Young Henry Spelman, who had earlier been sent to live among the Powhatans to learn their language, related that before the trading began, Powhatan had ordered him and a young Dutchman of whom he was also fond to take refuge in another village so he would be out of harm's way. The killing of Ratcliffe and his men thus appears to have been premeditated, probably in revenge for earlier English insults and assaults. Spelman claimed there were only two survivors.[59]

Captain John Smith had not brought peace and security to Jamestown, for Englishmen were not safe outside the walls of the fort, unless they defected and sought refuge with Powhatan. The English colonists, by their unreasonable demands for food in a time of scarcity and by the terrorist tactics they had used to seize the resources Powhatan refused to offer, had triggered a guerrilla war. As William Strachey, arriving at Jamestown less than a year after Smith's departure, explained Powhatan's war tactics, the paramount chief's men drove away all the deer around Jamestown, killed English livestock (Strachey claimed 600 hogs were lost), cut off all trade, destroyed fishing nets, attacked and destroyed English boats in night-time raids, and ambushed and killed Englishmen who ventured outside the fort. Strachey believed Powhatan was winning, and attributed his success to lack of piety on the part of the colonists, which had "provoked the wrath of the Lord of Hosts and pulled down His judgments upon them." It is more reasonable to conclude, however, that the fault lay, not in their lack of prayer, but in their lack of understanding of the adversary. The persistent belief that through inspiring fear Christians could gain Indian acquiescence and even inspire love had been proved false first at Roanoke and again at Sagadahoc. It was even less effective in dealing with Powhatan.[60]

CHAPTER 4

❧

"A World of Miseries": The Virginia Colony, 1609–1614

A contemporary critic of the Virginia enterprise, on reviewing the first 15 years of the colony's existence, declared that the place deserved the "name of a slaughter house." He estimated the English mortality rate at 80 percent. Although no exact estimate is possible, there is no doubt that a substantial majority of the early settlers perished within a few years of their landing on American soil. Conditions were particularly grim during the half decade after John Smith's departure. Jamestown's commanders were troubled by defections of a number of angry and desperate settlers who found life on the other side of the cultural divide more promising than the prospect of dying of hunger or arrows at the English fort. Smith recorded some of the early desertions, attributing them either to the greed of gold seekers or the malice of foreigners. However, most of those who fled Jamestown were driven by something more fundamental: the desire to survive.[1]

To hold the colony together, its leaders resorted to extreme measures. A law promulgated on their advice by the Virginia Company in London in 1610 forbade any settler, on pain of death, "to run away from the Colonie, to Powhatan, or to any savage Werowance else whatsoever." George Percy described the enforcement of that law in 1611 at the English outpost at Henrico by Sir Thomas Dale: "Some he appointed to be hanged. Some to be broken upon wheels, others to be staked and some to be shot to death." We do not know exactly how many were executed. We do know that the defections continued. In 1612, the Spanish ambassador to England reported to Madrid that he had learned that between 40 to 50 Englishman were living in Powhatan's villages and had married Indian women. His account is imprecise but nonetheless credible. One recent scholar notes:

[T]he weight of evidence forces the conclusion that a significant number of the poorer elements at Jamestown saw desertion to the Indians as the most extreme indictment of the colony and as the most effective means of winning freedom for themselves. Of those who were granted the opportunity of returning with pardon few accepted, and some went to great lengths by fleeing from one tribe to another to ensure they would not be reclaimed.

In addition to privation, the "poorer elements" resented the harsh discipline imposed by the "better sort" who ran the colony.[2]

From November 1609 until the following May, Powhatan maintained a sustained siege at Jamestown. These are the months remembered in Virginia histories as the "Starving Time." Of the 220 settlers at the fort at the beginning of the siege, only 100 remained alive at its end. Some died of disease or Indian arrows, but most starved to death. With the collapse of trade relations with the Powhatans, Jamestown, as its leader George Percy related, once again "felt the sharp prick of hunger . . . a world of miseries ensued." Only a small enclave of 30 men at the mouth of the James River, in an enclosure they called Fort Algernon, survived the siege unscathed, ignored by the Indians and sustained by a number of hogs. At Jamestown, desperate men stole food from the common store, "for the which," Percy noted, "I caused them to be executed." Soon, to survive, the settlers ate their horses, "as long as they lasted," then "were glad to make shift with vermin, as dogs, cats, and mice." Next they ate "boots, shoes, or any other leather some could come by." The survivors foraged in the woods for "serpents and snakes and to dig in the earth for wild and unknown roots." However, as they ventured outside the fort's walls, "many of our men were cut off and slain by the savages." As the desperation and horror of famine deepened, the colonists, looking "ghastly and pale in every face," did "those things which seem incredible, as dig up dead corpse out of graves and to eat them, and some have licked up the blood which hath fallen from their weak fellows." The "most lamentable Act," Percy wrote, was that a man named "Collines murdered his wife, ripped the child out of her womb and threw it into the river, and after chopping the mother into pieces . . . salted her for his food." Collines confessed his guilt under torture and was burned at the stake. Percy also related that one starving settler, Hughe Pryse, took to "blaspheming, exclaiming, and crying out that there was no God, alleging that if there were a God he would not suffer His creatures, whom He had made and framed, to endure those miseries, and to perish for want of food and sustenance." Percy regarded it to be a mark of "God's indignation" at such an outburst that the very same day Pryse, foraging outside the walls, was killed by Indians and "his corpse rent to pieces by wolves or other wild beasts, and his bowels torn out of his body," whereas another victim of Indian arrows, "a corpulent fat man" with far more flesh on his bones was found with his corpse intact.[3]

In May 1610, some 135 new colonists, survivors of a shipwreck that had left them marooned on Bermuda for a year, arrived at Jamestown. They were led by Sir Thomas Gates who now, under orders from the Company in London, assumed command. The fort was no longer defensible. The new governor's close associate

William Strachey reported that "we found the palisadoes torn down, the ports open, the gates torn off their hinges, and empty houses." Many of the houses, once occupied by settlers now dead, had been demolished and burned as the survivors refused to go outside the gates "to fetch other firewood." They had good reason, as "it is true that the Indian killed as fast without the bounds of their blockhouse, as famine and pestilence did within." Gates was so appalled that he spoke, during his first address to the survivors, of the possibility that they would need to evacuate the colony and return to England, a statement greeted, as Strachey recalled, "by a general acclamation and shout of joy on all sides." The new settlers who had arrived with Gates "were disheartened and faint when they saw this misery," and had little desire to remain.[4]

Although John Smith's tactics in dealing with Indians often had been heavy-handed and provocative, he made an effort to balance terror with diplomacy. His successors in the conduct of Indian affairs have been described aptly by one historian as "spoiled aristocrats whose incompetence, pride and paranoia, cruelty and cowardice, gave the Powhatans a chilling preview of domination by England's best." Not even friendly and cooperative Indians were exempt from their terrorism. After the November trade mission to Powhatan had ended in the killing of Ratcliffe and of most of his company, Percy dispatched a party of some 36 men under the command of Francis West, a younger brother of Privy Councilor and future governor Thomas West, Lord de la Warre, to seek help from the Patawomecks on the lower Potomac River. Against the wishes of Powhatan, the semi-independent Patawomecks sold a fairly substantial supply of corn to West and his men. However, the English turned on their hosts, beheading and mutilating two tribesmen and enraging the rest. Percy related that as they sailed by Fort Algernon at the mouth of the James River, "Captain Davis did call unto them, acquainting them with our great wants, exhorting them to make all speed they could to relieve us." West and his men ignored Davis and sailed home to England, without delivering any of the food so desperately needed at Jamestown. The colony was left in "extreme misery."[5]

In a promotional pamphlet published in 1610 to answer charges of mismanagement, the Virginia Company tried to place the blame for the Indians' hostility on Francis West's atrocity against the Patawomecks. However, the officers appointed by the Company were hardly peace makers. To cite another example of their provocative belligerence and cruelty, in Percy's account, we read that Sir Thomas Gates commanding at Jamestown in 1611 seized ostensibly friendly Indians who came to the fort "bringing victuals with them" and had them executed "as a Terrour for the rest." Gates suspected that they were spies. Strachey added that the prices they asked for the food they brought conveyed a "contempt" the English could not "well endure." Powhatan periodically sent Indians to Jamestown to offer to trade. The English there may or may not have been right in suspecting treachery, but as they invariably either drove away or killed those envoys, we have no way of determining whether a peaceful accommodation with Powhatan would have been possible in 1611. It is recorded that Powhatan offered, on several occasions, to accept a small English settlement limited to the immediate Jamestown vicinity, but that was a condition the Company was not willing to consider.[6]

Gates had arrived in Virginia armed with a patent that abolished the government under which Percy was currently serving as president and put in its place a governor endowed with absolute authority. Gates was empowered to deal with dissension through the imposition of martial law and, upon its declaration, could impose the death penalty at his discretion. The Company sitting in London now mandated a new Indian policy. Although earlier the Company's council had called for an alliance with Powhatan and had instructed Newport to crown him, the paramount chief was now declared an enemy. The council hoped he could be captured by Gates and removed from power. If that were not feasible, then Gates should make all the *werowances* directly tributary to King James, and thereby end Powhatan's presumed "tyranny" over them. The council recognized that Indian alliances were essential. However, although previously Jamestown had offered to fight on Powhatan's side against his enemies, the Company now directed Gates to make friends with the lesser *werowances*, particularly those on the fringes of his empire and also with the distant tribes that periodically waged war against Powhatan. The Indians of Virginia, the London Company imagined, waited eagerly for liberation from Powhatan. They were, presumably, not only prospective allies, but would soon be willing subjects. After the new policy was in place, the *werowances,* at each harvest, could be expected to send Gates substantial tribute in corn, provide "many baskets of Dye," and also "many dozens of skins . . . you shall quietly drawe to yourselves an annual revenue of every Commodity in that country." Gates was also advised that he could draw on Indian labor in the building of colonial settlements, as each village chief would send "some many of his people to work weekly" as part of the tribute owed the English liberator. Those expectations, inspired perhaps by the example of the labor system developed by the Spanish in New Spain, proved utterly unrealistic.[7]

The company's instructions reminded Gates that "the most pious and noble end" of this venture was "the conversion of the natives to the knowledge and worship of the true god and their redeemer Jesus Christ." To that end, the governor was directed to take some Indian children from their homes and educate them in "your language and customs." However, the council saw a serious obstacle to Indian salvation and to English security in the influence of the native "Priests," who would continue to "poison and infecte their mindes" if not silenced. Unless he dealt with them, Gates was warned, "you shall never make any great progress in this glorious worke, nor have any Civill peace" in Virginia. The council advised the governor that as those Indian shamans were "murtherers of Soules and sacrificers of gods image to the Devill," it would not be "cruelty nor breache of Charity" to put them to death. They were beyond redemption, being "so wrapped up in the fogge and misery of their iniquity." Gates's instructions also called for strict security measures to guard against Indian "treachery." Trade in weapons or in iron implements that could be fashioned into weapons was to be made the subject of "some sharpe lawes." Overall dependence on Indian trade was to be minimized.

Every effort should be made to achieve self-sufficiency. Such trade as the colonists might carry on with Indians was to be conducted only within the fort. The London council directed that the fort itself be moved to a new and more defensible site, and Jamestown be used only as a river port.[8]

Those instructions, let it be repeated, revealed a serious lack of understanding of the true situation in Virginia. It is not surprising that during his short governorship, Gates achieved none of the objectives laid out for him. Jamestown once again faced the prospect of starvation as the meager food supplies Gates had brought with him ran low. No crops had been planted at Jamestown that spring. Although the settlers had earlier cleared fields outside the walls, they could not be cultivated because of Indian raids. There appeared to be no way, given Indian hostility and English weakness, that the settlement could find enough food to survive. Smith's method of coercing trade was no longer workable, given the anger inspired by English atrocities and the weakness of the English garrison. Accordingly, on June 7, after only a few weeks at Jamestown, Gates abandoned a plan to move the settlement to a more defensible site at Port Comfort, and decided the time had come to return to England. After blocking a move to burn the place down, Gates ordered the heavy guns buried by the fort gate, the rest loaded onto ships, and "at the beating of the drum," summoned the men to board.[9]

What one eminent historian has called "the Jamestown fiasco" should have ended then, on June 7, 1610. However, as the small flotilla was lying at anchor at Mulberry Island waiting for the tide, Gates and company saw a longboat approaching from Port Comfort, and learned of the arrival of a new governor, Thomas West, Lord De La Warre, who had been appointed as Gates replacement in an obscure political deal in England intended to protect the influence over the Virginia venture of Robert Cecil, Earl of Salisbury. (In accordance with custom, we shall henceforth refer to Thomas West as Delaware.) The company also sent some 300 new settlers and a supply of food, munitions, and other necessities. Landing at Jamestown on June 10, Delaware found the place, as he related in a letter to Lord Salisbury, "very noisome and unwholesome," and attributed much of its misery to the "idleness of our own people." A man of influence, a privy councilor and a veteran of the wars in the Netherlands, Delaware was an avid promoter of American colonization, He had been named to the Council for Virginia in 1609. After reading aloud his commission to the Jamestown survivors and formally relieving Gates as governor, he revoked Gates's evacuation order and went about the task of rebuilding the settlement and placing it on a firm military footing. He named his predecessor the colony's lieutenant general.[10]

William Strachey, who served as secretary of the colony for a little less than a year, returning to England in late 1611, described the layout of Jamestown as consisting of palisades, with a watchtower equipped with cannon at every corner, several streets lined with houses, and a central square with "a marketplace, a storehouse, and a *corps du guard*, as likewise a pretty chapel," now "ruined and unfrequented." To underscore the rebirth of Jamestown as an outpost of Christian civilization in the wilderness, Strachey wrote at length of Lord Delaware's plan to repair the chapel, which

> shall have a chancel in it of cedar with a communion table of black walnut, and all the pews of cedar with fair broad windows to shut and open, as weather shall allow, of the same wood, a pulpit of the same with a font hewn hollow like a canoa, with two bells at the west end. It is so cast as it be very light within.

To enhance and maintain its beauty, Governor Delaware ordered that "it be kept passing sweet and trimmed up with divers flowers." There were to be three sermons a week, two on Sunday and one on Thursday. The church bell twice a day would direct that "each man addresseth himself to prayers." Those prayers were of no little importance to Delaware, who held that England's presence in Virginia not only required God's aid, but also was part of His great plan for mankind. Before leaving London, he had secured the publication of a sermon by the Puritan preacher William Crashaw, a sermon that called on the newly appointed governor to remember that there was "a time when we were savage and uncivil, and worshipped the devil," but had gained the blessings of civilization from the Romans and the gift of eternal salvation from "the Apostles and their disciples." Delaware's charge, Crashaw proclaimed, was to be both a Roman governor and a Christian missionary to the lost souls in America and thereby defeat the devil "in his own kingdom."[11]

His mission, as Delaware understood it, also depended upon the upholding of that respect for hierarchy that he regarded as essential to true civilization. The Company had been appalled at reports of the dissension that had previously wracked the colony. Thus, they had granted their new governors the power to declare martial law and execute troublemakers. Delaware relied also on pomp and circumstance to convey the necessary message. Strachey related that when the governor

> goeth to church, he is accompanied with all the councilors, captains, other officers, and all the gentlemen, and with a guard of halberdiers in His Lordship's livery (fair red cloaks) to the number of fifty, both on each side and behind him; and being in the church, His Lordship hath his seat in the choir in a green velvet chair with a cloth, with a velvet cushion spread on a table before him, on which he kneeleth; and on each side sit the council, captains, and officers each in his place, and when he returneth home again, he is waited on in his house in the same manner.

On his arrival, Lord Delaware found no house in Jamestown worthy of a governor, so he lived aboard ship.[12]

The supply ships that accompanied the new governor had not brought provisions adequate to last through the coming winter. The Company had previously sent around 600 hogs and a large flock of chickens to provide a secure source of meat. The planners assumed they were still available to provide essential protein. However, those animals that the Indians had not killed had been slaughtered and eaten during the previous winter's "Starving Time," along with horses, mares, cats, dogs, and whatever vermin could be caught. Writing to London on July 7, 1610, Delaware reported "there was not above one sow we can hear of left alive, nor a hen nor chick in the fort." In June, the governor had agreed with Sir George Somers's proposal to return to Bermuda to "fetch 6 months provisions of flesh and fish, and some live hog(s)." In the meantime, he tried to harvest some of that great wealth of sturgeon Gates reported swarming in the river by Jamestown. It was to little avail. He then sent fishing parties into the bay, where they fished the waters between Cape Henry and Cape Charles. Delaware reported that the fisherman netted "so small a quantity and store of fish" that they could only feed themselves during the trip, and brought next to nothing back to Jamestown. Strachey reported that the men did not really know how to fashion effective fishing nets, or how to use them. Regarding the Indian trade that once had provided not only grain, but venison and fish, Somers, writing in June, advised Lord Salisbury that although the Indians seemed to be afraid to come to the fort to trade, "the truth is they had nothing to trade withal but mulberries." In his letter of July 7, Delaware advised London that if the plantation were to survive, "a necessary quantity of provision for a year at least must be carefully sent with men" more able than "the distempered bodies and infected minds" then occupying Jamestown. He added that the colony, weakened by disease, was almost out of medicine, with a three-week supply, at best, remaining. His report was countersigned by Gates, Wenman, Percy, and Strachey. In response, the Company, determined to protect its investment, undertook a major fund-raising effort, dispatching two major resupply expeditions during the year that followed.[13]

Although troubled by poor health throughout his time in Virginia, Lord Delaware proved to be a tough, resourceful commander. He saw the conflict with Powhatan as a holy war, and believed that with the new manpower he brought to the colony, he could soon go on the offensive. Many of the men who had accompanied him to Virginia were veterans of Ireland or of the continental wars, as the Company had emphasized military experience in its recruiting. For all of the men at Jamestown, the governor initiated regular and rigorous military drills, demanded regular church attendance, and forbade personal association with Indians in any form. Delaware declared that his immediate objective was "to tame the fury and treachery of the savages." In exhortations to the troops, he compared Virginia's Indians with the Canaanites of the Old Testament and cast the English in the role of Israelites claiming their promised land while serving as the righteous instruments of God's punishment of the heathen. However, although his instructions had directed Delaware to regard Powhatan as an enemy, he was also advised to seek friendly relations with those Indians who either already opposed him or who might be willing to assert their independence. The ancient imperial strategy of divide and rule, not the doctrine of total race war, shaped the London planners thoughts on Indian pacification. Moreover, the Company repeated in its charge to Delaware the premise it had emphasized for Gates: The salvation of the Indians was "the most pious and noble end of this plantation." To facilitate their conversion, the Council suggested to Delaware that he consider sending some Indian children to London for instruction. England's imperial visionaries harbored a very unrealistic view of the appeal of their religion to "savages," and some have doubted their sincerity in any case. At least one of Virginia's founders regarded all talk of Indian salvation hypocritical. The Company's promoters, John Smith declared, made "religion their color, when all their aim was present profit."[14]

For the first few weeks, Delaware bided his time, focusing on the reconstruction of the fort and the preparation of his men for combat. Hearing that Powhatan was not only heavily armed with English weapons, but had been instructed by the Dutch renegades on their use, he avoided contact for a time. However, on July 6, one of Gates's men, Humfrey Blunt, while trying to recover a longboat, was seized by Indians, "who led him up into the woods and sacrificed him." Gates, enraged, persuaded the governor of the need to take revenge. An armed party accordingly was dispatched to Kecoughton on the lower James River, where one of Powhatan's sons was *werowance*. After disembarking, Gates staged a demonstration of English drumming and dancing to lure the Indians out into the open, then attacked, killing five immediately and wounding several others. Some of the fleeing Indians, in Percy's words, having sustained "extraordinary large and mortal wounds" were later found dead in the woods. The raid killed 20 villagers and left the remainder homeless. Ironically, the victims, one recent historian comments, were "the only villagers who had fed Englishmen all winter." Strachey, in his report of this action, noted that the *werowance* got away, "but left his poor baggage and treasure to the spoil of our soldiers, which was only a few baskets of old wheat and some other of peas and beans, a little tobacco, and some few women's girdles of . . . grass silk." (The spoils were not always so sparse. Elsewhere, Strachey noted that the looting of Indian villages often furnished decoration for the bare cabins at Jamestown, as the soldiers brought home "a delicate wrought, fine kind of mat" that served "to dress their chambers and inward rooms, which make their houses so much more handsome.") At the site of the devastated Indian settlement at Kecoughton, which lies within the later city of Hampton, Gates's men began the construction of a small fort they named after Prince Charles.[15]

In mid July, a Paspahegh attack on the blockhouse commanding the entrance to Jamestown was repulsed after four of its defenders were killed. Delaware responded with a diplomatic offensive, sending emissaries to Powhatan to ask that he punish those of his people who had assaulted Englishmen. The emissaries assured Powhatan that "the lord governor and captain general did not suppose that these mischiefs were conceived by him or with his knowledge, but conceived them to be the acts of his worst and unruly people." Powhatan should issue a general order forbidding such acts and also either punish past perpetrators himself or turn them over to the governor. He was reminded that he had "upon his knees received a crown and a scepter" that bound him to obedience to King James.

Duty to his sovereign now also required obedience to Delaware's order that he surrender any Englishmen who might be living with his people, as the governor spoke for the king. Powhatan was unimpressed, sending word, as Strachey recorded, "that we should depart his country or confine ourselves to James Town." Otherwise, "he would give in command to his people to kill us, and do unto us all the mischief which they at their pleasure could and we feared." Powhatan ended by saying he would receive no more messengers from Jamestown "unless they brought him a coach and three horses, for he had understood by the Indians which were in England how such was the state of great werowances and lords in England to ride and visit other great men."[16]

Shortly thereafter, Powhatan's men, in twos and threes, started visiting Jamestown daily. Delaware was convinced they were spies seeking out signs of weakness preparatory to another attack and siege. He ordered them to stay away. Some then took to hiding in the grass or thicket outside the wall, where they would lie in wait and ambush those who came out "to gather strawberries or to fetch fresh water." Strachey wrote that in the days that followed, "they killed many of our men." In one skirmish, two Indians from Paspahegh were captured. The English recognized one of the captives as "a notable villain," who had participated in several ambushes. Delaware ordered "his right hand struck off," then told the newly mutilated Indian to take a message to Powhatan. The paramount chief was to be warned that if he did not immediately surrender all the Englishman living in his domain and turn over all the English weapons in his possession, Lord Delaware would not only kill the other Paspahegh, but execute every other Indian he could capture and burn all "cornfields, towns and villages."[17]

Predictably, Powhatan's response was defiant. Percy tells us he returned "no other than proud and disdainful answers." Delaware retaliated. In August, raiding parties from Jamestown struck several nearby villages, slaughtering men, women, and children indiscriminately; burning houses; and looting cornfields. At Paspahegh, Percy kidnapped a wife of the *werowance* and two of her children. However, on the voyage downriver back to Jamestown, as Percy related, his men "began to murmur because the queen and her Children were spared." After conferring with his officers, Percy ordered them to throw the children overboard. They did so, and then used them for target practice, "shooting out their brains in the water." Arriving at Jamestown, Percy fell into an argument with Captain James Davis, his second in command, over the disposal of the "queen." Davis wanted her burned alive, but Percy, tired of "so much bloodshed that day," ordered her put to the sword. Lord Delaware, for his part, was irritated that she had been brought back to Jamestown alive. A few days later, Davis attacked the Chickahominys, stealing their corn, setting fire to their houses, and destroying their "Temples and Idolls." An attack on the Wariscoyans followed soon thereafter. It was less successful, in Percy's eyes, than the earlier actions. The Indians there, "all fled and escaped," so the English had to be satisfied with "cutting down their corn, burning their houses, and such like." The commanders of that raid, Samuel Argall and Edward Brewster, incinerated two villages.[18]

Commenting on Delaware's August offensive, historian J. Frederick Fausz writes:

> These successful summer raids of catharsis and convenience translated England's *ad terrorem* tactics from the Irish wars of the late sixteenth century, specifically the use of deception, ambush and surprise, the random slaughter of both sexes and all ages, the calculated murder of innocent captives, and the destruction of entire villages—into a frontier idiom for the first time.

Fausz concludes that the raids, mounted against "relatively unthreatening people living within a twenty-mile radius of the colonial capital," were intended to remove the danger of starvation at Jamestown, deprive the Powhatans of provisions, and free "colonists from farm fields for use on the battlefield." Lord Delaware clearly did not intend to bow to Powhatan's demand that he remain within the confines of the Jamestown region.[19]

Actually, he had little choice. Although enough food had been seized during the August raids to avert starvation, terrorism and theft would not solve Jamestown's economic problems. The colony was expected not only to achieve self-sufficiency, but also to yield a profit to investors. The Company in London was very disappointed by the "smallness of the return" that Delaware sent home that summer. The value of the lumber he sent with the returning ships did not come close to defraying the cost of the supplies he had brought with him. The Company considered abandoning the venture as a bad investment and summoned Sir Thomas Gates home for consultations. Sir Thomas, as William Strachey recorded, swore that Virginia was a land of plenty and enumerated the riches to be had there. They included many types of wood: "oak, wainscot, walnut trees, bay trees, ash, sarsafrase, liveoak green all the year, cedar and fir." The land's forests could provide invaluable supplies of naval stores "of pitch and tar, of clapboards, pipe-starves, masts, and excellent boards of forty, fifty, and sixty length and three foot breath . . . one fir tree is able to make the mainmast of the greatest ship in England." Gates also rhapsodized about "the incredible variety of sweet woods, the mulberry trees which in so warm a climate may cherish and feed millions of silkworms and return us in a very short time as great a plenty of silk as is ventured into the whole world from all parts of Italy." The land was rich in iron ore, and could also provide "a kind hemp, or flax, and silk grass" for "all manner of excellent cordage." The river that ran by Jamestown, Gates avowed, swarmed with sturgeon, "the land aboundeth with vines"; the woods were filled with beavers, foxes, and squirrels; and "the waters do nourish a great increase of otters" that could provide "precious furs." There were, in addition, "dyes and drugs" to be had in Virginia. Native corn yielded a far greater return than any grain in England, and transplanted orange trees flourished. No doubt lemons, sugar cane, almond, rice, anise seed, and other commodities that could not be grown in the British Isles could be cultivated in Virginia. The land was, Gates declared in summary, "one of the goodliest countries under the sun."[20]

Some of Gates's testimony was fanciful. Neither silkworms nor orange and lemon trees ever flourished in Virginia. However, the Company was impressed by his report, invested more resources in the venture, and mounted a public relations campaign. Preachers at St. Paul's Cross, the great open-air gathering place by the cathedral, proclaimed England's divine mission in America and sought to refute the stories of misery, starvation, and savagery told by survivors returning from Jamestown. Some sermons equated criticism of the Virginia venture to the persecution of the early Christians. In a more secular vein, writers hired by the Company extolled Virginia as a worldly paradise.[21]

Determined to meet the expectations and demands of the investors, Delaware, in November 1610, dispatched a force of some 200 armed men up the James River to the falls. Their mission was to verify reports of iron mines in the interior, find other sources of mineral wealth, and, in compliance with the Company's instructions, build a new, better located settlement to replace Jamestown as the primary English city in Virginia. To assist in the search for mines, the Company had engaged a number of professionals led by a Swiss immigrant who called himself William Faldoe, but whose real name was Volday. Faldoe/Volday was an imposter, and according to Captain John Smith, a turncoat. The venture itself was unproductive. At the village of Appamatuck, scantily clad women led by Opossunoquonuske their "queen" (*weroansqua,* feminine equivalent of *werowance*) lured all 14 of Delaware's mining experts onshore, offering, as Percy recorded, "to feast them. . . . Our men like greedy fools accepted thereof, more esteeming a little food, than their own lives and safety." In response to an appeal not to alarm the women, they left their weapons in the boat and entered Indian lodgings expecting food and entertainment. Several were killed on the spot; others, sorely wounded, made their escape, but, with one exception, "within two days after also died." Percy believed the Appamatuck were avenging the killings at Kecoughton several months earlier. Ironically, the sole survivor of the Appamatuck massacre was the drummer who had lured the Kecoughtons to their deaths. In retaliation, the English burned the village and slaughtered 20 of its inhabitants. The "queen" was shot while fleeing into the woods, and, as Strachey recorded, suffered a miscarriage. Throughout the remainder of its westward trek, hostile Indians harassed the English party. With much difficulty the governor built "Lawarre's fort" at the falls, and spent a hard winter there. Powhatan's warriors raided the makeshift settlement repeatedly. Their loud invocations of the wrath of their war god unnerved the defenders. The sources do not reveal how many Englishmen died at the falls that winter, but do indicate that conditions there were grim. Percy remarked laconically that at Fort Lawarre "neither sickness nor scarcity was wanting."[22]

Among the sick was the governor himself, who after several months moved back to Jamestown, and then returned to England. In a letter to the Company responding to critics who raised questions about his early and unexpected departure, Delaware related that he suffered from poor health throughout his time in Virginia. He had been afflicted "with a hot and violent ague" shortly after his arrival. He was bled by the resident physician, and after about three weeks appeared to have recovered. However, he soon "began to be distempered with other grievous sicknesses which successively and severally assaulted me," including scurvy, and the "flux," which was marked by severe diarrhea and violent stomach cramps. He also suffered a recurrence of the ague and was afflicted with gout. His health broken, Delaware left Virginia in June 1611, after a year's residence, placing George Percy in command as interim governor. In a summary and defense of his governorship, he reported to the Council of Virginia that the colony's settlers were no longer in danger of starvation, with "at least ten months victuals in their store house." They were now able to grow corn, as their fields were defended by three small forts built at strategic points outside of Jamestown. He related that he had imported cattle which were flourishing, ready to calf and yielding "milk . . . a great nourishment and refreshing to our people." The colony now awaited the arrival of "two hundred swine" he had ordered. As to Indian affairs, Delaware placed particular emphasis on the success of Sir Samuel Argall, who in a series of probes in Chesapeake Bay in autumn and winter 1610 to 1611 had opened up trade relations "with petty kings in these parts" willing to defy Powhatan. Once again, for "a piece of iron, copper, etc." Indians would not only "truck great quantities of corn," but show "our people certain signs of amity and affection." Delaware reported that although Powhatan "still remains our enemy," the *werowance* at Potomac was "a king as great." Trade on the Potomac River would bring great wealth to the Virginia Company, Delaware declared, for on its banks "are grown the goodliest trees for masts that may be found anywhere in the world; hemp better than the English, growing wild in abundance." To the North could be found "mines of antimony and lead." The ailing Lord Delaware sailed with Argall for England in June 1611. He never fully recovered his health, but nonetheless tried to resume his work as colonizer. He died on his way back to Virginia in 1618.[23]

Delaware's assessment of Indian relations underplayed the continuing danger. The Potomac tribes cultivated by Argall would come to play a major role in ending hostilities and promoting English security, but at the time of Delaware's departure, they were not an effective counterweight to Powhatan, who remained dominant in the region. His raiding parties had continued to harass Jamestown throughout his governorship. A major attack occurred on March 29, a day after Lord Delaware's departure for England. On that day, one Lieutenant Puttock, an officer much despised by the Paspaheghs because of his recent killing of one of their elders, was in command at the blockhouse that protected the route from the mainland across the peninsula to Jamestown fort. From the woods, Puttock heard the mocking taunts of Paspaheghs hidden in the underbrush. Disobeying his standing orders to remain in the blockhouse, Puttock charged the woods with all 20 of his men. They soon faced a force Percy, probably with some exaggeration, claimed numbered 400 or 500 warriors. Whatever their number, they quickly dispatched Puttock and all his men, who fell studded with arrows that had flown, Percy wrote, "as thick as hail . . . the ground thereabouts was almost covered with them." As the English died, the Paspaheghs made "both the air and the woods" ring with their victory cries, then, as Percy ordered a counterattack from Jamestown, withdrew.

Although victorious in that engagement, the Paspaheghs decided life near James-town was far too vexatious. By May, they had left the vicinity. The English found their village site deserted, "overgrown with shrubs and bushes."[24]

On May 12, 1611, Sir Thomas Dale took command of the colony, bringing with him from England 300 new settlers and a herd of cattle "besides great store of armor, munitions, victuals and other provisions." In August, with the return of Gates from England, his forces were further augmented by some 270 more, some of them men of previous military experience. The colony's planners in London had determined to establish a powerful armed bastion in Virginia. Richard Hakluyt had expressed their disenchantment with peaceful persuasion of Indians when he declared in 1609, "if gentle polishing will not serve, then we shall not want hammerours and rough masons enough, I meane our old soldiours trained up in the Netherlands to prepare them to our preachers hands." But the colony was hardly on a war footing. Dale, a severe disciplinarian who had served previously as the colony's marshal, had been shocked by the conditions he found upon his return to Virginia. Discipline had collapsed; the men were idle. Rather than attending to the needs of agriculture and war, they went "bowling in the streets" of the dilapidated capital. Dale informed the council in London that the storehouse, the church, the stables, the munitions house, and the powder house were all falling down, and the settlement lacked a source of clean water, all of which required "much labor and many hands." Accordingly, he introduced a stringent new set of regulations that put all colonists to work under rigid military discipline, assigned to work gangs and summoned by beat of a drum, as Dale explained, "some to plant, some to sow corn, and others to build boats and houses." They were permitted little leisure until released by the drum at the day's end.[25]

Under the arbitrary powers granted governors under the new patent, Dale was authorized to impose the death penalty for murder, rape, adultery, blasphemy, disrespect for the Bible, private trading (even with other Englishmen), killing any domestic animal (even a chicken), plucking ears of corn or even grapes, and for committing any other act of theft no matter how petty. There were some lesser penalties. Swaggering, for example, was punished initially with the requirement that the offender apologize to all on bended knee. (The third offense brought life-time enslavement in the galleys.) However, the code emphasized capital punishment, and it was enforced with severity by the new governor. It is recorded that Dale ordered a man who had filched a couple of pints of oatmeal put to death in a singularly cruel manner. To fit the punishment to the crime, he first ordered that a needle be thrust through the man's tongue, after which he was chained to a tree and allowed to starve to death. Dale's contemporary critics later protested that, under his rule, freeborn Englishmen for minor disciplinary infractions were shot, starved, hung, burned alive, and broken on the wheel. But in London, many of Jamestown's sponsors agreed with Ralph Harmor that there was no other way of dealing with the "dangerous and incurable" sluggards who were endangering the settlement's survival. Captain John Smith agreed, writing that without Dale's severity, "I see not how the utter subversion of the Colonie should have been prevented." Later historians have also disagreed in their assessments of Dale and his measures. Some see him as the colony's savior, emphasizing the particular problems Dale faced; others, as a sadist whose cruelty far exceeded all rational need. Most, however, concede that he was a man of great determination.[26]

Not surprisingly, conflicts with the Indians continued. The cost was high. It is estimated that around 150 of the colonists died during the second half of 1611 as Dale resumed efforts to build new settlements upriver. That death rate amounted to more than a fifth of the Englishmen in Virginia. Percy included in his narrative a story that tells us much concerning the mental state of Dale and his warriors. Attributing the strange event he related to "the savages' sorceries and charms," he wrote that as the governor and his closest advisers were "sitting in an Indian's house, a fantasy possessed them that they imagined the savages were set upon them, each man taking one another for an Indian." They fell "pell-mell upon one another, beating one another down and breaking one of another's heads, that much mischief might have been done but that it pleased God the fantasy was taken away whereby they had been deluded." Percy's account exposes the fear and paranoia of men who believed that they confronted satanists in the wilderness.[27]

Dale mounted an aggressive campaign against Powhatan intended, as he explained to the Earl of Salisbury in a letter dated August 17, to drive him out of the area or force him to enter into "a firm accommodation with ourselves." He proposed to secure mastery over a tract of land on both sides of the river extending some 150 miles inland, a tract then containing "the principallest seats of Powhatan." Dale told Salisbury that he would fortify the mouth of the James River at Port Comfort, establish a major agricultural center at Kecoughton, and take over Powhatan's "chief town" at Werowocomoco for "my second plantation." His major project would be to "plant a new town" at Henrico 80 miles upriver from Jamestown, "a convenient strong, healthy and sweet seat" for a new capital. He also intended to occupy the site at the falls where earlier efforts at English occupation had failed. After he was in "full possession of Powhatan's country," those new settlements "would afford many excellent seats for many a thousand householder." No longer would Virginia be settled by a mere "handful of wretched and untoward people." As for Powhatan, with a proper application of force, he could be persuaded "either . . . [to] join [in] friendship with us or . . . leave then to our possession his country, and thereby leave us in security." Dale asked that 2,000 more men experienced in war be dispatched to Virginia to join in his campaign of occupation and conquest. His objective was the destruction of Powhatan's power and the annexation of his territory.[28]

The several hundred reinforcements Dale received in 1611 fell far short of his request, but they did give the English in Virginia an adequate army for the first time. Unlike their predecessors, Dale's soldiers were well supplied, being fully equipped not only with guns, but also with armor. In early June, Dale's first strike fell on the Nansemonds, who occupied a strategically critical position near the mouth of the James River. Although Dale's 100-man company was outnumbered by about two to one by the defenders, Indian arrows for the first time proved ineffective. In a pitched battle on a field near their village, the Nansemonds lost a fifth of their number to musket fire, but killed no Englishmen and wounded only a few. Percy related that "not being acquainted nor accustomed to encounter . . . men in armour," were astounded when "they did not see any of our men fall as they had done in other conflicts." In desperation, they resorted to

> exorcisms, conjurations and charms, throwing fire up into the sky, running up and down with rattles, and making many diabolical gestures with many necromantic spells and incantations, [imagining] thereby to cause rain to fall from the clouds to extinguish and put out our men's matches and to wet and spoil their powder. But neither the devil whom they adore nor all their sorcerers did anything to avail them. For our men cut down their corn, burned their houses, and, besides those they had slain, brought some of them prisoners to our fort.[29]

With the Nansemonds now subdued and the Paspaheghs driven from the region, the lower James River was reasonably secure. Dale accordingly turned his attention to the construction of a fortified city at Henrico, which would serve as a hub for the new English settlements he hoped to establish throughout the region. Alexander Whitaker, the Anglican minister who accompanied Dale's expedition related that Powhatan sent a warning that if the English tried to move upriver, he "would destroy us after a strange manner." Mulling over Powhatan's threat to use sorcery against them, Dale's men were on edge. Whitaker recalled that during a preliminary probe of the upper James River, Dale's party, encamped near the falls and at prayers, heard "a strange noise . . . coming out of the corn towards the trenches of our men like an Indian *hup hup!* with an *oho oho!* Some say they saw one like an Indian leap over the fire and run into the corn with the same noise, at the which all our men were confusedly amazed." In their befuddlement, they themselves "could speak nothing but *oho oho*" and began assaulting one another, using "the wrong end of their arms." After a few minutes, they recovered their senses and "began to search for their supposed enemies, but, finding none, remained ever after very quiet." Whitaker was reminded of another strange incident, during the Nansemond raid when, marching past an Indian town, they saw a "mad crew dancing" as one of their shaman "tossed smoke and flame out of a thing like a censer." One of their Indian guides told the English that "there would be very much rain presently, and indeed there was forthwith exceeding thunder and lightning and much rain within five miles, and so further off." Writing to the Reverend William Crashaw in England, Whitaker declared that such occurrences "make me think that there be great witches among them, and they very familiar with the devil." The devil's presence was manifested in many ways. Percy gives us another example, relating that when Dale led his occupation force to the site of Henrico, his men were "assaulted" repeatedly by warriors led by a flamboyant shaman the English called "Jack of the Feathers," who took to the field covered in bird feathers and wearing swan wings on his shoulders "as though he meant to fly." The chroniclers of Jamestown spoke often of God's special protection against Indian sorcery and witchcraft. Whitaker, for example, related that the rain at Nansemond failed to spoil English gunpowder.[30]

When Dale arrived at the site of Henrico, he constructed a palisade around "seven English acres of land," then built five watchtowers and some "poor cabins." Although Company promoters in England were soon extolling Henrico as an elegant place with a stately church, fine brick homes, and even a hospital, it was actually, as one historian notes, "little more than a few rickety huts surrounded by a fence." Dale admitted that some of his 350 men that first winter lived in holes dug in the ground. The promoters' claim that Dale's fortifications at Henrico could hold out "against the whole world" was hyperbolic in the extreme. Powhatan's warriors, with regularity, shot "their arrows into the fort" over the walls or through openings, wounding some of the men inside. On one occasion a small Indian raiding party broke into the enclosure itself. Most casualties were sustained outside the walls. Percy wrote of those who "having employment without the fort did come home short and were slain by the savages." Dale related that a number of his men were ambushed and then flayed "alive with mussel shells."[31]

Conditions within Henrico were grim. Giving testimony to the settlement's poverty, Dale claimed that he had no choice but to enforce without mercy a strict code of discipline, as otherwise the men "would starve one another by breaking open houses and chest(s) to steal . . . corn from their poor brother." The food shortage grew more acute as Indian raiders killed or drove off the cattle. Dale tried to pasture outside the walls. At Henrico, as at Jamestown, thieves faced painful execution, as did those who in their hunger and desperation had tried to seek refuge with the Indians and had been apprehended. Fortunately, Powhatan did not mount an all-out attack; he was reluctant to place too many of his own men at risk. As historian James Horn explains his problem,

> a frontal attack would have been disastrous, costly in lives, and would only have underscored the Englishmen's superiority in weaponry and armor. His bowmen's prodigious four-foot arrows, capable of passing straight through an enemy's body, could not penetrate English corselets or shirts of mail, and Indian war clubs were no match for muskets and cannons.

Could Powhatan have wiped out Henrico? Probably. But he was not willing to suffer the casualties necessary to do so. Nor could he sustain an indefinite siege, given the limitations of a subsistence economy. As winter approached, he regrouped his forces among the Pamunkey on the York River. In December, Dale's assault on the Appamatuck villages some five miles from Henrico encountered little opposition.[32]

Just as Powhatan backed away from his determination to eliminate or subjugate or, at a minimum, contain the English within the narrow confines of Jamestown, so Dale now modified his own professed intention to destroy Powhatan as an independent force. The extension of the war to reach the paramount chief's strongholds would be costly, and word from London apparently indicated that it would not be supported by the Company. The 2,000 new troops Dale advised would be needed to finish the job were not forthcoming, and the governor complained about the low quality of many of the men who were sent to him, describing them to Salisbury as "profane," "riotous," and "full of mutiny and treasonable intendments." The Virginia venture had earned a very checkered reputation at home, as disgruntled former colonists spread word of Dale's brutality toward Englishmen and Indians alike, and told stories of hunger, misery, and savage war in an unforgiving wilderness. From London, the Spanish ambassador wrote to Philip III of a story he had heard of two felons who, offered the choice of hanging or resettlement in the colony, declared immediately that they "would much rather die on the gallows here, and quickly, than to die slowly so many deaths as was the case in Virginia." Funds dried up as investors worried about prospective losses, and sometimes questioned the moral basis of the enterprise as well.[33]

The Company's promoters had appealed to Christian idealism, holding up Virginia as a sacred undertaking ordained to save the Indians' lost souls. However, a promotional tract published in 1612 titled "The New Life of Virginia," indicated uneasiness about the past conduct of Indian affairs. The anonymous author, later identified as Robert Johnson, the treasurer of the Company, had been disturbed by reports of unnecessary violence against Powhatan's people. He insisted that colonists remember that Virginia's main reason for existence was "to bring those infidell people from the worship of Divels to the service of God." He warned that if they tried to achieve that great objective "by stratagems of warre, you shall utterly lose it, and never come neere to it, but shall make your names odious to all their posterity. Patience and humanitie" not "iron and steele" were the key to transforming "their crooked nature." Indian children should be educated "with gentlenesse" and their elders won over "by wisdom and discretion" and made "equal with you English in case of protection, wealth and habitation." Any colonist who harmed an Indian should be punished, as Indians also were entitled to justice. Only kindness, Johnson averred, would "open the springs of earthly benefit" to the "savages" and bring "safetie to yourselves." Although the colonists did possess the right of self-defense, use of force against Indians should be the very last resort.[34]

Sir Thomas Dale's conduct of Indian affairs as governor had hardly been characterized by such restraint. He was sensitive to criticism, and in one letter to a London preacher expressed gratitude for the reverend's past "encouragements to persist in this religious warfare," assuring him that in all his actions he had worked constantly for "God's glory." In his 1613 letter from Henrico, Dale warned the Indians plotted constantly "to kill our men," and proposed to his London sponsors another punitive nighttime raid "when their corn is ripe." But he acknowledged and endorsed the Company's concern for Indian salvation, and added that he would not engage in campaigns of total extermination, but "will save all the children I can get and send them to yourself and such other of you that will see them educated in the fear of God."[35]

Dale relied on Whitaker, the preacher he had brought to Henrico, to provide reassurances about the religious nature of the enterprise. Whitaker's sermon, "Good Newes from Virginia," was published as a promotional tract in London in 1613. The body of the sermon consisted of the argument that the survival of the colony in the face of hostility from hordes of savage adversaries gave evidence that the enterprise was part of God's great plan. The Almighty clearly intended that those who cast their lot with Virginia would prosper. In a few paragraphs concerning the Indians, Whitaker spoke of the need for compassion for "the miserable condition of these naked slaves of the devil," and repeated the now-familiar stories of satanic rites and human sacrifice. But he also sought to refute those who portrayed Indians as beyond redemption. Although "they esteem it a virtue to lie, deceive and steal, as their master the devil teacheth them," they were still God's creatures, with "reasonable souls and intellectual faculties as well as we." Indeed, they were not only "of body lusty, strong and very nimble," but also in mind "quick of apprehension . . . exquisite in their inventions and industrious in their labor." Whitaker restated the familiar comparison of Indians to ancient Britons. Once again, the English were cast in the role of Roman civilizers and apostolic evangelizers.[36]

Whitaker's sermon reflected much of that ambivalence about the real nature of Indian character that long had permeated English thinking about New World ventures. However, although some of the earlier writers often had drawn a sharp contrast between noble and diabolical savages, with the intent to wage holy war in defense of good Indians against bad, the Virginia experience suggested a different dynamic, one reliant on the transformation of all Indians from savage satanists to civilized God-fearing Christians. It was a dynamic that held out the hope of peace and coexistence through Indian acquiescence, but also the possibility and justification of an exterminatory race war should efforts to transform the Indians' "crooked nature" fail. Although some suspected that most "savages" were not salvageable, all Company spokesmen in London and all commanders on the ground in Virginia still paid lip service at least to the possibility of Indian redemption. More to the point, they recognized the costs and risks of an unlimited Indian war and were acutely aware of their ongoing need for Indian trading partners and Indian military allies. The latter would be crucial should an anticipated Spanish invasion or French incursion into their North American domains materialize. I noted earlier that Lord Delaware had boasted about the new alliance with "the *werowance* at Patamack" (Potomac) whose power he mistakenly believed to be greater than Powhatan's. Dale, for his part, stressed in his 1611 report to London the prospect of a lucrative fur trade with "the savages in the northern rivers." More immediately, he spoke of plans to obtain corn and fish essential to avert English starvation from commerce with those tribes. During the colony's early years, none of the Virginia commanders envisioned a land free of Indians. But that view of the colony's future would, within a little more than a decade, win wide support not only among the colonists but within the leadership of the company in England.[37]

The task of opening up new trade outlets and forging new alliances fell to Sir Samuel Argall. A skilled mariner, Argall was hired by the Company in 1609 to locate the shortest and safest route to Virginia, and successfully plotted one that ran North of the Spanish-dominated West Indies. After delivering Lord Delaware to Jamestown in March 1610, Argall undertook an extensive Atlantic coastal exploration that took him all the way to Cape Cod. He spent the fall and winter of 1610 and 1611 in Chesapeake Bay, where he established trading relationships with "the petty kings in these parts" of which Delaware boasted in his self-exculpatory report to the Company. Argall had captained the ship that had brought Delaware back to England, but he did not long remain there. Returning to Virginia, he related that "from my arrival until the first of November, I spent my time in helping to repair such ships and boats as I found here decayed for lack of pitch and tar, and in pursuing Indians with Sir Thomas Dale for their corn." The latter venture was fraught with difficulties. Not only did those few Indians in the region willing to trade ask outrageous prices for a handful of corn, but coercion was risky. Accordingly, on the first of December, Argall, his ship now "fitted . . . to fetch corn," went farther afield hoping for a friendlier reception. Entering the Potomac River, he spotted a hunting party on the shore led by Iopassus, the *werowance* of the Pasptanzie. Iopassus in previous years had traded with both John Smith and with Argall. He was eager to resume his relationship with the English, declaring, Argall related, that he was "very glad of my coming, and told me all the Indians were my great friends, and that they had a good store of corn for me." Argall loaded his ship with some 1,400 bushels of the precious grain. He also "concluded a peace" with several other local *werowances,* giving and accepting hostages in a token of good faith. (In a marginal note of his account of this exchange, Argall specified that he left with the Indians "Capt. Web, Eugene Swift, Rob. Sparks & two boys.") Upon returning to Point Comfort at the mouth of the James River, he set his men "to the felling of timber for the building of a frigate," then used the new ship for more extensive exploration. In the interior, he found and slaughtered some stray cattle (the animals were probably survivors of the herd the Indians had driven from Henrico), located what appeared to be a mine, and, most significant, learned from "several Indians my friends that the Great Powhatan's daughter Pocahontas was with the Great King Patawomeck."[38]

Argall decided to kidnap Pocahontas. Powhatan, he reasoned, to secure her freedom would release all the English captives he held, give up the English arms and tools he had acquired, and, at long last, supply the colony with ample grain. Landing again on the lower Potomac, Argall called for Iopassus and Eugene Swift, and when they arrived demanded that the *werowance* help apprehend Pocahontas, warning that if he did not deliver her "into my hands, we should no longer be brothers nor friends." Deeply shocked, Iopassus protested that "if he should undertake this business, Powhatan would make war on him and his people." However, after Argall promised to fight on his side, the *werowance* agreed to take up the matter with "his brother, the great king of Patawomeck," who put the matter before his council that, as Argall related, "after some few hours' deliberation concluded rather to deliver her into my hands than lose my friendship." The reasons for the betrayal of Pocahontas were no doubt more complicated than

Argall suggests here or even knew. It is likely that long-accumulating resentments of Powhatan among these tributaries on the Northern fringe of his domain, combined with the continuing appeal of their trade goods, played some role in this astounding development. The Potomac tribal leaders were no doubt also mindful of Powhatan's failure to prevent English fortification of the mouth of the James and his inability to dislodge their substantial settlement at Henrico. The dangers of loss of "friendship" with the English were no doubt carefully weighed. There had clearly been a shift in power relations on the Potomac. Powhatan's failure to block English expansion had undermined his authority in the more distant parts of his domain. Word of his evacuation of Werowocomoco no doubt raised questions about his ability to cope with the intruders.[39]

Ralph Hamor, telling the story of Pocahontas's abduction, related that the wife of the sachem Iopassus was enlisted to lure Pocahontas aboard Argall's ship anchored in the Potomac. The young girl herself had been eager to visit the English again, so she readily agreed. Argall, the sachem, and his wife entertained the paramount chief's daughter at dinner. They all spent the night, Pocahontas being lodged in the gunner's room. Unaware of Iopassus' treachery, she was astonished to learn the next day that she was a prisoner, and, despite Argall's reassurances that she would be freed as soon as her father liberated the Englishmen he was holding and returned some stolen weapons and tools, "began to be exceedingly pensive and discontented." Argall, writing to an English friend in April 1613, related that after Pocahontas was in his custody, "an Indian was dispatched to Powhatan to let him know I had taken his daughter, and if he would send home the Englishmen which he detained in slavery, with such arms and tools as the Indians had gotten and stol'n, and also a great quantity of corn, that then he should have his daughter back." He reported that Powhatan agreed to the terms he set, freeing seven Englishmen, returning three guns, a broad-axe, and a long whipsaw, and delivering a canoe full of corn. Argall, after delivering Pocahontas to Gates at Jamestown, resumed his explorations of the Potomac, where he found the Indians eager to trade. In July, Argall led an assault that destroyed a French Jesuit outpost at Mt. Desert Island in Maine, sending several prisoners back to Virginia.[40]

Argall's assumption that Powhatan had accepted his terms was mistaken. Ralph Hamor provides the full story. The paramount chief first claimed he could not act without the advice of his council, adding that he was personally reluctant to lose the services of the Englishmen who worked for him. He added that although English swords and guns were of no particular use to him, they "delighted him to view and look upon." Three months then passed without any further word from Powhatan, then at the urging of his council he sent seven of his eight English captives to Jamestown, each of whom carried "a musket unserviceable." His messenger informed the English that Powhatan would send some more guns and 500 bushels of corn when his daughter was released, "and forever be friends with us." That response fell far short of Jamestown's expectations. Powhatan had delayed too long and now offered too little. The English quite rightly suspected that he had a large arsenal of weapons that he had no intention of giving up. He also had many more whites living in his villages. (One obstacle to their repatriation was the very real possibility that those who were not prisoners, but defectors, would be executed should they be returned.) The English sent word to Powhatan that although his daughter would be treated kindly, he could not expect to see her again until he complied with English demands. Powhatan made no reply.[41]

Tired of waiting, Sir Thomas Dale in March 1614 mounted a 150-man armed expedition into Powhatan's territory on the Pamunkey River. He carried with him Pocahontas, and sent word that she would be released if he were given 500 bushels of corn and the remaining English captives, weapons, and tools. Should the Powhatans not comply, Dale, as Hamor related, promised to "burn their houses, take away their canoes, breakdown their fishing weirs, and do them what other damage we could." Powhatan's reply was defiant. He advised the invaders to remember what had happened to Captain Ratcliffe. To Dale's consternation, several of the Englishmen whom Powhatan had sent back to Jamestown some months earlier now "ran to him again." As Dale's boat made its way upriver through a narrow channel, the Indians onshore "let their arrows fly." Dale retaliated by landing, looting, and burning 40 houses, and killing "five or six of their men." The expedition then proceeded upriver, where Dale burned down another village, "killed or hurt their men, and took away their goods." He told the survivors that the Powhatans could have peace if they granted his demands "with love."[42]

Powhatan then sent word that the Englishmen who had defected had now ran away from him because they were "fearful be put to death" by their erstwhile countrymen should they be returned to English custody. (Given Dale's previous executions of deserters, that was not an unrealistic fear.) He promised to apprehend them and turn them over the next day, along with the weapons and tools Dale demanded. However, "the next day they came not." Dale then marched on Powhatan's capital at Matchut on the upper Pamunkey, where he delivered an ultimatum. Because it was the planting season and everyone needed to attend to their crops, he would take no further action that day; however, if Powhatan had not satisfied his demands by harvest time, the English would return "and destroy and take away all the corn, burn the houses upon that river, leave not a fish weir standing, not a canoa in any creek thereabout, and destroy and kill as many of them as we could."[43]

Dale's ultimatum reflected a continuing, aggressive determination to incorporate Powhatan and his people into the colonial economy as food suppliers and to neutralize his power as a military threat. In 1614, Powhatan's ongoing resistance to trade was no longer the result of scarcity. The drought was over, as the success of Argall's trading efforts on the Potomac indicated. The issue now was purely one of self-respect and independence. The colonists' demands were humiliating. For the English, however, Powhatan's past behavior had not been reassuring. Their lingering suspicion of his motives, their ongoing fear that he plotted the extermination of the colony, drove their policy toward the paramount chief. In demanding that Powhatan return stolen English weapons and tools, Argall, Gates, and Dale sought to provide some measure of security against an attack by depriving Powhatan of the military technology that might provide a crucial margin of success in a new onslaught. The presence in Powhatan's villages of Europeans also worried the English leaders. They believed some of those defectors in the past had not only helped arm Powhatan, but provided instruction in the use and repair of weapons. The terms set for Pocahontas's release required essentially that Powhatan disarm. His complaint that the few old guns and swords in his possession were pleasing to look at but of no real use was not persuasive; it was provocative. Dale declared recovery of the weapons stolen by the Powhatans a matter of honor, as he kept them "as monuments and trophies of our shames." As always, the basic issues were autonomy (which Powhatan was determined to keep) and subordination (which the English demanded of him). The governor was convinced, as he wrote a friend in London in 1614, that "killing their men, burning their houses, and taking their corn" was the divinely ordained means by which the English would win peace, and the "good opinion" of the savages. Once again, the colonizer invokes the old formula: fear and love.[44]

The Virginia colony did enjoy several years of interracial peace after Dale's raid, but not as a result of his threats. In a letter boasting of his achievement of the "good opinion" of the Indians through his severity, he noted in passing that the conversion of Pocahontas to Christianity and her marriage to an Englishman provided "another knot to bind the peace the stronger." For once, the governor understated the case. That conversion and that marriage were of crucial importance to the termination of hostilities in Virginia, as Powhatan regarded Rolfe's offer to marry his daughter as the proffer of an unconditional peace treaty, setting aside the humiliating terms previously advanced.[45]

It was not Pocahontas's first marriage. She had previously been married to a young man named Kocuom, about whom nothing is really known, except that he was a warrior of middling rank (a captain, according to Strachey) and that they lived together at Powhatan's capital Orapax. We know nothing about how that marriage ended, nor can it be ascertained whether there were any children. In the early years of the Jamestown settlement, Pocahontas had been a frequent visitor. Still a child and a bit of a tomboy, she had amused the newcomers by doing cartwheels in the streets. As relations between the two peoples worsened, however, Powhatan restricted his favorite daughter's contacts with the enemy. In his later writings, Captain John Smith claimed that she often snuck away to warn the English of her father's malign intentions and complex plots. This cannot be verified and is rather implausible. Strachey, writing in 1610, indicated that she no longer visited the English, but for two years had been living with her husband.[46]

During Pocahontas's long confinement at Jamestown, the colony's governor Sir Thomas Dale took a particular interest in seeing to it that she was "instructed in Christian religion." He reported with great satisfaction that she "made good progress," soon "renounced publicly her country idolatry," "openly confessed her Christian faith," and was baptized. Dale's agent in her conversion was the Reverend Alexander Whitaker, who wrote, in a letter Hamor quoted, that the governor "had labored a long time" to bring the young woman to Christ. We would like to know more, to understand just what Pocahontas understood her conversion to mean. However, the record provides only the bare fact that she was baptized a few months after her capture. We can well imagine that she found her father's apparent indifference to her situation and her isolation within the confines of Jamestown fort highly disconcerting. One account has her raging against Powhatan for valuing her less "than old swords, pieces and axes." She allegedly told some of Powhatan's councilors, whom she met in March when she accompanied Dale, in his visit to Powhatan, that she preferred to stay with the English, who "loved" her. Her previous encounters with Englishmen, friendly for the most part, no doubt made her adaptation to her new circumstances less difficult than that experienced by most captives. Had she come to identify with her captors rather than her own people? Contemporary English sources indicate that this was the case. However, they were hardly objective. Her conversion remains rather surprising.[47]

No less remarkable was her marriage to an Englishman. In March, as the English withdrew from Pamunkey territory, Powhatan had sent Dale some vague assurances that his terms would be met, but the English heard nothing further and assumed that, once again, the paramount chief would not keep his word. Pocahontas remained a captive. However, the resumption of war was averted by a most unexpected development. As Ralph Hamor tells the story, "long before" the expiration of Dale's deadline, the governor was approached by John Rolfe, "a gentleman of approved behavior and carriage" who said that he had fallen in love with Pocahontas and wished to marry her. In making that request, Rolfe was defying a well-established taboo. The Reverend William Symonds, in the sermon to the Virginia Company, had warned that the colonists must rigidly observe the Old Testament injunction that God's people in Canaan "keepe to themselves. They may not marry nor give in marriage to the heathen, that are uncircumsized. . . . The breaking of this rule may breake the neck of all good succese of this voyage." The colony's leaders shared Symonds's fear. They regarded Indian women as sexually wanton, morally depraved, diseased (many were said to be bearers of sexually transmitted diseases), barbaric, satanic, and potentially treacherous. They constituted both an immediate security risk and a long-range danger, a danger that Englishmen in their embraces would lose their moorings, abandon "civility," and become as pagan and savage as the Indians themselves.[48]

John Rolfe shared that anxiety. In his letter to Dale, he acknowledged, as a serious barrier to his proposed union, "the heavie displeasure which almightie God conceived against the sonnes of Levie and Israel for marrying strange wives." However, Rolfe argued that his marriage would be "for the good of the plantation," presumably by bringing peace with the Powhatans, and that it would serve the great end for which Virginia had been founded: "the glory of God." In marriage, Rolfe declared, he could bring "the true knowledge of God and Jesus Christ" to "an unbelieving creature, namely Pocahontas." He acknowledged that union with a savage women under most circumstances might endanger his own spiritual well-being, but insisted that in this case it would work "for my owne salvation," because he would be doing the Lord's work in assisting in his wife's conversion.

Rolfe's letter tells us much about the wall of prejudice and fear separating the English from the Powhatans.[49]

Pocahontas, for her part, told "her brethren" of her love for Rolfe, and sought her father's consent. Dale and Powhatan both quickly agreed to the marriage, with the Indian leader sending "an old uncle of hers, Opachsco, to give her as his deputy in church and two of his sons to see the marriage solemnized." The ceremony occurred on April 5, less than a month after Dale's incursion into Powhatan's territory. Of that marriage, Hamor commented: "Ever since we have had commerce and trade not only with Powhatan but also with his subjects round about us; so now I see no reason why the colony should not thrive apace." The immediate result of the marriage was the elimination, for a short time, of the barriers of association. John Smith, after interviewing a number of former colonists returned from Virginia, noted that by 1616 trade had been fully resumed, and Englishmen and Powhatans even undertook joint hunting expeditions. Indians and whites, he wrote, lived together "as one people." Governor Francis Wyatt, when he took office in 1621, was surprised to find that Indians freely visited English homes, dined at their tables, even "lodged in their bedchambers."[50]

That intimacy, however, had strict limits. Unlike the pattern of racial relations that came to prevail in Spain's New World colonies, no *mestizo* class emerged in Virginia. In 1705, the wealthy Virginia planter and amateur historian Robert Beverley, in his *History and Present State of Virginia,* declared that much of the interracial bloodshed that marred the colony's first century could be attributed to the settlers' failure to take Indian wives. "Intermarriage," he wrote, "had been indeed the Method proposed very often by the *Indians* in the beginning" to secure peace and friendship. They believed that those who refused to marry their daughters "were not their Friends." Had the English responded positively to those overtures, Beverley argued, "the Abundance of Blood that was shed on both sides wou'd have been saved." Intermarriage, he continued, would have secured not only peace, but also the conversion of the Indians to Christianity and their preservation as a people. Instead, "all those Nations of Indians . . . are now dwindled away to nothing." Had they remained and joined with the English in marriage, Beverley declared, Virginia, her population augmented, would have enjoyed "much Success and Prosperity" in place of the "Frights and Terrors" that marred the colony's early history, and would have been far more attractive to prospective English settlers.[51]

Robert Beverley's vision of a Virginia populated by *mestizos* was shared by few of his fellow colonists. Despite the marriage of Rolfe and Pocahontas, Indian maidens were not esteemed as prospective wives by respectable Englishmen in the colony, and those who did engage in illicit romances that crossed the color barrier were the object of scorn. Popular prejudice was finally codified in 1691 in the passage of a law that prohibited not only racial intermarriage of any sort, but interracial sexual contact as well. Moreover, Beverley underestimated the problem. As Rolfe's singular example exemplified, to the English, intermarriage was acceptable only if the Indian marriage partner renounced Indian identity and embraced Christianity and civilization. Beverley's assumption that the Powhatans would have welcomed the opportunity to become English through marriage had such a possibility been generally available is highly questionable. Although Powhatan was no longer an active enemy, he remained disaffected and never accepted his prescribed role as a subject of England's king. When Governor Dale, a month after the Pocahontas–Rolfe wedding, sent Ralph Hamor to ask Powhatan for the hand of his 12-year-old youngest daughter in marriage, as a means of binding the two people yet closer together, Powhatan refused. Although he offered as an excuse a promise he had made that the young girl would marry one of his *werowances,* his response hinted at unease with any further family connection with the English. Hamor reported that he seemed rather irritated at the suggestion that there was need of a further token of goodwill. Powhatan remembered past slights, insults, and humiliations, and made a pointed reference to past bloodshed even as he assured Hamor of his intent to keep the peace. When Hamor asked that he release from his service an Englishman named William Parker who wanted to be repatriated, he complied with reluctance and ill grace; asked that Dale send him a substantial present including "ten peeces of copper," a shaving knife, two combs, a cat and a dog; and then renewed his threat to move far from the English. His dislike of the colonists was palpable even as he observed the proper rituals of hospitality in receiving and entertaining Hamor and his party. Powhatan was an angry man, even though he protested that he was too old to wage war and now loved peace. His brother and ultimate successor Opechancanough was even more resentful, and less committed to coexistence. The English, as a condition of peace, forced on the Powhatans a treaty that required their acknowledgment that they were subject to the authority of the Crown. Although the language of that treaty has not survived, it probably followed the outline of the agreement with the Chickahominys, negotiated at the same time. Under that treaty, the text of which we do have, Indians were required to pay tribute, to supply warriors to the English on demand, do no harm to either Englishmen or English livestock that wandered into Indian territory, but remain outside English territory unless specifically invited. There is no doubt that Powhatan leaders resented such terms. However, the tensions festering beneath the surface were not simply, or even primarily, the reflection of past conflicts and current humiliations. There were deep cultural incompatibilities dividing the two peoples. It is to those matters that we must now turn.[52]

CHAPTER 5

~

"Upon Doubtful Terms": Virginia, 1616–1622

In 1616, Pocahontas, now renamed Lady Rebecca, and her husband sailed for England. Her visit, as one historian notes, "was a propaganda venture subsidized by the Virginia Company of London." Its purpose was to emphasize the presumed triumph in the wilderness of English civility and Christian civilization by showcasing the Company's prominent convert. Pocahontas quickly won the approbation of the king's wife, Anne of Denmark, and a prominent place in her entourage. As Indian royalty, she was widely celebrated in London society. Beverley tells us that she "was publicly treated as a prince's daughter; she was carried to many plays, balls, and other public entertainments, and very respectfully received by all the ladies about the court." On all those occasions, she behaved not only with "much decency," but with "so much grandeur in her deportment that . . . she gained the good opinion of everybody." In the expectation that Pocahontas's conversion would pave the way for the Christianizing of the Powhatans, the Virginia Company awarded the Rolfes a substantial grant to undertake in Virginia through Lady Rebecca's godly and virtuous example "the winning of that People to the knowledge of God, and embracing of true religion." It was not to be. Before the ship carrying them back to Virginia cleared the English channel, Pocahontas died, probably of dysentery, and was buried at Gravensend on March 21, 1617. Disaffected from her own people, she had been reluctant to leave England. John Rolfe returned to the colony and reported to London that he found "the Indyans very loving, and willing to parte with their children" so that they might be trained by the English in civility and true religion. Events would demonstrate that he was mistaken.[1]

The Company in London regarded Rolfe's venture as a matter of the highest importance. Colonial planners consistently warned that no long-term relationship with Indians would be possible without their conversion and subordination.

In 1613, as the Powhatans continued their armed resistance, preacher William Crashaw had declared there was no "other known place of the world" where Satan so "visibly and palpably reigns." There could be no lasting peace with devil worshippers. However, he held out to Virginia settlers the hope that "god will tread Satan under your feet shortly." Crashaw had asked that missionaries "consecrating those heathenish earths with their happy bodies" be sent at once to the colony. The promotional literature issued by the Company in its fund-raising ventures repeated that plea as it continued to stress the sacred nature of the Virginia venture. One broadside, issued in 1615, contained an engraving of Indians calling upon the subscribers to "Bring Light, and sight, to Us yet blinde; Lead us, by Doctrine and Behaviour, Into one Sion, to One Savior all." With the endorsement of King James I, funds were solicited to found a "University of Henrico" to be devoted, as the Company put it, to "the training up of the children of those Infidels in true Religion, morall virtue, and civility."[2]

Neither the squadrons of missionaries nor the Indian college envisioned in these promotional ventures materialized. The colonists were preoccupied with their own pursuits and had little interest in committing time or scarce resources to the project. Nor were the Powhatans eager to renounce their ways. The Reverend Mr. Purchas had tried to convert the Powhatan priest and councilor Uttamatomakkin during the latter's visit to London, by warning that he committed blasphemy by honoring Okeus, a mere "idol." Purchas reported that the Indian would "hear no persuasions to the truth." As one historian notes, Purchas's arguments "left Uttamatomakkin bewildered and furious. He demanded to be returned to his homeland 'in the first ship' available." In Virginia, Indians, for their part, adamantly refused to give up their children to English indoctrination and training. Governor Yeardley, in a New Year's report to the Company in 1622, provided a very succinct explanation: Indian "feare of hard usage by the English." The Powhatans, who were loving and indulgent parents, found the English attitude toward children cold, severe, and, at times, cruel. They found it almost incomprehensible that children should be removed from their own families and subjected to the harsh discipline of strangers. We have already recorded at some length the derogatory stereotypes of Indian savages harbored by colonists. The Powhatans had their own images of the Other, and saw in them no reason to abandon their own ways. They had had more than a decade of bad experience with those intruders who periodically stole their corn, burned their fields and villages, slaughtered noncombatants, seized their land, and treated their leaders with contempt. There was little about the English that appealed. They were, as the Powhatans saw them, arrogant, rude, greedy, violent, unpredictable, cruel, and, in their claim to follow a god of love, hypocritical. They were also parasitical, being unwilling or unable to feed themselves. Because of their power, they needed to be placated from time to time. But contrary to the fond English expectation that they would command the Indians' affection as well as their fear through demonstration of their superior virtues, the Powhatans perceived little that they considered admirable.[3]

The tensions inherent in the relationship of two peoples, each of whom regarded the other as not only inferior, but also as despicable and treacherous, was severely exacerbated by some fundamental changes in the nature of the English economy in Virginia. During the early years, the colony was not economically viable. Some income was generated by the exportation of timber, pitch, tar, and sassafras, but efforts to grow silkworms and establish a glass industry ended in failure. Contrary to the hopes of both investors and colonists, there were no gold or silver deposits in Virginia. The one commodity that would be the source of great wealth at first seemed quite unpromising. The tobacco grown by the Powhatans, *Nictotiana rustica,* was described by William Strachey as an inferior strain, "poore and weake, and of biting taste." There was no demand for it on the London market. Around 1610, John Rolfe experimented with the planting of another variety, *Nictotiana tabacum,* from Trinidad. Although it flourished in the local soil and was popular with English settlers in the colony, it did not initially do well in England. In 1615 to 1616, London merchants bought only 2,300 pounds of Virginia tobacco. The Spanish, by contrast, that year sold them more than 57,000 pounds of tobacco from the Caribbean; however, this situation changed rapidly. Virginia tobacco exports reached 20,000 pounds in 1617, doubled during the next two years, and reached 1,500,000 pounds in 1629. The impact of the new tobacco boom on the English settlement in Virginia was immediate and extreme. When Samuel Argall arrived at Jamestown to assume the governorship in 1617, he found the fort almost derelict, only five or six houses occupied, the bridge to the mainland broken, "the marketplace, and streets and all other spare places planted with tobacco," and most of the inhabitants "dispersed all about planting tobacco." The Virginia Company in London, three years later, declared tobacco a "deceivable weed," deplored the diversion of men and resources from other more essential enterprises, and warned that tobacco profits "might soone vanish into smoake." That complaint was reiterated repeatedly in the Company's correspondence with the colony during the next few years. The Company advised the Virginia settlers to diversify by building an ironworks, producing naval stores, planting vineyards, making salt, and catching fish—to little avail. Drawn by the tobacco boom, some 4,600 new settlers since 1617 had poured into the colony, establishing numerous new farms and plantations committed to the growing of the "deceivable weed." The new colonists, the Company complained, more often than not were interested only in short-term profit and did not regard Virginia as their permanent home. They did not heed Company instructions to achieve self-sufficiency, having "utterly neglected not only staple Commodities but the verie necessities of mans life." For several years before the expansion of tobacco cultivation, the colonists had actually produced a food surplus, selling corn to the Indians often in exchange for land. But in June 1620, Governor Yeardley complained that he could not feed many more new settlers. If immigration was not soon restricted, the colony, he warned, might face starvation again. Clearly, the colony was reverting to the old pattern of over dependency upon food supplied by Indians. Yeardley, on June 20, 1620, wrote to the Company of his acute need for "a store of blue and white beads" to use to buy corn from the Indians.[4]

Despite the ongoing need for Indian supplies of corn, the English continued to take from the Powhatans much of their prime farmland along the James River, thereby inflaming old resentments. Tobacco cultivation, which exhausted the soil in three years, required new land—a lot of it—and the new planters in their quest for quick wealth often assumed that Indians, being "savage," had no real claim to ownership. Even before Pocahontas's marriage to Rolfe, several tribes in the Powhatan Confederation residing on or near the James River had been displaced and forced to relocate in the interior, including the Kecoughtons, the Paspaheghs, the Arrohatecks, and the Appamatucks. The process was accelerated as new English settlers, attracted by the prospect of quick wealth from tobacco, flocked into the colony. The English population quadrupled between 1618 and 1622. The pressure on Indian lands was intensified by the Company's decision, in 1619, to grant land to adventurers who would establish, and populate, with English immigrants, new plantations outside the existing English settlements. Those who availed themselves of this new opportunity for enrichment often clashed with the Indians, violating, as one disgusted settler informed the Council, "the equity of God & natures lawes" by their avaricious and sometimes murderous behavior. Indians, he related, were cheated, robbed, and sometimes killed. These new plantations were beyond the easy reach of the governor's supervision. This inability to control the frontier, which time and time again in the history of British colonization and American expansion, and would undercut policies intended to ensure peace with Indians, had its beginnings at Jamestown.[5]

The Powhatans, by 1622, had lost most of their access to the banks of the James River and were forced to cultivate less fertile inland fields or relocate elsewhere in the region. Only the Southern Shore of the James from Nansemond down to the Chesapeake Bay remained under Indian occupancy. However, as historian Michael Oberg has noted, "the result was more than the loss to the natives of their prime farmlands, for the English had occupied the link between the two major Powhatan subsistence areas: the hunting and foraging territories inland, and the food-producing and reed-gathering regions along the rivers." The loss of river access was serious, because "waterways provided a critical source of food and means of transportation for the Powhatans . . . their best agricultural soils were located most often on narrow strips of land bordering the rivers and streams." The disruption of the supply of game as English farmers occupied new territories created hardship. Equally serious was the destruction of Indian crops by English domestic animals, and the clashes between Englishmen and Indians that often ensued. The evidence indicates that the Powhatans were much less prosperous than they had been before the founding of Jamestown. In 1617, Governor Argall reported to London that "Indians [are] so poor they cant pay their debts and tribute." The English denial that Indians had any permanent right to land, being "uncivilized," added insult to injury. Powhatan's old policy of trying to defend his lands by confining the English within a circumscribed territory through periodic attack on settlers outside Jamestown was now a thing of the past. The old paramount chief, weary of war, grudgingly tolerated their expansionism and continuing lack of regard for his people's territorial rights.[6]

Other members of the Powhatans' ruling caste were not so inclined, but bided their time. Their anger was reinforced by continuing incidents of violence. These are poorly documented, because the English provided few details and probably left some unrecorded. But there are hints. One finds in the records of Parliament a very suggestive response to a petition from one Captain John Bargrave that alleges that the captain hired a "very disordered crew" that "committed outrage and repine upon the pore Indyans." What exactly did they do? There are no specifics, other than a reference to stealing Indian corn. There is also no record that anyone was punished for any "outrage." Although less common than during the earliest years of the colony, the record indicates that seizures of food continued. The largest scale theft occurred in 1619, when colonists short of provisions had mounted a raid on the Patawomecks and commandeered some 800 bushels of corn. There were also some killings on both sides, but we do not know how many because the details are lost.[7]

Despite the anger of his people, Powhatan's death in spring 1618 did not, initially, appear to threaten the peace. John Rolfe, recently returned to the colony, reported Powhatan's passing to his English sponsors and assured them that "the Indians continue in peace. Itopatin his second brother succeeds him, and both hee and Opechancanough have confirmed our former league." The new paramount chief, originally named Opitchapan, now took the name Itoyatin (as it is now generally spelled). He was an old man, described by Purchas as "decrepit and lame." From the outset, Powhatan policy was dominated by his younger brother Opechancanough, who initially shared power with him then succeeded him in 1621.[8]

Opechancanough had played a major role during Powhatan's reign, and toward its end there were rumors that he had become so powerful that Powhatan had "gone southward" out of fear that he would be deposed by his younger brother. These rumors are probably unfounded, but the impression they conveyed of Opechancanough's dominant presence were not. Shortly after his return to Virginia in spring 1617, Governor Argall reported that Powhatan, now infirm, had turned over the task of governing the Confederation to his two younger brothers, of whom Opechancanough was the dominant partner. Described by one early Virginia historian as "a man of large stature, noble presence and extraordinary parts," he was both an able if Machiavellian diplomat and a formidable warrior, who "caused all the Indians far and near to dread his name." In 1616, he intervened very shrewdly in a dispute between the English and the independent Chickahominy tribe. That tribe had agreed, in 1614, to an alliance with the English that committed them to supplying an annual tribute in corn. However, two years later, when crops were poor, they failed to meet that commitment and, as Opechancanough whispered to the English, also violated the treaty by killing some English livestock. Thus provoked, Governor Yeardley mounted a punitive expedition that yielded no corn but resulted in killing and hostage taking. Opechancanough then called on the Chickahominys, negotiated a truce, and secured his own election as their chief, thereby bringing them within the Powhatan Confederacy—an accomplishment that had eluded the great Powhatan.[9]

During the Chickahominy negotiations, Opechancanough took pains to assure the English that he was serving their interests. This was disingenuous. His objective in this, as in other ventures, was to create a personal power base that could be used ultimately to rally opposition to the appeasement policy. The price for peace that Powhatan in his old age was willing to pay was too steep for his more vigorous, and embittered, younger brother. Long-festering grievances were exacerbated by bad times. Not only were there crop failures that made English demands for food tribute exceedingly onerous, but in 1617 an epidemic of the "bloody flux" struck Virginia, resulting, one English observer noted, in "a great mortality among us, [but] far greater among the Indians." Two years later another epidemic of unknown nature but marked by intense fevers again caused great mortality, this time "chiefly among the Indians," but also among the newer English settlers who, according to the Company's subsequent complaint, had not been properly cared for by the colony. Both epidemics had been brought to Virginia in English ships. It is not unlikely that Opechancanough and those who shared his convictions blamed the newcomers for their misfortunes. Whatever their understanding of the origins of the diseases that now decimated their villages, they knew that the coming of the English had made their lives far worse.[10]

Samuel Argall, the governor whose landing at Jamestown in spring 1617 brought the "bloody flux" to Virginia, issued a decree restricting use of firearms, a restriction necessitated by a shortage of gunpowder. Several years later, a report from several disaffected "Ancient Planters" related that in response "the Indians, perceiving our forbearance to shoot as formerly, conclude that our pieces were as they said, sick, and not to be used." Thus emboldened, some Indians attacked and killed six white settlers, thereby "breaking that league which before was so fairly kept." Assessing the state of Indian relations in 1619, the critics of the colony's management declared them

> upon doubtful terms. Neither did we ever perceive that they at any time voluntarily yielded themselves subjects or servants to our gracious sovereign, neither that ever they took any pride in that title nor paid they at any time any yearly contribution of corn for the sustenation of the colony, nor could we at any time keep them in such good respect or correspondency that they and we did become mutually helpful or profitable each to other; but to the contrary whatever at any time was done upon them proceeded from fear without love, for such help as we have had from them has been procured by sword or trade.

In a little more than 100 words, the "Ancient Planters" had summed up the failure of Indian policy in colonial Virginia. One is struck, however, by the lack of irony in this statement: the absence of any acknowledgment of the defect at the heart of the fear and love formula for Indian relations.[11]

Although he continued to profess his friendship for the English in his dealings with the colonists, Opechancanough on several occasions refused requests from the colony's governors for a new treaty of peace. The 1614 agreement had defined the Powhatans as subjects of the English king. If Virginia authorities expected the new principle chief to swear an oath of fealty, they were destined to be very disappointed. For several years he refused to even talk about the matter. In November 1618, the peace was breached in two separate incidents, resulting in the killing of 11 colonists. Opechancanough disavowed responsibility for those attacks, blaming Chickahominy renegades. He assured the English that he would bring the assailants to justice, but did not keep that promise. In fact, the assailants were not Chickahominies, but Pamunkeys, directly subject to Opechancanough. Around this time, Nemattanew, a Pamunkey warrior–shaman the English called Jack of the Feathers, who as we noted earlier had played a prominent part in the resistance to English expansion a decade earlier, emerged as a major figure in Opechancanough's entourage. In 1619, unconfirmed reports held him responsible for several killings of Englishmen. Late in that year, however, Jack of the Feathers called at Jamestown to convey a request from Opechancanough that the English contribute 8 to 10 armed men to a punitive raid against a tribe in the interior above the falls that had allegedly killed some Powhatan women. Asked for advice, the governor's council reacted cautiously. Perhaps this would be an opportunity to win over Opechancanough, who continued to refuse to make "any treaty at all notwithstanding all the Arte and endeavour the governor could use." Perhaps the Powhatans, who refused to give up any of their own children, might permit the English to seize some from the enemy to take back to the colony for religious instruction. However, the council worried that Opechancanough might be scheming against them, seeking to use this presumed collaboration to inflict a "treacherous disaster upon us." They finally decided the risk was minimal and advised Governor Yeardley to cooperate in the hope of promoting "amity."[12]

Yeardley's predecessor Samuel Argall, a veteran of the first Anglo-Powhatan war who served as governor from May 1617 to May 1619, had felt little confidence in the good intentions of Opechancanough or his people. Early in his administration, he issued a proclamation that prescribed the death penalty for any settler who taught an Indian to use a gun, and for any Indian who received such instruction. The governor also forbade any "familiarity" with Indians, including private trade, and ordered all communities to maintain protective stockades. Argall envisioned a policy of security through racial separation in Virginia, in effect rejecting the London Company's hope that conversion could be expedited through careful but close association with the "salvages." Opechancanough, for his part, found the policy denying his people access to muskets offensive and continued English encroachments on Powhatan lands alarming. Argall had ignored his complaints. Opechancanough, who remembered past insults and outrages all too clearly, as noted earlier, had declined to discuss reaffirmation of the peace treaty with the colonists. He was also adamant in refusing to allow Indian children to live with the English, suggesting as an alternative that they should invite whole Indian families to live with them in their settlements. That was a proposition the planters, ever suspicious of Indian "treachery," did not care to entertain. In any case, even if the Indian families Opechancanough proposed to relocate among the English harbored no malign intent, the presence of adults would hinder the objective of the enterprise: the transformation of their next generation "into civilized Christian subjects of the King."[13]

The first Virginia House of Burgess, which met in summer 1619 on the summons of Governor Yeardley took up, among other matters, the issue of Indian residence within territory settled by the English. It was guided by the premise, as its resolution stated, that "they are a most treacherous people . . . quickly gone when they have done a villany." Accordingly, legislation prescribed that no more than five or six Indians were to be allowed to live in a settlement at any one time, and in each instance only with the consent of the governor. They were to be guarded constantly and were required to live in a separate house. Colonists were not permitted to entertain Indians in their homes. To minimize the danger, the Burgess prescribed a speedy hanging for anyone who supplied an Indian with a gun, powder, or shot. No one was allowed to visit an Indian village, travel more than 20 miles from home, or be absent more than 7 days without official permission. Given the Indian danger, the Burgess declared that no plantation should be established more than 10 miles from its nearest neighbor. However, to maintain "present peace," the Burgess also passed legislation against the mistreatment of Indians. "No injury or oppression," the Burgess resolved, was to "be wrought by the English against the Indians." All tribes were covered by that declaration, with the Burgess stating explicitly that the Chickahominys, a tribe Argall had proposed be driven out of Virginia, were not to be attacked unless they broke the peace again. Those who stole from Indians must make restitution. Freemen were to pay fine of five pounds (a very substantial amount). Servants were to be publicly whipped. The records do not disclose how frequently these laws were enforced, if at all.[14]

The Burgess responded to a complaint from Opechancanough by summoning Captain John Martin to answer charges that his men had seized a canoe loaded with corn and forced Indians who did not want to trade to accept some copper beads for its contents. The Captain promised to guarantee "the good behavior of his people towards the Indians." However, in its capacity as a court, the Burgess heard another case that exposed its deepest feelings about relations with Opechancanough. The case involved a complaint against Henry Spelman. Robert Poole, who was also an interpreter, charged that Spelman, during a visit to Opechancanough's "courte" had spoken "very unreverently and maliciously against the present governor." Although the Assembly could not determine exactly what Spelman had really said, they seized upon his admission that he had told Opechancanough that a new governor would soon arrive in Virginia. Thereby, the Burgess concluded, he had undercut the incumbent governor's authority "both with Opochano and the Indians" and placed "the whole colony in danger of their slippery designs." The Burgess ordered Spelman reduced in military rank and decreed that he should "perform seven years of service to the Colony in the nature of Interpreter to the Governor." The recorder of these proceedings noted that Spelman was unrepentant and unappreciative of the Burgess's leniency, and that there were many, resentful of his attitude, who favored a sterner penalty. Governor Yeardley, however, attributed Spelman's indiscretion to his immaturity and pardoned him. Not long thereafter, Opechancanough accused Poole of stirring up trouble between his people and the English. John Rolfe reported to London that Opechancanough remained a friend, whereas Poole had proved to be a scoundrel. Other Virginia settlers were less sanguine and remained fearful of the Powhatans' "slippery designs."[15]

Virginia's colonial government did not maintain a consistent policy in its dealings with Opechancanough. Argall's successor, George Yeardley, promptly modified Argall's restrictive measures and supplied some Indians with muskets. The closer associations that had characterized the two peoples immediately after the marriage of Rolfe and Pocahontas now resumed, as Indians and Englishmen once again visited, traded, and sometimes hunted together. In 1621, Opechancanough and Yeardley agreed to a renewal of the 1614 treaty of "Peace and League." Yeardley saw continuing tensions with the Powhatans as a deterrent to the expansion of the highly lucrative Virginia tobacco enterprise, an enterprise in which he was personally deeply involved. Planters not only needed to be free of worry about Indian attacks, but, having committed more and more land to single-crop cultivation, were once again dependent upon Indian trade to supply the foodstuffs needed for the burgeoning English population. The Virginia Company, in 1620, expressed renewed concern that the neglect of corn cultivation in the English settlements could reduce them "into an extremity of being ready to starve." Yeardley, however, no doubt understood that the resumption of the coercive food levies of the past could reignite the Anglo-Powhatan war. Unwilling, because of his own involvement in the tobacco business, to force colonists to grow more corn, he relied on the cultivation of Opechancanough's goodwill to keep trade relations open. At one point, he sought Opechancanough's consent to a land grant, a gesture that later earned the disapprobation of the officers of the Virginia Company in London, who complained that "a sovereignty in a heathen infidel was acknowledged, and the Company's title thereby much infringed."[16]

The Company was dissatisfied with the management of affairs in Virginia. Argall and Yeardley had not only failed to place the colony on a firm footing of economic self-sufficiency, but no progress had been made in the conversion of the Indians. A new governor, Sir Francis Wyatt, assumed office in November 1621. The Company, in its instructions to the new governor and in its communications with the colony, stressed once again the dangers of overreliance on tobacco. Wyatt was ordered to see to it that the colonists faithfully observed the "divine lawes" as embodied in the rituals and teachings of the Church of England, so that "their example may be a means to winn the Infidells to God." He was directed to encourage a closer association of Indians and Englishmen, in the expectation that "the better disposed of the Natives" would assist in the "more generall conversion of the Heathen." The Company urged the Virginians to welcome Indian families into their settlements as a means of advancing their conversion, but also warned to guard against the treachery of the unregenerate savages.[17]

Governor Wyatt was assisted by George Thorpe, a former member of Parliament and gentleman of the king's privy chamber. Thorpe had long been interested in the work of conversion. Five years prior to his voyage to Virginia, he had taken into his care and sought to educate a young Indian boy who had been brought to London by Sir Thomas Dale in 1616. (Like most Indians living for a time in England, the lad did not survive, succumbing to illness in September 1619.) Thorpe's interests were not, however, purely philanthropic. He had invested heavily in Virginia land and saw humane treatment of the Powhatans not only as a good work worthy of a Christian, but also as an eminently sound business proposition. His decision to leave wife and family behind and settle in the colony was impelled, in part, by the need to manage directly his American plantation, "which had fallen on hard times." Wyatt and Thorpe undertook a program of reform that included efforts to promote economic diversification, improve relations with the Indians, and nurture the "Indian college." Wyatt and Thorpe both shared the Virginia Company's determination to make clear to the native peoples "theire love and hartie affection towardes them." The Company had directed Yeardley, in 1619, to proceed with the construction of "a college for the training up of the children of those Infidels in true religion moral virtue and Civility," and had also dispatched to the colony 50 new settlers specifically charged with the responsibility of taking Indian children into their homes. Nothing came of these directives. The Powhatans were not cooperative. Wyatt was sensitive to the need to improve relations with Opechancanough and his people, and insisted that colonists who abused Indians be punished in accordance with the laws passed by the House of Burgess. The new administration encouraged closer personal relations intended, in the words of the governor's instructions from the Company, to see to it that the Indians would "thereby . . . grow to a likeing and love of civility and finallie be brought to the knowledge of God and true religion."[18]

Thorpe, appointed overseer of the Indian college's lands, believed that past hostilities were largely the result of English misconduct, and deplored the prejudice and malice he found in Virginia. The Indians, he declared, were of "a peaceable & virtuous disposition." The problem was the settlers, as "scarce any man amongst us that doth soe much as afforde them a good thought in his hart and most men with their mouthes give them nothing but maledictions and bitter execrations." Indians had been falsely accused of "all the wronge and injurye that the malice of the Devill or man can afford." Thorpe was determined to redress that. Learning that Indians were afraid of the mastiffs on the college lands, he had the dogs killed as a sign of goodwill.[19]

Many, probably most, of the Virginia colonists believed that Wyatt and Thorpe were ill advised. Their misgivings were spelled out in a letter to the Virginia

Company from the Oxford-trained Reverend Jonas Stockton (or Stockam) of Elizabeth City. The colonists, he complained, had already tried to convert over the Indians by kindly persuasion, only to be met with "derision." They could be controlled, he argued, only by brute force. Moderate means were useless. No progress in winning them over would be possible until "their Priests and Ancients have their throats cut." Stockton found nothing about Indians worthy of commendation, noting that the young Englishmen "we have sent . . . amongst them to learne their Language . . . returne worse than they went." Captain John Smith, publishing Stockton's letter in his 1624 history of the colony, declared that he was right.[20]

Thorpe sought to prove the Indian haters wrong by cultivating interracial harmony "by kinde usage." He sent elaborate presents to Opechancanough, among them an English–style house, the doors and locks of which reportedly entranced the paramount chief. He sought to persuade Opechancanough that, as Christians, his people would enjoy the same material amenities that had made the English a people to be envied. He explained to his London correspondents that by appealing to their material desires, the Powhatans might be brought to desire eternal salvation as well. Thorpe asked that he be sent supplies of English clothing and "householdstuffe" to use as gifts to inspire Indians. He held the highest hopes for the work envisioned for the Indian college, which would wean the children of the Powhatans away from "savagery." However, despite a substantial infusion of funding from England, Thorpe's efforts failed. Like others before him, he was unable to persuade the Indians to give up their children, even though generous payment was offered for any young people they might send to live with the English.[21]

Thorpe was among the first to die at the hands of Indian insurgents in the spring of 1622. He had no sense that he was in danger, no premonition that an Indian attack was imminent. The previous winter, he had met with Opechancanough and came away from that meeting with the belief that the paramount chief was about to convert to Christianity. Opechancanough, he related, told him that he now realized that Indians had not been following "the right way," as the English god was clearly far more powerful than theirs. He promised to abandon the *huskanaw* [male initiation] ceremony to cease offending the English, and asked for religious instruction. He also promised to negotiate a new peace agreement with Governor Wyatt, and suggested that Indian and English families henceforth might live together. He also declared that he would not oppose new English settlements within his own territory as long as they did not encroach on areas where his people had established villages. Thorpe and his countrymen accepted Opechancanough's observations and promises at face value, because they accorded perfectly with their vision of Virginia's future.[22]

Although Thorpe saw Opechancanough as a leader well aware of his weakness and vulnerability, and accordingly eager to appease, in fact "the Powhatans were probably stronger than at any time since the arrival of the English." They occupied well-defended, consolidated villages in the Pamunkey and York river basins North of Jamestown, and now enjoyed, through Opechancanough's diplomacy, the loyalty and support of the Chickahominys and Nansemonds. He had forged a stronger alliance system than Powhatan ever commanded, and was a potentially formidable adversary, but few English observers realized the extent of his power. A report in 1621 by an observer of his review of warriors during his "annuall progress through his pettye provinces" contained a mocking note about how the principal chief had bestowed his highest praise on a worthy whose only exploit was the killing of seven muskrats.[23]

One development that might have alerted the English to impending danger in spring 1621 was the decision of the Powhatan leaders to adopt new names. Opechancanough became Magopeesomon. (For convenience and clarity, I will continue to use the old name.) His elder brother, the paramount chief Itoyatin, previously Opitcham, became Sasawpen. Such name changes sometimes betokened incipient hostilities, as *werowances* assumed the roles of war chiefs. Although name changes might have been innocuous, there was one fairly clear sign of continuing Powhatan disaffection and defiance. The shaman warrior Nemattanew, whose animosity toward the English and their ways was unmistakable, remained high in the councils of Opechancanough, Itoyatin, and their fellow *werowances*. Wearing a feather costume that covered his entire body and gave the impression, as one English observer put it, that he intended to take flight like a bird, Nemattanew was believed to have supernatural powers that rendered him immortal; he claimed to possess an ointment that made him invulnerable to bullets. Some authorities regard him as a prototype of later Native American revitalization leaders. Although the sources do not permit reconstruction of his worldview or message, one thing is clear: Nemattanew's prominent presence in Opechancanough's entourage strongly suggests that the latter's repudiation of native deities and ceremonies was far from sincere.[24]

Early in Wyatt's administration, Indians from a friendly tribe on the Eastern Shore reported that Opechancanough had tried to buy from them a quantity of poison for use against the English. That rumor was followed by one that warned of a plot to use the occasion of Powhatan's temple interment to gather warriors to "sett upon every Plantation of the colony." However, after several uneventful months, the rumors were discounted. At the beginning of the new year, Governor George Wyatt declared that Indians and whites in Virginia lived "in very great amytie and confidence."[25]

The sudden and violent resumption of interracial war in Virginia in 1622 surprised the colony's English supporters, who generally assumed that the danger was past. Unaware of what had happened in the colony less than a month before he spoke, the Reverend Patrick Copland, in London on April 18, 1622, preached a sermon of "Thanksgiving for the Hapie Success of the Affayres of Virginia the Last Year." Although conceding that during the colony's early history settlers had been killed by Indians, Copland assured his listeners that God had moved quickly to "mollfie the hearts of the Salvages" and had long since "staid the fire that it doe not burne, and the hungry lyons that they do not devore." Copland added with satisfaction that some Indians had even voluntarily given up "their own warme and well seated and peopled habitations" to make room for the English. Copland was not alone in his misconceptions. The Virginia Company the year before had decided not to appoint a marshal in charge of the colony's defenses on grounds that there was "no present necessity or use for such an officer." Although the colonists in Virginia never felt entirely secure, they were, for the most part, preoccupied with their individual quests for wealth and took little note of the Company's decision.[26]

Less than three months after Copland delivered his sermon, word reached London that one-third of the colonists had been killed in an Indian uprising. English commentators were quick to assign blame. Typical was the judgment of Samuel Purchas who, acknowledging no English provocation, declared that "the true cause of this surprise . . . [was] the instigation of the devil." Indians, Purchas reminded his readers, were "a bad people, having little of Humanitie but shape . . . more brutish than the beasts they hunt, more wild and unmanly that the unmanned Country which they range rather than inhabit." They were, he declared in concluding his invocation of the old devil worship motif, "captivated . . . to Satan's tyranny in foolish pieties, mad impieties, busie and bloudy wickedness." Purchas thus reveals the underlying British mind-set—a mind-set that denied Indian right to the land (they "range rather than inhabit") and attributed their hostility to dispossession to their bondage to Satan.[27]

We turn now to the event that, it is now believed, triggered the attack. Sometime between fall 1621 and March 1622, Nemattanew was accused of killing an Englishman named Morgan, who owned a plantation not far from Jamestown. He had apparently persuaded Morgan to travel with him to Opechancanough's capital on a trading expedition. A few days after their departure, Nemattanew reappeared, wearing Morgan's cap. Questioned by English servants on Morgan's plantation, he told them their master was dead. Morgan's men then tried to restrain the Indian holy man, planning to take him before George Thorpe, who was authorized to hear such cases, but in the struggle that ensued, they shot Nemattanew. In English accounts of his dying moments he allegedly begged his captors not to reveal he had been killed by a bullet, and asked to be buried among the English. John Smith, writing two years after the event, related that "at the losse of this Salvage Opechankanouh much grieved and repined, with great threats of revenge, but the English returned him such terrible answers, that he cunningly dissembled his intent, with the greatest signes he could of love and peace, yet within fourteene daies after he acted." He unleashed a devastating attack on the English settlements.[28]

The killing of Nemattanew is now generally regarded as the incident that precipitated that uprising in 1622, but in itself, that event cannot explain the resumption of hostilities. Indeed, without other more fundamental difficulties, it would have been nothing more than a regrettable but minor incident. However, given the long-pent-up tensions between the two peoples, Nemattanew provided an aggressive, flamboyant, and provocative symbol of resistance. One is struck, in the accounts of his death, by his bold, indeed reckless, defiance. Wearing the cap of an Englishman he had apparently killed was risky behavior, but it appears that he believed himself endowed with a sacred power that conferred immunity from gunshot. Opechancanough's response to his killing is explicable only if we assume that the paramount chief, the dead holy man, and their people shared a common rage against the English. The reasons for their anger are not hard to find. As we have seen, one can easily produce a long catalogue of insults and atrocities against Indians going back to the first months of the English colony's life. One can also catalogue Indian outrages, as Smith and other English chroniclers often did. However, those catalogues in and of themselves explain very little. The Virginia tragedy was not simply the result of bad character on either or both sides. Its roots are far deeper, grounded in mutual cultural misunderstanding, suspicion, and intolerance, as well as conflicting economic interests. Both sides assumed the superiority of their own way of life and expected the subordination of the other. Although the Powhatans were forced by events to abandon their efforts to incorporate the newcomers into their own polity, and accept co-existence, the English remained convinced that coexistence was possible only through Indian submission.

Englishmen during the 17th century did not interpret human affairs in purely secular terms. They easily saw in Indian insubordination the hand of the devil, and routinely characterized Indian culture as diabolical in origin and nature. To compromise with savages was to appease the devil himself, and although such compromises might be necessary over the short haul, long-range strategy required the extirpation of Indian religion and the reformation of their mores. Without equivocation, English theorists of empire advocated cultural genocide. The proposal to kill all Indian "priests" could not be put in operation for practical reasons. However, no English colonial planner advocated toleration of their religious practices. Such toleration, they believed, would bring divine wrath down upon the English themselves. It must be emphasized that the advocates of the extirpation of Native American religious beliefs and practices did not regard themselves as hostile to Indians. Their mission, as they saw it, was to deliver Indians from savagery and thereby save souls. Those who look for evidence of genocidal intent in the early documents of colonization in the sense of direct advocacy of physical extermination will not find them. They will, however, easily find characterizations of Native American life and culture that are so harsh, so dark, that they serve easily to rationalize the devaluing of native life. The potentially genocidal aspect of colonialist thinking and writing emerges from the conviction that those Indians who do not accept the blessings of civilization and Christianity remain in the thrall of a depraved, indeed diabolical, way of life. English plans for Virginia's native inhabitants involved, not only placing them under English rule and occupying and transforming their land, but also eliminating their belief system through a radical reeducation of children separated from parents and family.

The 1622 uprising had its roots in bitter memories of extortion and violence. Opechancanough and his advisers placed killing of the holy man Nemattanew in that larger context. The incident itself occurred at a time when the level of violence between the two people was actually relatively low. However, English contempt for Indian culture, their lack of respect for the land rights and political sovereignty, and, perhaps most provocative, their ongoing campaign to eliminate their religion and transform their culture, combined with increasing economic privation, all contributed to the underlying tensions that led to the Powhatans' decision to strike the colony.

The uprising, as we shall see, inspired the English to abandon the policy of coexistence and conversion, and embark upon a program of genocide and ethnic cleansing. The colonizers had regarded Indian recalcitrance as evidence, not of a justifiable defense of their independence, but as collusion with Satan. Hence, when they met resistance to their tribute demands and land seizures, John Smith and his contemporaries and successors had felt justified in the use of terror as a means of forcing compliance. The intention was not originally to exterminate, only to subdue. However, the perception of resistance as satanic in origin could and did ultimately lead to the justification of exterminatory violence.

The second Anglo-Powhatan war was not triggered by religious and cultural tensions alone, however. The economic relationships of the two peoples were problematic from the outset. During the early years, the Indian was needed as a trading partner. Without the food he supplied, the colony would starve. Moreover, colonial planners expected Indians to provide some commodity, hopefully some precious metal, that would enable the colony to prosper. However, Indians not only had no gold or silver, but they also often proved reluctant to trade, so foodstuffs, all too often, were obtained at sword point. The English, as they developed their own agricultural economy, made little use of Indians as a source of farm labor. Their fields were cultivated by immigrants often under indenture. Official policy, although erratic, usually discouraged or even outlawed employment of Indians. Unlike the pattern in Spanish and French colonies, as immigrants poured into the colony, the Indian in British North America was essentially marginalized.

For the Powhatans, whose economy was based upon horticulture, hunting, and fishing, the English presence was destructive, as many of their fields were lost, their hunting grounds invaded, and their crops uprooted by rampaging pigs and cattle. In the official history of the "massacre" issued by the Virginia Company, Edward Waterhouse, while attributing the tragedy to the wiles of Satan, acknowledged that Opechancanough and his people were also driven by "the dayly feare that possest them, that in time we by our growing continually upon them, would dispossesse them of this Country." The Powhatans from 1607 onward had been given good reason for that anxiety. The records kept by the English, as we have seen, contain incident after incident in which they acted upon their basic belief that Indians had no right to land, property, or sovereignty. Opechancanough's uprising was not just an act of retaliation for Nemattanew's death. It was a response to English violations of their territorial, political, economic, and cultural integrity.[29]

CHAPTER 6

❧

"A Plantation of Sorrows": Virginia, 1622–1635

In mid July 1622, the Reverend Joseph Mead, prominent Cambridge theologian and classical scholar, picked up a most disturbing rumor about the Virginia colony. It was said, as he related to a correspondent, that some 300 or more colonists had been "massacred by the Indians at the instigation . . . of their wicked God Ochee." Only the intervention of "our God, who is the best God" had kept the rest from perishing "in like manner." Mead reported that the Jamestown settlement itself had survived only because it had been forewarned by a young Indian convert who had been asked by a friend to help "cutt all the Englishmen's throats" at a feast they planned to stage outside the English fort. When several hundred murderous Indians arrived ostensibly to escort the English settlers to that gathering, their prospective victims fell upon them and "beat out their brains, scarce any escaping." The story of the aborted feast Mead told was false, as were some other rumors then making the rounds, among them that the Indian uprising occurred on Easter Sunday, that Pocahontas's husband John Rolfe was among the first victims, and that the Indian assailants took no prisoners. However, the death count he related was fairly accurate.[1]

During the first few months after the uprising, details were hard to come by. Governor Wyatt's report to the Virginia Company, which had arrived in London shortly before Mead heard of the catastrophe, declared that on Friday, March 22, "it hath pleased God for our manyo[ld] sinns to laye a most lamentable Afflictione uppon his Plantacion, by the treachere of the Indyans." Wyatt declared that, had God not been merciful and thwarted the attack at crucial points, the Indians would "have Swept us away at once through owte the whole lande." He reported that there were more than 300 casualties, and that numerous plantations had been abandoned. He warned that the colony was facing a serious food shortage and, indeed, was now in danger of "a relapse into an extreme famine." London must send food immediately. He also asked that he be sent engineers trained in the building of fortifications and a supply guns and munitions. Wyatt also called for a change in policy. The disaster they had just suffered, he declared, was the result of previous encouragement of the uncontrolled and indiscriminate expansion of settlement. English plantations in Virginia henceforth must be restricted to areas easily defended. Wyatt asked the Company to cease granting land patents to individuals, but delegate that prerogative to "the directione & appoytment of the Governor and Counsell here." He resolved to build in Virginia a well-protected stronghold that could withstand the onslaughts of "our worst Enemies."[2]

Wyatt's letter was brief, containing little specific information. In August, however, Edward Waterhouse, Secretary of the Company, published a more detailed report that included, for the benefit of English readers, a brief summary of the events that past March, a list of the places attacked, and of the names of the dead. His purpose, as he explained, was to correct the "varied and misreported stories" then circulating in England. His main point was to stress that the tragedy occurred, not because of English weakness, but because of Indian treachery. Calls for the abandonment of the colony should therefore disregarded. Governor Wyatt, he reported was indeed forewarned, but not in the manner related in the Mead story. The warning came too late to permit immediate action to forestall the attack. The dramatic preventive blow against the Indians outside the fort at Jamestown related in Mead's letter never actually occurred. The day before the Indians struck, according to Waterhouse, a young Indian boy named Chanco, then staying on a plantation some three miles from Jamestown, was visited by his brother and told of a plan to kill all the colonists. Chanco's assignment was to murder his host, Richard Pace, the next day. His brother assured Chanco that throughout the colony that day Indians would be visiting and killing all the English. Chanco, however, frightened and confused, told Pace about the plot. Pace posted an armed guard at his plantation, then hastened to the capital to alert the governor in the early morning hours of March 22. On very short notice, Wyatt sent a alarm to some nearby settlements, but most were struck unaware that Friday morning.[3]

Although there is no mention in Waterhouse, or in any other account from Virginia, of any Indian effort to attack Jamestown, the outlying villages and plantations on the James Rivers were not so fortunate. Early in the morning, Indians by the score arrived at those settlements carrying bundles of fish, game, and other foodstuffs, which they offered to trade. They were generally welcomed by the settlers, many of whom were still seated at their breakfast tables. Then, as Waterhouse's report related, the Indians grabbed whatever instruments were at hand— hammers, axes, tongs—and began slaughtering their hosts, "not sparing eyther age or sexe, man, woman, or childe." In some cases, they mutilated the dead, "defacing, dragging, and mangling their dead carkasses into many pieces, and carrying some away in derision, with base and brutish triumph." The killings at individual farms and plantations were accompanied by all-out onslaughts on village settlements mounted by Pamunkeys, Tanx-Powhatans, Appamatucks, Weanocs, Chickahominys, Quiyoucannocks, Kiskiacs, Warraskoyacks, and Nansemonds.

Opechancanough had succeeded in forging a formidable coalition, united by the determination to abandon Powhatan's appeasement policy and take back the land. Their military strategy, combining infiltration and mass hit-and-run assaults, was brilliantly executed. Waterhouse's estimate of the death toll at 347 turned out to be slightly exaggerated, because he assumed the attackers took no prisoners. At least 20 women did survive as captives, and some were later repatriated. However, by any standard, the morning of March 22 was catastrophic. Around a third of the English population had been killed in a few hours, and others displaced. As historian Frederick Fausz notes, "by their devastating attack, the Powhatans altered English settlement patterns and created a severe refugee problem that would kill hundreds more of the English in the year following the March uprising." Twenty-two English settlements along a 100-mile stretch of the James River had been hit. Seven were permanently abandoned. At Henrico, raiders destroyed the fledgling ironworks and killed George Thorpe and the tenants on the land committed to the Indian college. Their dismembering of Thorpe's corpse would figure prominently in English accounts of the uprising for many years to come, cited repeatedly in evidence of Indian ingratitude and brutality. The psychological impact of the Indian assault was devastating. John Smith, pondering the survivors' reports as he wrote his 1624 history of Virginia, found the colony plunged into a "labyrinth of melancholy."[4]

Although contemporary English commentators and later historians have claimed that Opechancanough's objective was to kill every Englishman in Virginia, several key English settlements—Jamestown, Elizabeth City, Newport News, and the plantations along the Eastern Shore—were left untouched. The survival of the majority of English settlers they attributed variously to God's intervention, to the Indians' reluctance to attack fortified areas, or to their cowardice in fleeing whenever they encountered opposition. Those explanations are not persuasive. The Indians had the manpower to continue the assault, and after the success of the morning's surprise attack on March 22, they had a tactical advantage. They could well have taken more lives. A majority of settlers, as noted previously, survived the attacks. Some, in areas not hit, were not even aware they were occurring. Despite the carnage, as English observers conceded, some who might well have been killed survived. The colonists and their English sponsors attributed that good fortune to divine intervention, but there is another possible explanation. Although we cannot, in the absence of documentation about his thoughts and proclamations, say with certainty that Opechancanough did not intend to commit genocide through the total extermination of the English in Virginia, it is more likely that his intention was to revive Powhatan's old policy of confining the English within fixed boundaries. However, the survivors had no doubts about Opechancanough's intentions. Convinced he intended to wipe them out, they believed that only divine intervention had made it possible for anyone to escape.

Reports of the March massacre prompted an immediate and radical change in the Company's view of Indian policy. Although, previously, instructions from London had emphasized the importance of coexistence and the priority to be given to Indian conversion, the colonists were now enjoined to wage unlimited war against the Powhatans and seize all their lands outright. In a communiqué to the survivors dated August 1, the Company wondered how Virginia settlers could have suffered such losses "by the hand of men so contemptible." Echoing Governor Wyatt, the Company concluded that God had used the savages to punish them for their sins, which the company believed, included not only neglect of divine worship and excessive drunkenness, but "enormous excess of apparel." However, those whom the offended Almighty had used as the rod of His judgment must now be punished. Having demonstrated that they were "so cursed a nation, ungrateful to all benefit, and incapable of all goodness," the Powhatans should be shown little mercy. The colonists were directed "to roote [them] out from being a people." The colonists were to wage "a perpetual warre without peace or truce." Indians not under Opechancanough's sway were to be bribed with beads and copper to kill Powhatans and bring in their severed heads for reward. As for the Powhatans, those who were not killed were to be driven "so far from you" that there would no longer be any reason to fear them. The Company, dissatisfied with Wyatt's strategic retrenchment, ordered the colonists to retake the ironworks, the college lands, Henrico, Martin's Hundred, and Charles City. The Indians who had reoccupied those places were to be killed or driven out. Exceptions, however, might be made for Indian children, whose "mindes [were] not overgrown with evill," in the hope that they might be "reduced to civilitie and afterward to Christianitie," and then used profitably as servants to the English.[5]

The following May, the Company's directors abandoned any pretense of concern for the "convertings of the Infidells," declaring, in response to a complaint about mismanagement in Virginia, the conversion endeavor "an attempt impossible they being descended of the cursed race of Cham." The ideological rationale for genocide was now firmly in place. Company instructions applied most immediately to the Powhatans, but the new assumption that all Indians were cursed did not distinguish between friends and foes. The Virginia Company previously endorsed the once-commonplace affirmation that the native peoples were no less capable of civility and ultimate conversion than the ancient Britons. The belief that they were part of a universal and providential progression from savagery to civilization no longer informed their declarations about Indian policy.[6]

Waterhouse's report, published shortly after the August 1, 1622, letter was sent to Jamestown, explained to the English public the measures the Company had directed be used to revenge the dead and free the colony of Indians. He started by rejoicing that "our hands which before were tied with gentlenesse and fair usage, are now set at liberty by the treacherous violence of the Savages." In a highly fanciful portrayal of the land tenure situation in Virginia, Waterhouse claimed that previously the English had "possession of no more ground then their waste." They "now by right of Warre and law of Nations, could with a clear conscience invade the Country, and destroy them who sought to destroy us: whereby we shall enjoy their cultivated places . . . and possess the fruits of others labours . . . now their cleared grounds in all their villages (which are situate in the fruitfullest places of the land) shall be inhibited by us." Great benefits would come from emptying the land of Indians. In addition to access to cleared cropland, there would then be ample free range for English livestock, undisturbed by Indian predation, and an increase in the availability of game. With regard to the means to be used against the Powhatans, Waterhouse, echoing the earlier instructions to the colonists, declared that they would destroy "their Boats, Canoes, and Houses"; burn their corn; disrupt their winter hunts; and thereby create "famine." The Powhatans were to be chased from their villages by horses and bloodhounds, and torn apart by mastiffs, who would take "naked, tanned, deformed savages for no other than wild beasts."[7]

As a means of speeding the destruction of Indian independence, Waterhouse commended the Spanish practice of playing one Indian group off against another, and urged that local rivalries be exploited. However, no permanent alliances could be made with any Indian tribe. In contrast to earlier Company spokesmen who had deplored Spanish brutality and urged a more humane Indian policy for England, Waterhouse noted with admiration that the Spanish in the West Indies "by industry, patience and constancy" for 40 years "effected the great worke of theirs": the reduction of the local Indian population from more than 1,000,000 to less than 500. The Spanish, he declared, clearly understood that Indians were a people "by nature the most lying and inconstant in the world." He commended their example in presiding over the extermination of most of the Indians of the West Indies. The English in Virginia, in contrast, had made a near-fatal mistake. They had assumed Indians might be trusted and that they were capable of improvement. In reality, however, Waterhouse argued, no Indian could be trusted, because Indians as a race were of "more than unnaturall brutishness." They were more bestial than any animal, and did not deserve to live. By teaching that lesson, Waterhouse concluded, "this massacre must rather be beneficial to the Plantation than to impair it."[8]

Waterhouse's vehemently anti-Indian imagery was echoed and embellished in numerous ballads, broadsides, poems, and sermons during the next few years. The death of George Thorpe was a particularly popular subject. The most notable celebration of his martyrdom is found in a poem by Christopher Brooke, a friend, lawyer, and director of the Virginia Company. Brooke declared Indians had "no Character of God in them," but were "off-spring of Hells's damned brood," not descended from Adam, but of "a later Brood" not saved in Noah's Ark, but "since the generall Flood/ Sprung up like vermine of an earthly slime." They were not human beings, but "Rooted in Evill, and oppos'd in good/ Errors of Nature, of inhuman Birth/ The very dregs, garbage and spawne of Earth . . . Father'd by Sathan, and the sonnes of Hell." One is hard pressed to find in the annals of genocide a more vicious portrayal of a people.[9]

On October 7, the Virginia Company wrote again "to the Governor and Council in Virginia" to reinforce their demand that severe action against the Powhatans be taken to achieve "the rooting them out from being people upon the earth." Not only must the colony not be abandoned, but the Company reiterated that the areas evacuated after the attack must be reclaimed from the Indians. Governor Wyatt now might differ with London on matters of timing (feeling that the directors expected too much too soon), but not on the final objective. Writing to a friend in England he declared, "it is infinitely better to have no heathen among us, who were at best a thorne in our sides, than to be at peace and league with them." The Governor declared the "expulsion of the salvages" the colony's highest priority.[10]

One prominent colonist sounded a cautionary note. John Martin, a member of the colony's Council and former manager of the now defunct ironworks, circulated a letter, written on December 15, with the title "The Manner Howe to Bringe the Indians into Subjection" that rejected both genocide and unrestricted ethnic cleansing. He endorsed a program of severe retaliation against the Powhatans, recommending that they be harassed throughout the winter by an army of 200 armed men who would burn their towns, destroy their goods, and keep them in the spring from planting crops in their field, fishing in their streams, or obtaining food through trade. In addition, 10 shallops should be used in spring and summer to bar their access to rivers and bay. However, Martin, responding to those who took literally the demand that Indians cease being "a people upon the earth," argued against "an extermination of the savages yet." Holy Writ, in his particular reading, forbade it, because the Israelites were not permitted to kill all the Canaanites, for God not wanting the land to revert to wilderness, still had use for them. The Indians, Martin argued, could serve a useful function in the civilizing of Virginia, as, when subdued, they would provide a badly needed and very profitable source of servile labor. They could, he declared, be used to row English ships and assigned other menial "uses too tedious to set down." English policy should therefore be directed to their reduction and subjugation, not their extermination.[11]

Martin believed the colonists still had an obligation to seek their conversion. Few Englishmen, however, held out any hope for Indian salvation, even though, like Martin, they might still (from time to time) echo the old rhetoric. Samuel Purchas, in 1625, spoke for most when he declared that God Himself called for the "extirpation," not the deliverance, of the Powhatans. Only the least dangerous among them were fit even for enslavement. He declared that the Indians' "unnatural, inhuman wrongs," along with their presumably nomadic mode of life, gave the English just title to all the lands in Virginia. He did not distinguish between those tribes that had supported the uprising and those that did not.[12]

As Martin penned his recommendations in the waning days of 1622, the question of extermination of all the "savages" was an academic one, because the colony lacked the means to free the land of Indians. The survivors were short of guns and ammunition, and sent an urgent request to London for aid. The Company responded by sending some 42 barrels of powder and some obsolescent "old caste Armes. . . . Altogether unfit, and of no use for moderne service" that could be used against "that naked people" who has assaulted the colony. The colonists were also hungry, and many were sick as a result of malnutrition, exposure, overcrowding, and poor sanitation. Some 500 colonists would die during the coming year in what the Governor described as a "generall sicknesse"—more than Opechancanough had killed during the March uprising. Food supplies were sparse—starvation, a real threat. A rare glimpse of the conditions in Virginia a year after the massacre is provided in a letter dated March 1623 from Richard Frethorne, an indentured servant at Martin's Hundred, to his parents back home in England. He wrote of the prevalence of "scurvie, the bloody fix, and divers other diseases which make the bodie very poore and Weake," adding that the sufferers had little to comfort them, as their main food was a miserable "water gruel." Meat was not to be had. A small loaf of bread "must serve for 4 men . . . people cry out day and night." Half the company that had come to Martin's Hundred with him were already dead. More died each day. He begged his parents to either pay off his indenture, so he could go home or send him some food, perhaps some old cheese. He included in his letter instructions regarding how to package the cheese so it would not rot aboard ship. Frethorne ended by declaring that their answer to his plea would be "life or death to me." His letter confirms Governor Wyatt's warning that he did not have the resources to feed the refugees that streamed into Jamestown and Elizabeth City after the attack, let alone the new people the Company dispatched to Virginia. Some provisions were sent to Jamestown that spring, but in August the Company informed the Governor that it did not have the resources to send any food. In October, London decided, because of the food shortage in Virginia, to cancel its plans to send an additional 100 settlers to the colony. Wyatt had ordered the colonists to plant more corn and place no further reliance on Indian food supplies. However, the 1622 and 1623 harvests were far from adequate. Some corn was taken from the Powhatans in retaliatory raids, but not enough.[13]

The governor hoped that trade with Indians outside Opechancanough's orbit might make up the difference. Wyatt dispatched several expeditions to the tribes of the Chesapeake Bay. Because he was uncertain regarding their feelings, his instructions to each of the captains directed them to trade peacefully if possible, but use "force and violence" if needed to obtain "Corne, furrs, or other commodities." Captain Henry Spelman visited the Wicocomicos and found them friendly. Captain Raleigh Croshaw visited the Patawomecks, as did captain Ralph Harmor. Harmor apparently encountered opposition from the Nacotchtanks, enemies of the Patawomecks, who lived upriver on the opposite shore. He reported to London that he "slew divers" of their number because they "sought to Circumvent him by Treacherie." The Patawomecks, for their part, had rejected overtures from Opechancanough to join in the war against the English by killing their English visitors. However, Croshaw failed to persuade them to become English allies. Despite the tribe's neutrality, the Patawomecks appeared to be a promising trade partner. Accordingly, in May, Harmor was sent to the Potomac to assist Croshaw. Because his hosts had no surplus corn supplies to trade, he joined them in raiding their upriver neighbors. After Harmor's return to Jamestown, Croshaw remained behind, but apparently somehow antagonized the Patawomecks' *werowance*, and took refuge in a hastily constructed fort.[14]

In June, the Governor sent Captain Isaac Maddison to assist Croshaw in repairing relations with the Patawomecks. He was given very specific instructions to defend them against their enemies and guard their corn supply "to his utmost power." Maddison handled his assignment in an exceedingly stupid and brutal manner. Distrustful of all Indians, and persuaded by rumors, spread by the unscrupulous interpreter Robert Poole, among others, that the Patawomecks'*werowance* was plotting against him, Maddison attacked and massacred 30 or 40 villagers, and took the chief, his son, and several others back to Jamestown as hostages. The Patawomecks were forced to pay a substantial ransom in corn to get them back.[15]

The Potomac tribes did not prove to be reliable trading partners. Understandably, they resented the heavy-handed methods of the likes of Maddison. Indians, perhaps in reprisal for Maddison's depredations, wiped out a trading party several months later led by the more skillful interpreter and diplomat Henry Spelman, and also tried to seize an English pinnace on the Potomac River. In the fall, trade having failed to provide the food the colony so desperately needed, George Yeardley stole around 1,000 bushels of Indian corn by raiding the Powhatans. Other expeditions brought in another 3,000 bushels, some by trade, most by force. Those supplies, along with some food finally supplied by the Company, saved the colony from starvation, but barely. Control of access to Indian food supplies was so crucial, and private speculation such a threat, that Wyatt and his Council on March 24, 1624, in dispatching Captain William Eppes on a trade mission, authorized him to confiscate any Indian corn he might find in the hands of unlicensed English traders.[16]

Conditions in Virginia remained grim. The authorities dealt harshly with those who challenged their actions. We find in the surviving minutes of the colony's general court sessions several examples. For "base and detracting" remarks about Governor Wyatt, one Richard Barnes in was sentenced to "have his arms broken and his tongue bored through with an awl," after which he was forced to run the gantlet and was exiled from the colony. For complaining about the conduct of Captain William Tucker, who had reprimanded him for disobeying an order from the governor, John Heny was lashed (60 stripes), forced to pay damages to Tucker, and imprisoned until he made payment. Edward Newell was placed in the pillory in the marketplace at Jamestown with a "paper on his head shewinge the cause of his offense," then had both ears cut off. He was also sentenced to a year's servitude and disenfranchised. His offense: an informant had reported that Newell, in a conversation with a shipmate while anchored "at Damrell's cove in Canada," threatened to take vengeance against Governor Wyatt whom he blamed for the death of his brother, a ship captain executed on the uncorroborated testimony of a "scurvie boy" for attempted sodomy. For a milder but unspecified act of insubordination, one Richard Evans was fined "100 waight of tobacco," forced to lie in the marketplace tied "neck and heele, for three hours" and "be putt out of his place." There are no indications that such severity improved English morale. One settler a year after the massacre described the colony as "a plantation of sorrows . . . plentifull in nothing and wanting nothing but plenty."[17]

Wyatt was persuaded that the colony's prosperity could be restored only through the extermination or removal of the Indians. An early effort to bargain with them reinforced that conviction. Receiving word that Opechancanough was holding some English women taken at Martin's Hundred, Governor Wyatt in June had sent Captain Maddison to negotiate their release. He was rebuffed, and reported that the "insolent" paramount chief had expressed his contempt by doing some unspecified "dishonor" to a picture of the king. (We may be permitted to wonder if a more tactful English representative might have elicited a more favorable response.) Beginning in mid summer, Wyatt, having abandoned the less defensible English settlements and resettled their inhabitants, mounted a series of punitive raids against the Powhatans, striking, in addition to Opechancanough's Pamunkeys, the Weanocs, Quiyoucannocks, Nansemonds, Warraskoyaks, Tanx-Powhatans, and the Chickahominys. As the Indians generally fled their villages before the English forces arrived, direct casualties were light. The English treated those they apprehended with great brutality. Most of their atrocities were not recorded, but we do know that in one incident three Chickahominys who didn't get away in time were summarily beheaded. For the most part, Wyatt's forces found, as the governor explained to London, that their adversaries "were nott suddenlie to be destroyde wit the sworde by reasons of theire swyftnes of foote, and advantages of the woodes, to which upon all our assaultes they retire." However, the destruction by fire of Indian villages, boats, fish weirs, and corn supplies proved far more lethal. The English, the governor boasted, waged war against the Powhatans with "blud and crueltie."[18]

Waterhouse, in calling for the elimination of the Powhatans, had described them as a very vulnerable people because they lived in small settlements, rather than fortified centers, and could not defend themselves adequately against armed raiders. The casualty rates in the war that followed that March cannot be computed with any accuracy, but the data we do have indicate that Indian losses were disproportionately high. According to a report compiled in spring 1625, Indian raids after the massacre had claimed no more than 30 English lives. The remaining English settlements were well protected. Hunger and disease, not Indian arrows, accounted for around 95 percent of the colonists' fatalities. By contrast, although Governor Wyatt could provide not even an approximate body count, because most victims died out of sight, he claimed at the end of 1622 that more Indians had been killed during the previous spring and fall "then hath been slayne before since the beginnge of the colony." We have every reason to believe him.[19]

In March 1622/1623, Opechancanough asked for a truce, using as an intermediary Chanco, the young Indian who had warned Jamestown of his conspiracy a year earlier. According to Chanco, the Powhatan leader felt that enough blood had been shed, and admitted that his people were starving because the English had burned their villages and food supplies. Opechancanough may have been facing some internal dissension. There was an unconfirmed report several months later that his older brother, the former paramount chief Opitchapam had offered to betray him to the English. Opechancanough promised that if a truce were granted that would enable his people to plant their crops, he would set free some 20 English prisoners. A week later, before receiving a reply, the Powhatan chief released a woman named Boyse, who came home "appareled like one of their Queenes." Hoping for the return of the other captives, the colonists suspended hostilities. The Virginia Council explained to the Company in London that they would now permit the Indians to plant their crops undisturbed, to know their exact location when the war resumed. Overall, they hoped to make the Powhatans feel "as secure as wee were that we may follow their Example in destroying them." The English in Virginia in 1623 had no interest in a lasting peace with their Indian neighbors. A settler, William Capps, wrote to a friend in London to explain that it was generally understood that, although the Indians "would faine have peace," they would be attacked again "when the Corne is readie." "The last massacre," Capps declared, "killed all our countrie, besides them they killed, they burst the heart of all the rest." They would take vengeance on "the Heathen kennel of dogges."[20]

In May, the English invited Opechancanough and other tribal leaders to a peace conference at Patawomeck village on the Potomac River. The leader of the colonists' 12-man delegation, Captain William Tucker, was directed to obtain the release of the remaining English prisoners. He did so, but was also ordered secretly to administer to Indian attendees a deadly poison said to have been prepared by Dr. John Pott, an enterprising and powerful land owner and sometime physician later accused of augmenting his wealth by "foul and covetous means" that included cattle rustling. After a number of ceremonial speeches delivered by the chiefs, Tucker proposed a toast, offering the Indians flagons of sack containing Pott's lethal concoction. Tucker estimated that some 200 Indians were poisoned. Later estimates suggest 100 of those who drank the sack died of it. Another 50 were killed when Tucker ordered the English to fire on the sickened Indians. However, contrary to Tucker's initial report, Opechancanough himself escaped. Tucker's men mutilated the corpses of their victims, taking "parts of their heades" back to Jamestown. The Virginia Company, despite its directive that unlimited war be waged against the Powhatans, expressed displeasure at the deceitful tactics used at that massacre. The Virginia colonists felt, however, that considerations of honor had no place in their war against the Powhatans.[21]

On July, 23, 1623, Governor Wyatt unleashed a new offensive, sending some five armed bands into Indian country, killing, burning, and destroying the cornfields that, as the governor noted, had been planted that spring "in great abundance upon hope of a fraudulent peace." He had promised the Company that he would "geve them shortly a blow, that shall neere or altogether Ruinate them." Commanded by William Pierce, Nathaniel West, Samuel Matthews, William Tucker, and Isaac Maddison, the raiders burned the fields and villages of the Chickahominys, Appamatucks, Weanocs, Tanx-Powhatans, Nansemonds, and Warraskoyaks. In November, the governor personally led a new armed expedition, this one into the Chesapeake Bay region. While repairing relations with the Patawomecks, who once again promised to assist the English in their struggle with Opechancanough, Wyatt and his men attacked the Anacostans, their rivals and enemies. The pretext for that action was that they were presumably responsible for killing Spelman and his men the previous year. In fact, there is reason to suspect that the Patawomecks themselves were responsible, having taken that action in reprisal for Maddison's depredations. However, the Anacostans were enemies of the Patawomecks, whose favor the colonists once again wished to cultivate. In his November expedition, Wyatt mixed some diplomacy with his terrorism and theft, but diplomacy was secondary. In his report to London, Wyatt related that his troops had "putt many to the sword," as they destroyed an Anacostan village and burned "a marvelous quantity of corne," being unable to load the entire amount of grain into their boats. What is striking about this episode is the fact that the victims were not allied with Opechancanough. Although one historian sees the renewal of the alliance with the Patawomecks as evidence of "the mature development of a pragmatic Indian policy" based on recognition that "there could be some 'good' Indians who were not dead Indians after all," these and subsequent events suggest a more complex, and darker, reality.[22]

In the commission directing Ralph Harmor to proceed to the Potomac River to trade with the Indians in January of the following year, Governor Wyatt explicitly declared that the captain was not to use force to compel trade, or "to offer any violence to any except in his owne defense." A similar stipulation was placed in the orders issued to Raleigh Croshaw two months later. However, those orders applied only to the Chesapeake trade. The policy toward the Indians of the James and York rivers remained one of unremitting hostility. The House of Burgess, summoned in March 1624, adopted measures intended to put the colony on a full war footing. The Assembly forbad both private and public trade with Indians, demanding once again that the colony grow its own corn. It declared that "every dwelling house" was to be palisaded. All plantations were to maintain an adequate and serviceable supply of guns, powder, and shot, and were to keep a night watch. Gunpowder was not to be wasted in frivolous entertainments such as drinking bouts. All men were to carry arms when they went to work in the fields, and were to post a sentinel. On no occasion were residents to leave "in such numbers as thereby to weaken or endanger the plantations," but when they did need to travel, they were to do so in armed groups of sufficient size to repel Indian attack. Most striking, every year in July, plantations were to "fall upon their adjoining salvages," thus establishing an annual schedule for Indian killing. Soldiers injured during those raids were to be cured or, if incurable, maintained at public expense "according to his person and quality."[23]

That fall, Governor Wyatt led a band of 60 colonists on another raid into Powhatan country. This time, as they entered a large Pamunkey cornfield determined to cut it down, the English were confronted by an Indian force the governor estimated to number some 800 warriors from several tribes commanded, not by Opechancanough, but by his presumably deposed brother Itoyatin, now using the war name Sasawpen. (Opechancanough does not reappear in the records as the Powhatan's leader for several years. The reason for this is not known.) To Wyatt's surprise, his prospective victims did not run away, but fought with great courage and tenacity. There ensued a two-day pitched battle in which 16 English-men were wounded and a much larger but undetermined number of Powhatans killed. By virtue of their superior weaponry, Wyatt's forces prevailed, and they seized food supplies sufficient, the governor estimated, to feed 4,000 men for a year. He regretted that a shortage of gunpowder prevented a greater slaughter of Indians.[24]

The gunpowder shortage forced the suspension for some time of further military action against the Indians. The Company's charter was revoked in 1624, and a new patent redefined Virginia as a royal colony. The change had little immediate effect on local government. Former Governor George Yeardley replaced Wyatt when the latter returned to England to settle his late father's estate, and the same notables who had long controlled the colony remained in power. The notorious Dr. Pott was among their number. However, with the demise of the Company, detailed reports of interactions with Indians were no longer forwarded to London. Thus, many of the events of the second Anglo-Powhatan war are poorly documented. We do know there was a lull in hostilities, because the royal patent did not bring with it the military supplies the Virginians so badly needed. Despite the earlier resolution of the Burgess, the colonists did not raid Indian country at all in 1625 or 1626, but concentrated on fortifying their own enclaves and building up a large store of muskets, shot, and gunpowder. An order of the general court dated August 7, 1626, declared that "no planter shall remove from the plantation wherein he is seated, to seat himself upon any other" without a special order from the governor and "some of his council." The penalty: a substantial fine, to be paid in tobacco, and forced relocation to his original site. The court restated and expanded upon the regulations regarding defensive measures at the plantations passed by the Assembly in 1624. It now declared unauthorized absence from the home plantation for more than 24 hours forbidden. The "Commander of every Plantation" was ordered to conduct regular training exercises so his men "may be made more fitt for service upon any occasione." The court reminded the colonists that commanders who wasted powder, "in drinkinge Entertayments or the like" would be punished.[25]

The English strategy, for about two years, was essentially defensive. Extermination proving beyond their immediate reach, the colonists adopted a temporary policy of racial separation through boundary maintenance. Then, on July 4, 1627, the general court ordered a new raid. The planters on August 1 were directed to "go upon the Indians and cutt down their corn." Each settlement was assigned a specific target. "The good ship called the Virgin" was sent upriver toward the Pamunkey to mislead the Powhatans about English intentions. Raiding parties in August struck farther South, devastating the villages of the Tanx-Powhatan, Wyannoke, Appamamatucks, Nansemond, Chickahominy, Tappahannock, Warraskoyak, and Chesapeake. In October, a force led by Governor Yeardley struck the Pamunkey. The killing, Captain Francis West lamented, was hindered by "a common Scarsity of Shott." Otherwise, he boasted, they would have achieved the "utter ruine and extirpation" of the enemy. Shortly thereafter, the English entered some negotiations involving the repatriation of several English captives that led to an arrangement sometimes referred as a "peace treaty." As a condition for ending hostilities, the Powhatans apparently agreed to stay out of English territory and cease killing English livestock. Although this did constitute a sort of truce, the Virginia general court's minutes of April 24, 1628, make clear that they had not made "any peace or dishonorable treaty," and awaited a new opportunity to take their revenge.[26]

Continued Indian intrusions into areas settled by the English and continued killing of wandering livestock, along with the death at Indian hands of one colonist, provided the excuse to resume hostilities, with the colony's Council now resolving once again to pursue a policy of "perpetual enmity." On the last day of January 1628/1629, the court minutes recorded that "the Governor and Council therefore upon serious deliberation, have thought fitt and are of the opinion that in their judgment it is a safer Course for the Colony in general to prevent a second Massacre utterly to proclayme and maintayne enmity and warre with all the Indians of these partes." The Council accordingly declared "all the former treaties of peace be utterly extinct and disannulled." Warfare resumed, and although one report in 1630 claimed that more Indians were killed than at any time "since the great massacre," the altercations that occurred between 1629 and 1632 cannot be reconstructed. We do know that at one point the colonial government declared only the Accomacs of the Eastern Shore friends to the English, and therefore exempt from killing on sight. It is impossible to determine the number of Indian casualties in this, the second, Anglo-Powhatan war, but Rountree estimates their population at the end of the decade as no more than 5,000. They were now outnumbered by the English.[27]

The Indian policy that emerged after 1622 was genocidal in its impulses, but placed its primary emphasis upon a rigid racial separation that would ensure English safety through creating Indian-free regions. A very few former Powhatans who proved serviceable to the English were allowed to remain and work in the colony. The records include a directive to Virginia from the Company in London commending to the care of the colony "those Indians whom God used as instruments of revealing and preventing the total ruin of you." We know that one of those Indians was Chanco. The names and numbers of the other are unknown. A small handful of captured Indians were apparently enslaved. Frethorne wrote of two taken at Martin's Hundred. It is also recorded that Captain William Eppes owned an Indian slave. A puzzling entry in the records of the Virginia general court refers to the invention, by the Indian trader William Claiborne, of some "assured ways and means" for "the safe keeping" of captive Indians, whom he proposed to use as guides. The court, noting "there is one Indyan come in unto us," encouraged Claiborne's experimentation with that person, and gave him exclusive rights to his innovation. Others were encouraged to discover other ways of restraining and exploiting "any Indyan they shall attaine to." We do not know what it was that Claiborne had invented, but we do know there very few Indians, slaves or otherwise, permitted in English Virginia after 1622. The general rule was that Indians were banned from the colony and, unless on recognized diplomatic missions, could be killed on sight. This principle was incorporated in the short-lived 1627 truce. Fear of Indians was pervasive and prevented any extensive use of them as slaves. An episode recorded in the general court minutes illustrates this point. When a ship captain named Sampson deposited a cargo of Carib Indians at Jamestown, the authorities were puzzled as to what to do with them. The captain offered no help, saying, as the general court recorded, that "we should dispose of them as we shall please." When several of the Caribs ran away and hid in the woods, the authorities, fearful that they would join the Powhatans in robbing and killing Englishmen, ordered that they be apprehended and then "hanged till they be dead."[28]

The leadership at Jamestown envisioned, not only Indian exclusion from the areas occupied by colonists, but also, in time, the expansion of English settlement and the removal of Indians from the new areas they occupied. Settlers in 1627 were sent up the York River to occupy the abandoned Indian site they called "Chesiac," located above the modern city of Yorktown. This expansion/Indian removal policy was augmented by an act of the Assembly in 1630 that granted 50 acres and a tax exemption to those who agreed to occupy a new line of settlement extending from Chesiac to Jamestown. The following year, the Assembly mandated a labor levy of one man in every 40 to work on the construction of buildings and fortifications in the area. "By the next year," according to one authority, "a pale some six miles long running through Middle Plantation and joining two creeks, the one flowing into the James, the other to the James, had further strengthened the defenses raised against Indian incursions." Some 300,000 acres were now free of Indians. However, most of the territory that would be incorporated into the Virginia Colony during the next two decades remained outside that pale.[29]

Sir John Harvey, appointed royal governor in 1630, sought to provide a sound foundation for the peaceful and profitable development of Virginia's economic potential. He envisioned the securing of a self-contained and self-sufficient English territory protected, not only by a palisade across the top of the peninsula from the James River to the York, but also by a very well-armed and vigilant militia. He reorganized the colony's military forces, built up a store of arms and munitions, and demanded the fortification of all plantations. The colony's Assembly, summoned early in 1632, declared Indians "our irrecosilable enemie" and authorized commanders to kill those who might be found "lurkinge" near English settlements. No settler was "to dare to speake or parlie with any Indians either in the woods or in any plantation if he can possibly avoid it by any means," but should report the incident or, if possible, bring the Indian to the local commander. The penalty for unofficial conversation: one month's servitude for a freeman, a lashing of 60 stripes for a servant. (The Eastern Shore, where the tribes were not actively supporting the Powhatans, were exempt from the prohibition on private contact with Indians. The Assembly directed the planters there to "observe all good termes of amitie," but remain on guard.) The Assembly also prohibited all trade, public as well as private, with Indians. The governor, however, did not share the

Assembly's conviction that an unending campaign against Indians was in the colony's best interests. After the Powhatans, early in 1632, sent word that they were interested in ending the war, Harvey, late in summer 1632, over the objections of several members of the local governing council, agreed to abandon the policy of "perpetual enmity." The exact terms of the settlement are not known, but the evidence indicates that they involved the minimization of contact, and therefore of conflict, between the two peoples. The governor reported to London that once again "the country is on good termes with the Indians." He added, however, that "we stand at all Tymes upon our guarde." In that spirit, the Assembly in August declared that anyone who sold or bartered a gun to an Indian should suffer confiscation of all property and be sentenced to life imprisonment. Indicative of the continuing climate of distrust and fear, the colony's secretary in 1638 reported to London that the Virginians were acutely aware that "the savages" remained "ever awake to do them injuries."[30]

Indian policy in Virginia during the 10 years between Opechancanough's attack on the colony and Governor Harvey's peace agreement with the Powhatans underwent a series of transformations. The Virginia Company's fond expectation that all Virginians, English and Indian alike, sooner or later would become God-fearing Christian subjects of England's king had never had much appeal to those who actually lived in Virginia. After 1622, that particular vision ceased to play much, if any, role in English thinking about the colony's future. It had never had any appeal to Virginia's indigenous people. The Company's strident demands for total Indian extermination as a response to the massacre was no more realistic. During the 1620s, the colonists simply did not have the means to carry out such a program, although the documentary evidence we have suggest few, if any, moral reservations about doing so. The policy that did develop was one that now would be termed "ethnic cleansing." Convinced both of the undesirability of Indians as neighbors and of their own ability ultimately to live without their trade or labor, the colony pursued a policy intended to create in Virginia a region free of Indians. Those Indians who survived famine and sporadic killing in armed raids would be forced westward. That policy had its roots, as we have seen, in the colony's earliest days. Then and later, it was a prescription for ongoing conflict not only with Indians, but within the colony as well, as the frontier was periodically destabilized by both natives on the move and Europeans on the make.

Governor Harvey himself soon fell victim to this process. On May 7, 1635, the Virginia House of Burgess, acting on the recommendation of the colony's Council, removed him from office and named a local planter, John West, his interim replacement. Their indictment of the governor, which was promptly sent to sent London, charged him with tyrannical behavior. Although it is true that Harvey was often tactless and arbitrary in his dealings with local notables, their legal case against him has rightly been characterized by historian Miles Thornton as "a string of weak accusations, each of which Harvey later answered with no trouble." The governor's support of Lord Baltimore's Maryland ventures had irritated the vehemently anti-Catholic Indian trader William Claiborne and his allies. However, the fundamental source of discontent with Harvey is to be found in his land policy. Although the colonists during the administration of the Virginia Company had been granted numerous 50-acre "headrights," often in country recently occupied by Indians, Harvey was reluctant to make such grants. His interim replacement John West, in contrast, issued more than four times as many land patents in less than two years than Harvey had awarded in more than four. Although there were several reasons for Harvey's refusal to make more grants, avoidance of conflict with the Indians was an important consideration. As Thornton notes, Harvey's opponents wanted "to pursue a vigorously aggressive, expansionist policy toward the Indians, thus opening new regions to white settlement. Harvey, on the other hand, had sought to make peace with the surrounding tribes and to formalize the territorial status quo." Some well-placed Virginia insurrectionists, led by the former interim governor and notorious Indian poisoner Dr. John Potts, charged that Harvey, by ending the killing of Powhatans, was provoking "a second massacre" of Christians in Virginia. They demanded a restoration of the policy of "perpetuall enmity." However, Sir Francis Wyatt, appointed to a new term as governor in 1638, maintained the peace, even as prominent Virginians acquired more Indian lands and, in some cases, profited greatly from the Indian trade in deerskins and furs. A more aggressive policy, one designed to exterminate the indigenous population, would have been costly, dangerous, and disruptive of a lucrative commerce.[31]

Chapter 7

Another War and a New Policy

In a 1626 memorandum to the Company in London, Virginia's Governor Wyatt had noted that the Indians, bloodied by English raiders, were "infinitlye desirous" of peace. Wyatt, as we have seen, assured his correspondents that he only intended to lull the Powhatans by a false truce, then when their fields had been planted, would resume his depredations. He kept his word. Indiscriminate English killing of Powhatans for a decade after the massacre was constrained only by shortages of gunpowder, shot, and manpower. We do not know how many Powhatans were put to the sword or burned in their villages by order of Wyatt and his successors, nor can we estimate how many Indians succumbed to starvation or disease in the wake of those attacks. The leading authority on the Powhatans estimates that their numbers were reduced by around two-thirds during the first two decades of English settlement. Because of their vulnerability, the Powhatans were, as Wyatt had described them, eager for a settlement long before the colonists were willing to stop the killing. The peace, finally accepted by Harvey in 1632, lasted for some 12 years, but then the Powhatans struck again. The English were persuaded that the reason for the third war was inherent Indian treachery. A close reading of available sources suggest a different explanation.[1]

English pressure on Indian land after the deposing of Harvey was unremitting. The expansion of tobacco production constantly required new land not only to accommodate new planters, but also to replace soils rapidly depleted by single-crop production. The policy of containing English plantations within a defensive pale line was soon abandoned, as planters moved up the James and York rivers and occupied much of the Eastern Shore, displacing and sometimes surrounding Indian communities as they went. In that process, some Powhatan chiefdoms disappeared completely, their people absorbed by those that remained. Others moved farther inland, their numbers depleted, their old villages deserted.

The Virginia Assembly, by legislative order on October 11, 1639, established a process of allocation of "empty" land that facilitated and rewarded white settlement. The settlers were not allowed to purchase land directly from the Indians displaced by their new plantations. Their titles were granted by the colony on condition of occupation and cultivation. As to the former occupants, as Rountree has noted, "the government might or might not compensate the aborigines for the lands it took, depending upon its attitude of the moment toward 'barbarians.'" By the time the Powhatans launched an offensive against the colony in 1644, the English had taken most of the Confederation's former lands, and now laid claim to extensive land tracts on both the Rappahannock and Potomac rivers.[2]

Despite the provocations inherent in the English expansionist program, the Powhatans, acutely aware of their weakness, kept the peace for nearly 12 years. With the death of his elder brother, Opechancanough reappears in the records as the paramount chief, but for a time proved surprisingly conciliatory in his dealings with the colony. Unfortunately, we cannot estimate the number of clashes between Englishmen and Indians during the early 1640s, because almost all the colonial records for this period were destroyed during the American Civil War. There are indications of recurrent conflicts over English intrusions on the Indians' land and over the damage done by and to cattle and hogs that strayed onto their fields. One case of which we have a record is of particular interest. A planter named Burton killed an innocent Indian in reprisal for a theft committed by another tribesman. Opechancanough surprisingly urged the English court to be lenient, saying that he understood the killing had been a mistake, and in consequence Burton's fine was remitted. As one historian notes, in this and other cases, Opechancanough "swallowed his pride to keep the peace." Although we have neither numbers nor specific details, the problem of private reprisals against Indians for such things as killing wayward English livestock was sufficiently serious that the general Assembly passed a law requiring that such cases be referred to local militia commanders, who were to avoid violence but take a hostage from the offending tribe and then seek a settlement with the tribal leaders. The law did not achieve its objective. A new Anglo-Powhatan war broke out in spring 1644.[3]

The attack came on April 18, Maundy Thursday, a day Opechancanough may have chosen out of the belief that the English would be preoccupied with religious matters. This time, there was no advance warning. The plantations and villages outside the older palisaded settlements were hard hit. Within a few hours, more than 500 settlers were dead. However, because the English population then exceeded 8,000, this was, percentagewise, a far lower death toll than the colony had suffered in 1622. Opechancanough's Confederacy was now far smaller; its chances of success remote. After the initial assault, which left the colony's frontier dazed and terrified, Opechancanough's warriors withdrew and waited. Their leader was an infirm and crippled man estimated to be around 100 years old. His warriors carried him into battle on a litter. The reasons for his audacious act are obscure. Governor Berkeley later claimed that Opechancanough had been told about the civil war in England by some disloyal colonists. He presumably believed the colonists now would not be resupplied or reinforced by their London sponsors and, if cut off from the interior, would starve. Some scholars believe that misconception explains Opechancanough's failure to follow up on the April 18 attack, but this is conjecture. We have no direct evidence. We can safely say that the old chief no doubt hoped to avenge a lifetime of insults and injuries, and avert future danger of loss of land and sovereignty.[4]

The Virginia Assembly resolved to "for ever abandon all formes of peace and familiarity" with the Powhatans. Responsibility for the conduct of the war fell upon the newly appointed Governor, William Berkeley, the 36-year-old fourth son of a prominent English landed family, educated at Cambridge and trained in law at Middle Temple. Berkeley, unlike previous royal governors, had no prior experience in Virginia. He did have excellent London political connections, and with their help had skillfully engineered the removal of the veteran Governor Francis Wyatt. With equal skill he then cultivated Wyatt and other Virginia notables to secure a powerful political base in the colony. The bungling ineptness, the stubborn willfulness, and the brutal insensitivity that marred his final years as governor three decades later were not at all in evidence when he assumed office in 1642. In contrast to his equivocations during the Indian crisis of 1675, Berkeley, in 1644, acted decisively to counter the threat from Opechancanough. He designated William Claiborne "Generall and Chief Commander" of the militia and ordered him to take the offensive immediately. Acutely aware of the colony's perennial shortage of war material, in June, Berkeley sailed for England to seek assistance, leaving the colony in the hands of Deputy Governor Kemp. Shortly after the governor's departure, Claiborne led his army up the York River against the Pamunkey, burning their fields, killing those they could catch, and forcing Opechancanough and other survivors farther into the interior. Two other military expeditions struck Indian villages south of the James and in the Charles City and Henrico regions. After the return of Claiborne's army in late August, another smaller force raided the Chickahominys. In the fall, raiding parties were periodically sent out to strike and destroy Indian cornfields and food supplies throughout the region. By the time winter set in, the English, as Shea notes, had "a large area beyond the palisade cleared of hostile forces."[5]

But Opechancanough remained at large. To secure the Virginia settlements from future Indian raids, the colony built three palisaded blockhouses: Fort Royal on the York near the site of the now-deserted Pamunkey villages, Fort Charles at the James falls (near modern Richmond), and Fort James in Chickahominy country midway between the other two forts. A hundred men were assigned to each fort, with orders not only to guard against enemy incursions, but also to conduct raids against the Pamunkey and Chickahominy wherever they might be found. Provisions were made to arm the soldiers, provide them with pay, and guarantee medical aid if wounded, support if disabled, and benefits for their families if killed. (In fact, although several were wounded, no soldiers were killed during this war.) With these measures, Virginia moved away from exclusive reliance on a citizen militia and toward the creation of a professional military.[6]

Berkeley returned from England in spring 1645. Because of the Civil War in the homeland, he had not been able to secure English assistance in the war against the Powhatans, but did join for a time that fall in King Charles's war against Parliament. Assessing the situation in Virginia after his disembarkation, the governor learned that the previous year's raids, despite a shortage of gunpowder that limited their duration, had taken a heavy toll on the Indians. Word arrived in Jamestown, conveyed in a letter from an English captive, that Opechancanough wanted peace. The governor declared a truce and agreed to a meeting in June at Fort Royal; however, he had no intention of making peace. When the Indian delegation approached the fort, they were charged by the garrison. A number were killed or captured, but Opechancanough was not among them. The aged chief remained at large for another year, as English raiders once again burned cornfields and demolished makeshift villages. The end came in spring 1646, when the governor, alerted to his great adversary's whereabouts, led "a Party of Horse" that ran down a straggling group of Pamunkeys trying to carry him out of harm's way on a litter. The governor, taking his prisoner back to Jamestown and planning to send him to England in demonstration of his great victory, ordered that he be "treated with all the Respect and Tenderness imaginable," but that was not to be. As Robert Beverley related in his classic history of Virginia three quarters of a century later, Berkeley "could not preserve his Life above a Fortnight; for one of the Soldiers, resenting the Calamities the Colony had suffer'd, by this Prince's Means, basely shot him thro' the Back, after he was made Prisoner, of which Wound he died. He continued brave to the last Moment of his Life, and show'd not the least Dejection at his Captivity."[7]

At its March 1646 meeting, the Virginia General Assembly, on recommendation of Governor Berkeley, had repealed its earlier resolution of unending war against "our common enemies the Indians." The destruction of their villages, the governor reported, had left them scattered, "lurking up & downe the woods in small numbers," rendering almost impossible "a further revenge upon them." Accordingly, the military expedition the Assembly authorized and funded was ordered to seek a settlement, because "peace, if honourably obtained would conduce to the better being and comoditie of the country." The waging of exterminatory war against the Indian remnants was deemed simply too difficult, too expensive, and, given the vulnerability of isolated English settlement to Indian raiders, too risky. In October, the English accepted the surrender of Opechancanough's successor, Necotowance. The terms were harsh and represented a radical change in the relationship of what was left of the old Powhatan Confederacy and the Virginia colony. Necotowance now acknowledged that he and his people were subjects of the English king, and agreed to deliver each fall a tribute of 20 beaver skins to Virginia's governor. The treaty he accepted specified that the governor would now either name or confirm the appointment of his successors. He was to surrender all guns and return English prisoners, blacks, and any Indians formerly held as servants in the colony, as well as relinquish all claim to most of the lands formerly occupied by the Powhatan Confederacy.[8]

In return for Necotowance's submission, the colony promised protection "against any rebels or other enemies whatsoever." Necotowance was now, in effect, subject to an English protectorate. He and his people were to be allowed "to inhabit and hunt on the north side of Yorke River without any interruption from the English." However, that land grant was not unconditional; the governor and Council could authorize new English settlement within Indian country from "Poropotanke downeward" at their pleasure. They only needed to notify Necotowance that they were doing so. (He received that notification less than three years later.) Necotowance was required in the treaty to permit Englishmen to enter his territory at will to retrieve "cattle and hogs" and, if authorized by the governor, "to fell timber or to cut sedge." The Indians were to withdraw completely from "that tract of land betweene the Yorke River and the James River, to Kecoughton." Should any Indian be found in that area, they could be killed on sight by any Englishman. Messengers from Necotowance to Jamestown were required to call at Fort Royal and obtain a specially marked striped coat before entering the territory prohibited to Indians. One English observer recorded that Necotowance, presenting tribute in 1648 with five "petty Kings attending him," assured the English "that he had Decreed, that if any Indian be seen to come within the limits of the English Colony (except they come with some message from him, with such and such tokens) that it shall be lawfull to kill them presently, and the English shall be free to pass at all times where they please through His Dominions." The surviving records disclose that at least three Indians were killed for entering English territory without the proper garb. There were probably more. The laws the Assembly adopted to implement the treaty also forbade unauthorized English intrusions on Indian territory, but did not specify a penalty. The Assembly prescribed the death penalty for any Englishman killing an Indian wearing one of the official diplomatic coats. It also declared that any colonist who entertained or concealed Indians older than the age of 11 years would be put to death without benefit of clergy. Evidence on the enforcement of those laws is lacking. Although the peace agreement appeared to recognize Indian land rights on the upper York and James rivers, the English treated the land boundaries of 1646 as a temporary accommodation to end a war, nothing more. The Assembly directed that those who had previously been given land grants in the area North of the York set aside for Indians in the peace treaty were not to "seate or inhabitt" there until further notice. But their grants were not, revoked but were confirmed, with holders given three years after the promised future revocation of the settlement prohibition to make good their claim.[9]

Despite the treaty and the Assembly resolution temporarily banning white settlement in the areas specified for the Powhatans, settlers did not wait to occupy that territory. Governor Berkeley, hoping to prevent resumption of hostilities and spare the colony the expense of another military expedition, tried to slow down and control the process of Indian dispossession. In 1647, he ordered the evacuation of unauthorized settlements in the Northern Neck and "other remote and straying plantations on the south side of the Patomeck River, Wecokomoko, Rappahannock and Fleet Bay." A year later, he declared a moratorium on new settlements in Indian country prior to September 1649. However, Berkeley had neither the power nor the will to protect Powhatan lands from English incursions. He acknowledged colonists were driven by a pressing need for new soils for cultivation, because they were then hampered by "barren and overwrought grounds," and lacked "sufficient range" for livestock. Accordingly, in 1649, three years after the promulgation of the peace treaty with the Powhatans, the Virginia Assembly repealed the treaty prohibition on English settlement North of the York and Rappahannock rivers.[10]

Four years later, in 1653, the Assembly conceded that Indians, having now been driven off much of the land guaranteed to them by treaty, had been forced "into such narrow streights, and places, That they Canott Subsist either by plantinge or huntinge." Expressing the fear that such injustice might drive the Indians "to attempt some Desperate Course for themselves," the Assembly forbade any future settlements on land claimed by Indians without prior authorization from colonial authorities. The Assembly reaffirmed a 1650 law specifying that, before any new lands were occupied by English settlers, the colony should grant to each local *werowance* a land allocation of 50 acres for every "Bowman" in their tribe. However, only those allocations, not the original 1646 treaty boundaries, were guaranteed to Indian occupants by the Assembly's actions. Because the Indian population had been greatly diminished by war, disease, famine, and alcohol, there were only 725 bowmen left among the tributary Indians by a 1670 count. The effect of this Indian land allocation program was to free most of their remaining territory for colonization. As Rountree notes, in place of independent tribes, there were now "many separate Indian political units on reservations." Those communities were soon surrounded by white settlements. Anticipating the later reservation systems, "the lands allowed were adequate by English economic standards but grossly undersized for Powhatan use in hunting and foraging; the rapid increase of English settlers who cleared land and hunted for their own tables also decreased the game in the region. It is no wonder that by 1656 most Indians were facing starvation." Some limited relief was afforded by a law passed by the Assembly in 1655, providing that each Indian who brought in eight wolf heads would be given a cow.[11]

The 1646 treaty represented the realization of a long-standing English ambition. The idea of making Indians tributary of the English Crown had been proposed by the Virginia Company as early as 1609. The ludicrous attempted coronation of Powhatan had been an inept effort to execute that policy. Not long thereafter, Captain John Smith had attempted unsuccessfully to secure an agreement with Powhatan that would provide protection from the Monacans on condition that he cede some land near the falls of the James River, pay "a yearly tribute to King James," and acknowledge that Indian thieves and other malefactors who victimized colonists were subject to English law. In his later writings, Smith boasted that during his exploratory travels in Chesapeake Bay, he had received the submission of several dozen "Indian kinges" who were now loyal subjects of James I. Although those *werowances,* in fact, may have been subjected to some sort of ceremony (which they did not understand), Smith's claim was only another example of his hyperbole. In 1614, a treaty with the Chickahominys had promised protection from the Powhatans in exchange for tribute and an acknowledgement of English sovereignty. However, that agreement was soon superseded by the Chickahominy alliance with Opechancanough. The 1632 settlement of the second Anglo-Powhatan war was based on maintaining rigid barriers between Englishmen and Indians. It did not effectively negate Powhatan sovereignty. The 1646 treaty did.[12]

The year 1646 marked the end of the Powhatan chiefdom's dominance in tidewater Virginia. Several tribes previously allied with the Powhatans had remained neutral. Now the Pamunkey leader could no longer be considered a paramount chief, and the English subsequently negotiated separate agreements requiring the payment of tribute by tribes once part of the Powhatan Confederacy. As noted previously, only five other sachems accompanied Necotowance in his visit to Jamestown in 1648. He disappears from the record thereafter. His successor, Topotomoy, was killed eight years later while fighting against the Ricaheerians as an ally of his English overlords at the Battle of Bloody Run. The Virginia Assembly, in land allocations to the subject tribes beginning in 1649, recognized Topotomoy only as the sachem of the Pamunkey. He was succeeded after his death by his wife Cockacoeske, a very shrewd and astute leader who for some three decades would attempt, through manipulation of the English, to recapture some of the power her people had wielded during the early 17th century, when Pamunkey leaders politically dominated the Indians of the Virginia coastal plain. The Pamunkey now relied on English goodwill.[13]

The Virginia authorities were determined to keep all the Indians within the colony under firm control. In 1656, when the so-called "Ricaheerians," a band of unknown migrating Indians from the interior tried to settle near the falls of the James River, the Assembly declared that they "be in noe sort suffered to seat themselves there, or anyplace near us it having cost so much blood to expell and extirpate those perfidious and treacherous Indians which were there formerly." The colony sent 100 volunteers, augmented by an equal number of Pamunkey warriors, to expel the newcomers. When five Ricaheerian chiefs tried to parley, the commander of the English forces, Colonel Edward Hill, in violation of his orders to try to negotiate their peaceful removal, promptly murdered them. In the battle that ensued, the English fled from the field, leaving the Pamunkey to bear the brunt of Ricaheerian rage. It was during that battle, known as "Bloody Run," that Topotomoy, as we have noted, lost his life. Hill subsequently lost his militia command, condemned by the Virginia Assembly for "crimes and weaknesses." The Ricaheerians, undefeated, withdrew, with their subsequent whereabouts unknown.[14]

With the local tribes under firm control, the colony softened its Indian policy. The Assembly in 1655 declared Indian trespass in English territory no longer punishable by death, and although such intrusion was still regarded as a criminal offense, the offender was not to be maimed. Another resolution declared that "no Indians in our protection be killed," unless convicted of a felony on the testimony of two sworn witnesses. Prior to his temporary removal as governor in 1652 by England's commonwealth government, Berkeley had banned the enslavement of Indians. It is not clear just what effect that prohibition actually had. The surviving county records indicate that some Indians were held as slaves for their lifetime, and were sometimes transferred from owner to owner, both before and after the presumed outlawing of Indian slavery. One authority, after a thorough investigation of the records of the Eastern Shore, concluded that there were "scores of Indian slaves in Virginia," some of whom "were bought and sold in the late 1640s." Although enslavement of Indians may have been technically illegal, long-term indentured service was not. Eastern Shore records disclose arbitrary extensions of terms of indenture ("unduly perpetuated," according to one court finding), and it is reasonable to assume that such abuses occurred throughout the colony. In any case, in actual practice, as Rountree notes, "in the decades after 1646, the English did not draw a clear line between 'servants' (i.e., domestic employees) and slaves, either for Indians or Africans." Their treatment depended upon the whims of their masters. The number of Indian slaves and Indian indentured servants remained low. Even fewer were assimilated into the Anglo-Virginia workforce at the end of their indenture. Native Americans were economically marginalized in English Virginia.[15]

Once again, there was some talk in the colony of converting Indians. To that end, special provisions were made for Indian children, and their indentured servitude declared a means of their salvation. The Assembly twice—in 1649 and again in 1658—passed legislation guaranteeing that those brought in to the colony would not be enslaved. They were to be employed as servants, but could not be held in indenture beyond age 25. Their hosts were obligated to provide them with a Christian education. The Assembly, in 1656, reaffirmed earlier resolutions that encouraged Indian parents to send their children to live with the English, promising that they would not be mistreated nor enslaved, but would receive kindly instruction "in Christianity, civility, and knowledge of necessary trades." The parents were allowed to pick the family in which their child would be placed. The children were not to be sold or transferred to other families. That program was not particularly successful. Unlike New England, Virginia gained no reputation for the saving of Indian souls. The colonial records contain no references to prominent Indian converts. When Governor Thomas Culpepper mentioned Pamunkey professions of interest in Christianity in a report to London in 1683, he added that he did not believe they were sincere, given their treacherous character. When asked by the Board of Trade in 1696 for his assessment of the methods used in Virginia to convert Indians, New York's Governor Andros relied "none ever heard of."[16]

Berkeley, who had remained in Virginia and prospered as a planter and investor, resumed the governorship by election of the Assembly and subsequent appointment by King Charles II in 1660. Prior to his departure on a mission to England, he assigned to his deputy Francis Moryson the task of guiding through the Assembly a codification of Virginia's laws. The legislation subsequently adopted in 1662 contains a comprehensive statement of the governor's ideas about Indian policy. That policy was driven by his hope of minimizing conflicts with peaceful Indians within the colony. The statutes provided to all such Indians legal protection of both their property rights and personal security, declaring that "whoever shall defraud or take from them their goods and doe hurt and injury to their persons shall make such satisfaction and suffer such punishment as the laws of England or this country doe inflict, if the same had bine done to an Englishman." In a remarkably candid declaration, the Assembly noted that troubles with the Indians "proceed chiefly from the violent intrusions of divers English made into their lands." It therefore ordered that English settlers who had settled on Indian land without a title granted by the colony must vacate. The governor was given the power to investigate complaints of illegal occupation and forcibly expel squatters. The Assembly deplored the intimidation of Indians by land-greedy whites, and their defrauding by "corrupt interpreters" who exploited their lack of understanding of English. All too often, it found, Indians seeking confirmation of their land rights were later told that by making a mark on a piece of paper, they had given that land to an Englishman. The Assembly was distressed by the perennial failure to enforce prior laws against private purchases of Indian land and declared such purchases "hereafter made or pretended to be made being hereby declared invalid, voyd, and null, any acknowledgement, surrender, law or custom to the contrary notwithstanding." Moreover, colonists settling within three miles of an Indian village were placed under obligation to assist the Indians by fencing their corn field. Recognizing that Indians often had been placed in straitened circumstances by the "seating of the English" upon their former lands, the Assembly now guaranteed them the right to enter English territory to fish and gather wild plant food as long as they remained unarmed. The 1662 Assembly resolutions are remarkable in their candid admission that Indians had been victimized, and by their recognition that prior protective legislation had not been effective. The new legislation, however, would also prove to be ineffective.[17]

Governor Berkeley's interest in good relations with Indians was not entirely motivated by concern for the common good. Early in his governorship, he had entered into lucrative relationships with the colony's most prominent Indian traders. His biographer explains that those arrangements

with experienced traders enabled Berkeley to partake of a profitable trade for the venture of a nominal contribution from his purse. They, not he, purchased trade stuff; they, not he, packed merchandise into the forests; they, not he, dealt with the Indians for deer hides and other furs that constituted the native side of the exchange; they, not he, marketed the skins through their mercantile outlets to Europe; in short, they, not he, assumed all the great risks of a highly chancy business; and they paid Berkeley licensing fees in the bargain. For him a failed expedition merely meant no more than loss of investment capital. Failure could cost his partners not only their money but possibly their lives as well.

Berkeley's alliance with Indian traders was not only profitable; it brought political benefits as well, by allying him with some of the most powerful people in the colony. Among them, William Claiborne and Samuel Mathews—who "ran a trading network that stretched from the James River to Chesapeake Bay and London and back, which surpassed anyone else's for value of its traffic"—were most notable.[18]

During Berkeley's second administration, relations with the surviving core of the old Powhatan Confederation on the James and York rivers remained peaceful. The Pamunkey and Chickahominy had been broken as independent forces. The governor and Assembly on occasion intervened to protect them from the aggression of would-be English claimants of the lands the colony had granted to Powhatan survivors. However, given the reliance on local county courts in land matters, there were some crucial areas of conflict when the authorities at Jamestown had only very limited control of Indian affairs. One was the Eastern Shore; the other, the Northern Neck and adjacent frontier regions. It is to these trouble spots that we now turn.[19]

The Eastern Shore is a narrow peninsula, some six to eight miles wide and 75 miles long, bounded by the Chesapeake Bay on the West, the Atlantic Ocean on the East, and, after 1632, the colony of Maryland to the North. Two Algonquian-speaking Indian tribal groups—the Accomac in the Southern tip and the Occahannock in the North—inhabited the region, with a population estimated in 1621 at around 2,000. They had been very loosely aligned with the Powhatan Confederacy, but did not support Opechancanough in his wars against the English. The Accomac leader, known to the English as the "Laughing King," had warned Governor Yeardley of the impeding attack in 1622. Opechancanough, as you will recall, had allegedly tried to buy poison from the Accomacs to use against the English notables attending Powhatan's final funeral ceremony, but had been repulsed. During the second Anglo-Powhatan war, the proclamations of the colonial government identified the Accomacs as allies, exempt from the various anti-Indian measures adopted by the Burgess and Council. They were valued trading partners, producing a surplus of corn they willingly sold to the colonists.[20]

Because very few English settlers moved to the Eastern Shore during the 1620s—interpreter Thomas Savage being the most notable exception—the violent conflicts over land that characterized Indian-white relations along the James and York rivers were absent. Nonetheless, the contact of peoples on the Eastern Shore decimated the Indian population, which, it is estimated, by 1700, stood at mere 10 percent of its level a century earlier. Although they were never subjected to killing and starvation on the scale visited upon the core tribes of the old Powhatan Confederacy, the Eastern Shore natives, as Indians elsewhere, were sorely afflicted by diseases of European origin for which they had no immunity. It is believed that they were struck by a smallpox epidemic as a result of unrecorded contacts with European visitors some years prior to the founding of Jamestown. Continued contacts brought recurrent illnesses.[21]

An influx of English settlers during the 1630s brought loss of territory as well. Initially, the greatly diminished Indian communities were not adverse to yielding surplus land. However, disputes soon arose over their frequent exclusion from their former hunting and fishing territories, and over the destruction of their crops by English livestock. A petition from an Indian town to the county court in 1652 complained that white settlers had not only driven them from their traditional hunting territories, but were taking so much land even in "the very towne of Oanancocke" that they threatened to "utterly destroy the inheritance of themselves and of their posteritye." The petitioners asked that their consent be required before any further English settlement be permitted. However, as Governor Berkeley noted in a communication with local justices (discussed later) land-greedy settlers would frequently construe a limited sale as a patent for vast tracts of land. Four years later, the Accomac's "emperor" Wachiowamp petitioned the Northampton County Court for a land grant to protect his people from further dispossession. The court promised to provide such a grant, but never made good on that promise. In 1660, the Accomacs appealed to the Virginia Assembly. The Assembly resolved that they should receive a land grant, but did not honor their request for hunting and fishing rights on that land. Moreover, the authorized grant was never actually made. The Indians remained confined to a few shrinking plots of land. The only protected reservation area actually given to Eastern Shore Indians was a 1,500-acre plot granted by the Virginia General Assembly in 1641 to establish the village of Gingaskin in compensation for the removal of some Accomacs first from lands claimed by the wealthy planter William Stone, then from a tract owned in absentia by the son of the late Governor Yeardley. When Gingaskin was surveyed, it had somehow been whittled down to a mere 650 acres. Throughout the Eastern Shore, prominent planters patented vast tracts and often forced the relocation of the Indians within those tracts long before English occupation of the lands in question. Even the reservation set aside at Gingaskin was not immune, as court records indicate persistent attempts by English claimants to take portions of that land.[22]

Governor Berkeley was concerned about the mistreatment of the Indians of the Eastern Shore. In 1650, he wrote to the Northampton County Court to remind the justices that the friendship of the "Laughing Kinge Indyans" had been of great value to the English "in the last bloody Massacre." That friendship was now in jeopardy, the governor warned, because of "Acts of Rapine and violence" committed against Indians by those who were driving them from their homes by producing fraudulent land sale documents. Berkeley asked "in the Name of the Peace & Safety of the country that you Suffer noe land to be taken from them, But what shall bee allowed both in Justice and Convenience by the full court." The governor's admonitions were of little effect, and the victims of English land greed remained deeply aggrieved. That summer, the planters of Northampton County were alarmed by rumors of an Indian plot to poison English wells and then massacre the settlers. The plot was said to have been organized by the Nanti-cokes in neighboring Maryland, and allegedly had the support of several Accomac villages.[23]

In April 1651, in response to those rumors, Edmund Scarburgh, a wealthy planter and Indian trader, launched a preemptive strike against the Pocomoke, killing several and enslaving others. Scarburgh's rash action, which appears to have been motivated in part by a determination to eliminate trade rivals, alarmed his neighbors. The Northampton County Court, finding that Scarburgh had acted "in a hostile manner contrary to the known laws of Virginia," declared that he had "caused the Indians to gather themselves together in great multitudes to invade the country to the great danger of the peoples' Lives and estates." The court arrested Scarburgh and several of his followers, and sent them to Jamestown for trial. However, on that occasion, the accused managed to persuade the governor and Council that the Indian conspiracy was real, warranting their severe response. Scarburgh, for many years thereafter, used suspicion and fear of Indians to justify their exploitation and abuse. Throughout his long career as a trader, land baron, and Indian fighter, he terrorized, enslaved, and killed Accomacs. His fellow plant-ers often deplored his provocative actions and worried about Indian reprisals, but they were unable to control him. His blatant seizures of more Accomac lands to relieve his precarious financial situation led to rumors in 1670 of an Indian uprising. Finally, Governor Berkeley, who had clashed with him over several other matters throughout the years, responded to appeals from the aggrieved and threatening Accomacs by removing Scarburgh from his county court office and ordering his arrest. The governor declared of Scarburgh, "he hath contrary to my order & the peace long since established between us and the Indians unjustly & most tiranously oppresed them by murthering, whipping, & burning them, by taking their children by force from them who are their parents & many other waies to the apparent hazard of the said peace." Scarburgh died shortly thereafter. The governor's failure throughout the years to protect the Indian victims of his rapacity and brutality exposes the weakness of his Indian policy.[24]

The Eastern Shore's pattern of disregard for Indian land rights was also found in the North of the colony along the Rappahannock and Potomac rivers, where county courts entrusted with land patents and Indian relations proved unable, and often unwilling, to protect Indians from aggressive settlers. The Virginia Assembly in July 1653 had set aside a tract of land for the Rappahannocks. The Lancaster County Court confirmed that grant by treaty two months later, and promised to construct an English-style house for the Rappahannock *werowance*. However, that treaty was not honored by land-hungry settlers. Rappahannocks, angered by incursions on their remaining lands and by the devastation of their crops by unfenced English farm animals, resisted, offering, according to the set-tlers, "divers injuries and insolencys." The Virginia Assembly sent local militia units to the main Rappahannock village with instructions to settle the matter by peaceful negotiation. It is not clear that the militiamen made any serious effort to do so, but they did kill Taweeren, the principle Rappahannock *werowance,* and several lesser notables. In 1656, the local county court agreed to peace treaties that presumably guaranteed the land rights of the Rappahannocks and neighboring Mattaponis. The Virginia Assembly, two years later, directed once again that the usual land allocation of 50 acres be granted each bowman. It was to little avail. Northern Neck settlers were not inclined to respect directives from Jamestown. Land-hungry newcomers, in addition to chipping away at Rappahannock land, drove the Mattaponis from their seat on Piscataway Creek, burning the *werowance's* residence and terrorizing his people. Governor Berkeley rebuked the local militia commander and ordered restitution paid to the Mattaponis, but was unable to prevent their dispossession.[25]

In Westmoreland County, on the Potomac River, local officials in the furtherance of their land schemes deposed and imprisoned the Potomac *werowance* Wahanganoche on a trumped-up charge of high treason. The Virginia Assembly, in its March 1662 session, declared their action illegal. The four offenders—Giles Brent, Gerard Fowke, John Lord, and John Mason—were fined, ordered to pay damages to the chief, and forever barred from "bearing any office civil or military in this countrey." It is not known whether they ever paid the fines or damages, but county records do indicate that the malefactors continued to hold office, the Assembly's disqualification notwithstanding. They retained their power and prominence in Westmoreland County. Another example of antagonism between the government at Jamestown and frontier settlers is found in the trial of nine Rappahannock "kings" arrested by the local militia and charged with complicity in attacks on Englishmen. The governor and Assembly in 1664 concluded that the charges were unfounded and released the chiefs. The Rappahannock county officials, who wanted them hanged, were outraged.[26]

Overall, Berkeley's interventions on behalf of Indians were limited in scope and driven primarily by the need to avoid the expense and disruption of war. Except in the most extreme and provocative cases, the governor deferred to the local interests that controlled the county courts, and, when he declined to do so, his actions usually came too late to offer Indians much real relief. We must bear in mind that, although he favored a moderate and nonprovocative Indian policy, Berkeley had little personal regard for "savages." In common with other Virginians, he harbored a deep distrust of all tribes that had not submitted to English authority by signing treaties that relegated them to tributary status, and, as we shall see, was sometimes suspicious of the intentions the colony's Indian subjects as well. He was deeply alarmed by reports of "strange" Indians moving into the colony. Rumors of such intrusions, combined with reports of skirmishes between settlers and natives in the Northern Neck, led Berkeley, in June 1666, to advise Councilor Robert Smith that it was "necessary to destroy all those Northern Indians" before they could make common cause with the newcomers. An exterminatory war against them mounted by local militia, the governor advised, should be financed by sparing women and children and selling them into slavery. The Council ratified Berkeley's instructions to Smith, calling in a resolution adopted in July for the elimination of "the whole nation of the Doegs and Potomacks." It is not clear what action, if any, Smith and the militia in Rappahannock County undertook in response to that directive. Colonial records are mute. The threat from the "Northern Indians" Berkeley targeted for elimination had clearly been exaggerated. The colony's secretary Thomas Ludwell, who owned land in the Northern Neck, wrote to the Earl of Adlington that following February to report that Virginia was "very peaceable and undisturbed by any enemy except some few Indians from whom we cannot fear any great misfortune." The governor would not launch an actual war against frontier Indians for another nine years, but his letter to Smith makes it clear that Berkeley had no principled aversion to large-scale Indian killing if it could be carried out without undue risk or expense.[27]

CHAPTER 8

Bacon's Rebellion and Its Aftermath

In 1676, the royal governor of Virginia was deposed by a self-styled "General of the Volunteers" who demanded the destruction of all the Indian communities in Virginia. Although Bacon's rebellion had deep roots in the social tensions, political resentments, and economic deprivations that plagued the colony, the immediate chain of events that culminated in that surprising development began with an altercation the year before over some stolen hogs. Some 30 years after the event, Thomas Mathew, the Northumberland County planter at the center of the initial quarrel, seeking to endow his conflict with Indians with cosmic overtones, recalled that 1675 was marked with three portentous and frightening omens that foretold "Disasters." The first was a "large Comet . . . Streaming like a Horsetail westward" to the horizon. The second was a flight of pigeons covering a quarter of the sky and having "no visible End." The birds were so numerous that they broke down the branches of large trees when they roosted at night. The old Planters were alarmed by their appearance, because the previous time such flights were seen, the Indians "Committed the last Massacre." Finally, there was an infestation of flies "about an Inch long, and as big as the Top of a Man's little finger, rising out of Spigot Holes in the Earth." The swarm ate "the New Sprouted Leaves from the tops of Trees," then departed after a month. The meaning of those "three Prodigies" became clear, Mathew suggested, when "on a Sabbath day morning in the summer Anno 1675, People in their Way to Church" found Robert Hen, the overseer of his plantation at Stafford on the upper Potomac River

> lying th'wart on his Threshold and an Indian without the Door, both Chopton their Heads, Arms and other Parts, as if done with Indian Hatchetts. The Indian was dead, but Hen when ask'd who did that? Answered 'Doegs Doegs,' and soon

Died, then a Boy came out from under a Bed, where he had hid himself, and told them, Indians had come at break of day and done these Murders.

The omens, Mathew maintained, had portended Indian treachery and impending massacre.[1]

Mathew did not tell the full story. The royal commission, which in 1677 issued a report on "the late rebellion in Virginia," concluded that there had been no serious problem with the Indians on the Potomac before some Doegs and Susquehannocks crossed from the Maryland shore and seized some of Mathew's hogs in satisfaction of a debt Mathew, who regularly "cheated and abused" Indians, had refused to pay. In response the English pursued the Indians, freed the hogs, killed several Indians, and wounded others. In retaliation, the Doegs sent a war party that "killed two of Mathewes his servants, and came also a second time and kill'd his son." Mathew's representation of Doeg retaliation as an unprovoked expression of Indian malice was disingenuous.[2]

Mathew related that his neighbors quickly responded to the Doegs' "horrid Action." The Stafford County militia, commanded by Colonel George Mason and Colonel George Bent, pursued the Indian party back into Maryland. Soon after dawn, they found the raiders in a cabin, "which they Silently Surrounded." Brent, who spoke their language, called them to come out and parlay. When "the King came trembling forth and would have fled," Brent grabbed him by his forelock and demanded that he surrender "the Murderer of Robt. Hen." After the Indian "pleaded his Ignorance and Slipt loose," Brent shot him "Dead with his Pistoll." Then, according to Mathew, two or three shots were fired from the Doegs' cabin. The militiamen fired into the cabin; the Indians inside tried to flee and were shot down. Ten were killed, and a young Indian boy "of about 8 Years old," son of the "King," was taken prisoner. Meanwhile, the militia detachment led by Colonel Mason had surrounded another nearby cabin, whose sleeping occupants, awakened by the gunfire, also tried to get away. Mason's men killed 14 of them before an Indian rushed up to the Colonel, screaming that the victims were not Doegs, but members of another tribe allied to the English. Mason then "ran amongst his Men, Crying out, 'For the Lord's sake, Shoot no more, these are our friends the Susquehanoghs.'"[3]

The Susquehannock Indians were indeed allies, not enemies. They had been closely connected to the Virginia Indian trader William Claiborne. In 1642, after Maryland authorities ejected Claiborne from Kent Island, Susquehannocks attacked the newcomers' settlement at St. Mary's, triggering a low-scale war with the colony. However, beleaguered by their trade rivals and enemies, the Iroquois from the North, the Susquehannocks found it in their interest to make peace with Maryland and, in 1652, ceded to the English extensive land on both sides of the Chesapeake Bay. In 1661, Maryland and the Susquehannocks agreed to a treaty that specified that they would "assist one another against the Ennemies of either nacion." Under that treaty, the Marylanders provided 50 men to assist in the fortification of the Susquehannock stronghold. The new fortifications, which included artillery emplacements, proved formidable. Its defenders easily repulsed an Iroquois war party in 1662. The Susquehannocks then carried the war into Iroquois territory, inflicting heavy casualties in the their raids during the next few years. During the early 1670s, however, the tide turned, as Susquehannocks, in engagements that are poorly documented, suffered serious losses. The Maryland government, hitherto supportive of their war against the Iroquois, decided in 1674 to enter into a treaty with the Seneca, who were leading the Iroquois offensive. The Assembly that approved that policy change expressed some concern that it might lead to the outbreak of hostilities with their erstwhile allies. But the Susquehannocks, their numbers thinned by war casualties and disease, were in no position to challenge the colony. Hoping to develop new trade ties in the South and avoid further conflict with the expanding Senecas, they relocated on the banks of the Potomac River, finding sanctuary in an abandoned fort.[4]

The Governor of Maryland, Lord Calvert, and his Council protested the Virginians' murder on their soil of Indians under their protection. The Susquehannock protest was not expressed in words. They struck back. In a proclamation on August 31, 1675, Governor Berkeley and his Council reported that the Susquehannocks had joined with the Doegs in murdering "two more Englishmen," had cut down "severall fields of corn and Tobacco and distroyed severall stocks of cattle in the . . . upper parts of Stafford County." There were soon daily reports of "them appearing Armed in considerable numbers to the apparent indanger of the whole Country." The proclamation declared that militia commanders must "expel the Enimy," but it also called for a "full And thorough inquisition" into "the true causes" of Indian hostility. That investigation was entrusted to John Washington and Isaac Allerton. They were authorized to use the militia to "demand satisfaction" from the Indians for the recent killings and depredations, but the proclamation stressed that any action taken must be "necessary and just." Berkeley and his Council asked that Allerton and Washington provide regular reports of "theire several proceedings" and promised "further Orders" to secure the safety of the colony.[5]

Unfortunately, the instructions given Allerton and Washington were ambiguous. The proclamation did not clearly indicate that they were to negotiate a settlement with the Indians if possible, nor did they ask the commanders to look into the possibility that rash English actions, not the Indians' malice, might have been responsible for the current difficulties. As it turned out, Allerton and Washington conducted no investigation of the circumstances behind the earlier killings, nor of the more recent incidents. Instead, they waged war, mobilizing local militias and calling on Maryland's governor to provide further support. Calvert supplied 250 Maryland troops under the command of Major Thomas Truman. On September 26, 1675, 1,000 armed Englishmen arrived at the Susquehannock stronghold in Maryland. Five chiefs responded to Major Truman's call for a parley, but there was no real parlay. As soon as they denied responsibility for the recent killings, the English commanders seized the Susquehannock leaders and executed them. (The lower house of the Maryland Assembly later censured Truman for his part in this affair, but the upper house refused to support that action.) After the murder of the chiefs, the Virginia and Maryland forces besieged the fort; but, lacking artillery, their seven-week siege failed. One night the Indians, undetected, killed 10 of the guards sleeping outside the walls, abandoned their stronghold, and disappeared. The campaign against them had failed on all counts. The governor had hoped for a settlement of the problem of frontier security. Instead, he got an Indian war. Berkeley was furious, and raged against Washington and Allerton for their treacherous killing of the chiefs. He later declared in an address to the General Assembly: "If they had killed my Grandfather and Grandmother, my father and Mother and all my friends, yet if they had come to treat of Peace, they ought to have gone in Peace." However, the frontier did not share his belief that Englishmen should be bound by principles of honor in dealing with "savages."[6]

In January 1676, Susquehannock raiding parties, after slaying around 60 settlers in Maryland, crossed the Potomac River and struck English settlements on the Rappahannock, killing some 36 people in their first assault on Virginia soil. The Susquehannocks withdrew after that raid, sending peace envoys to Berkeley, who rejected their offer to negotiate. There followed a wave of violent frontier incidents, as Indians of unknown tribal affiliation apparently joined the Susquehannocks in raiding on the upper York and James Rivers, killing settlers, slaughtering livestock, and burning houses and fields. Among the dead on the James was "Mr. Bacon's Overseer, whom He much Loved, and one of his Servants, whose Blood Hee Vowed to Avenge if possible." Initially, the governor appeared to share Nathaniel Bacon's desire to avenge the dead. He rejected a Susquehannock peace feeler and mobilized the militia, placing it under the command of Sir Henry Chicheley, an elderly, former royalist soldier then serving as lieutenant governor. He ordered Sir Henry to pursue the raiders with a force of 300 men, but then, in a serious political blunder, revoked the order and decided to assume a purely defensive posture. He advised frontier settlers to gather together, 10 men to a house, and be prepared to withstand Indian attacks. In effect, they were on their own.[7]

The reasons for Berkeley's abrupt change in strategy have been a matter of some controversy. However, we know from Berkeley's surviving correspondence that he was troubled by reports from New England where, as he wrote Thomas Ludwell, "the Indians . . . have burned divers considerable Villages (which they call townes) and have made them desert more than one hundred an fifty miles of those places they had formerly seated." Berkeley feared an Indian conspiracy that would engulf the entire Atlantic seaboard, declaring the recent problem with the Susquehannocks, the result of "infection" from New England. With regard to the immediate situation in Virginia, he informed Ludwell that "Our Neighbour Indians [by which he meant the Pamunkey and other tributaries] are pretty well secured," but were not to be trusted, "for it is no doubt but that they alsoe would be rid of us if they could." He was, accordingly, taking precautions, confiscating all the shot and gunpowder in the possession of those dependents. However, on the matter of striking those Indians who had recently attacked Englishmen, Berkeley was fearful that if the militia pursued the raiders, they might well blunder into a larger war—one that might end in a disaster comparable with King Philip's war in New England. The behavior of the frontier militia over the previous few months demonstrated to Berkeley the need to keep men such as Brent, Mason, and Allerton under tight control. Other motives have been attributed to Berkeley, by his contemporary antagonists, and by later historians, including concern for not disrupting the very profitable Indian trade monopolies enjoyed by his close associates. Recent experience, however, gave the governor ample reason to be wary of leaving Indian fighting to the county militias. There was real danger of a general Indian war.[8]

The fragile nature of the colony's relationship with the local Indians was illustrated in the Pamunkey response to the demand that they honor their treaty obligations and furnish men to serve as scouts in a campaign against the intruders. Shortly after the first Susquehannock raid, the Pamunkey "queen" Cockacoeske was summoned to appear before a committee of the governor's Council at Jamestown. The Pamunkey leader was a woman of striking appearance and imperious manner. One of the chroniclers of Bacon's rebellion described her as entering "the Chamber with a Comportment Graceful to Admiration" and "a Majestick Air." She wore a crown of white wampum three inches broad and an elaborately decorated deerskin robe. Although reasonably fluent in English, she insisted upon communicating with the Council through an interpreter (said to be her 20-year-old son). When the Council asked her what assistance the Pamunkey would provide in the war against hostile Indians, Cockacoeske, "with vehement passion," reminded the Council that 20 years earlier, her husband and 100 Pamunkey warriors had died fighting for the English and had never received any compensation from the colony. The chairman ignored her complaint, offering, "as our chronicler recalled," "no cold word toward asswaging the Anger [and] Grief her Speech and Demeanor Manifested" or even "taking any notice of all she had said." Instead, he continued to press her to provide men to serve with the English. She finally, very reluctantly, promised to send six. Told that was not adequate, "she sitting a little while Sullen, without uttering a Word between, Said 'Twelve' though she had a hundred and fifty Indian men in her town." She then "rose up and gravely Walked away, as not pleased with her Treatment." Cockacoeske would soon have additional reasons to be angry.[9]

Berkeley called the House of Burgess into session on March 7, 1676, and laid before them the problem of dealing with the Indians. At his urging, the Assembly, sharing his worry that the colony might soon be struck "by a generall combination of all from New England hither," vested control of all military operations in the governor, forbidding any action that did not have his explicit approval. The Burgess resolved that the frontier was to be protected by nine strategically located forts, supported by a mobile force of 500 rangers who would be on the lookout for hostile movements, but could strike only when ordered to do so by Berkeley. New taxes were to be levied in support of fort construction and the ranger force. Settlers were forbidden on pain of death to sell arms to Indians. Only Indian traders licensed by Berkeley were permitted to sell other goods to "such Indians as are amongst us in peace."[10]

As the Assembly deliberated and did the governor's bidding, stories of new kill-ings and of incipient massacre spread through the colony. Mathew recalled that "in these frightfull times . . . no Man Stirrd out of Door unarm'd, Indians were (ever and anon) espied, Three, 4, 5, 6 in a party Lurking throughout the Whole Land." It was widely believed that the Susquehannocks and their local allies had sent envoys to other tribes, some several hundred miles distant, and had offered substantial pay if they would join in a campaign of extermination against the Eng-lish in Virginia. It was also rumored that a great Indian strike force was already assembling at a secret location on the upper James River. The story was without foundation, but the panic it inspired was real. Berkeley's program struck many, perhaps most, Virginians as woefully inadequate to deal with the danger.[11]

However, the events that led to the governor's removal and to a civil war were the product of much more than a disagreement over how to fight an Indian war. Virginia in 1676 was, in the words of historian Stephen Saunders Webb, ruled by a colonial regime that "was incorrigibly corrupt, inhumanely oppressive, and inexcusably inefficient, especially in war." Although those close to the governor lived well and enjoyed ample privileges and amenities, including monopoly of the lucrative Indian trade, and, for those who held office, substantial salaries and exemption from taxation, most staggered under a tax burden that consumed from one-quarter to one-half of incomes much diminished by decreasing tobacco prices. Most lived lives of severe privation as they struggled to meet the exac-tions of an arrogant and insensitive ruling clique. As Webb notes, "without money enough to buy food themselves, the planters could not afford to pay their rul-ers' taxes." Virginia in 1676 was a land of diminishing opportunity, as wealthy speculators close to the governor engrossed more and more land, and the landless class grew in size. When Berkeley described Virginia as a place where "six parts of seaven at least are Poore Endebted Discontented and Armed," he provided the key to understanding the rebellion that ruined his career. The governor himself had lost the political finesse that had made his early administration so successful. To quote Webb again, Berkeley, during the later years of his governorship, was a man of "vile and vindictive temper . . . coarse and abusive language, and arrogant and overbearing manner."[12]

It was not just personal resentment of Berkeley or doubts about his compe-tence as a military commander that led to his undoing. It was widely believed that his plans to fight Indians were not only inadequate, but his forts and his rangers (many believed) offered no real protection to settlers on the frontier, and were intended to impose a new tax on the already overburdened people to pro-vide a boondoggle for his "favorites." The royal commissioners charged with the investigation of the causes of the rebellion against Berkeley later summarized the response to his program as follows:

> The unsatisfied People finding themselves still liable to the Indian Crueltyes, and the cryes of their wives and children growing grievous and intolerable to them, gave out in Speeches that they were resolved to Plant tobacco rather than

pay the Tax for the maintaining of Forts, and that the erecting of them was a great Grievance, Juggle and cheat of no . . . use or service . . . merely a designe of the Grandees to engross all their Tobacco in their owne hands.

The true solution to the Indian menace, Berkeley's critics believed, was to unleash the county militias and hunt down and kill the offending Indians, thereby not only eliminating the danger, but also removing the need for new taxes. Even more damaging to the governor was the rumor that he was personally profiteering from the Indian trade and was willing to sacrifice the lives of his countrymen to avoid disturbing his Indian trading partners. The charge was unfair, but it was widely circulated and was a major source of popular anger against him. In a letter to Thomas Ludwell in July 1676, Berkeley noted sadly that it was said "through the whole country that I was a greater frend to the Indians then to the English."[13]

In April, critics of the governor's strategy circulated "the Humble Appeal of the Volunteers to all well minded and charitable people," arguing that the proposed forts would be "so scantly manned" as to be useless in countering the invasion they thought imminent. The petitioners called for an immediate hard-hitting offensive mounted by the settlers themselves. The governor ignored their appeal. A new petition, signed at Charles City by settlers, some of whom had abandoned their upcountry lands out of fear of massacre, asked permission to name militia officers and then wage offensive war against the enemy. Berkeley, denying their request, told them they would be defended by his army. The petitioners claimed when they presented their appeal to him in person, the governor had denounced them as "fools and loggerheads," and, screaming "a pox take you," expelled them from his presence. Some of the petitioners also later asserted that Berkeley then issued a decree forbidding any future petitions of that sort. Although untrue, the rumor that he threatened to impose a "great pennalty" on anyone who might persist in calling for a new plan to counter the Indian menace did him much damage at the time, and has been accepted by a number of historians.[14]

The settlers gathered at Charles City were so alarmed by reports of "several formidable Bodies of Indians" moving down the James River toward them that they disregarded the governor's orders and assembled a volunteer force to counter it. However, they lacked both official sanction and a commander. As the royal commission's report later related, they soon found their commander. At Henrico, a young planter named Nathaniel Bacon had gathered with some friends to converse about "the Sadness of the times . . . and the fear they all lived in, because of the Susquehannocks who had settled a little above the falls of the James River, and committed many murders upon them, among whom Bacon's overseer happen'd to be one." Bacon's companions suggested that they cross the James River and visit the volunteers who had assembled at Jordon's Point. Bacon agreed, and, "taking a quantity of Rum with them to give the men to drinke," they made the trip. At the close of the conversations that ensued, the volunteers proclaimed Bacon their leader. As the commissioners related, they "cryed out a Bacon! a Bacon! a Bacon!" Bacon's friends urged him to accept command, resolving that "they would allso go along with him, to take Revenge upon the Indians, & drinke damnation to their Soules to be true to him." They would seek a commission from the governor, but if Berkeley did not agree, they would march against the Indians anyway. The governor did not agree, and when Bacon did not back down, declared him a rebel. Bacon then led a popular rebellion that deposed the governor and tried, ineffectively, to wage total war against all Indians.[15]

Although acclaimed by later generations as a man ahead of his time, celebrated in historian Thomas Wertenbaker's often-quoted phrase as "the torch bearer of the American Revolution" fighting for the rights of the common people, Bacon was an improbable revolutionary. He was the son of a wealthy Suffolk land owner. An indifferent student given to "some extravagances," Bacon had failed at Cambridge and spent three years during his late adolescence on a grand tour of Europe under the tutelage of John Ray, one of England's most gifted scholars. After a bout with smallpox, he reentered Cambridge, earned a master's degree, and, in keeping with family tradition, pursued the study of law at Gray's Inn, London. Apart from a few bare facts, we know little about his character or convictions. We know that his father-in-law, Sir Edward Duke, found him so offensive that he disinherited his daughter when she married him against his will. We know also that soon after his marriage, he was implicated in a scheme to cheat another young man of his inheritance and, in consequence, was sent into exile in Virginia by his father. Equipped with some 1,800 pounds (a substantial fortune in the 17th century), Bacon, in 1674, bought two plantations on the upper James River. His family background ensured him preferment. A cousin of the same name was a prominent councilor and militia colonel. He was also related to the governor and to the governor's wife. Berkeley soon made the 27-year-old newcomer a member of his governing Council and favored him with a license to trade with Indians. Bacon was no democrat. The royal commissioners described him as "ambitious and arrogant." Historian Stephen Saunders Webb adds that "his was the arrogance of ancient privilege." However, the sources at our disposal do not give us a very clear picture of this man. No portrait of Bacon has survived. The commission report described Bacon as "indifferent Tall butt Slender, black haired and of an ominous pensive melancholy aspect." With regard to his convictions, the commissioners suggested he was some sort of heretic, reporting that he was given to "a Pestilent and prevalent Logicall discourse given to Atheisme in most Companyes." This is not very revealing, however, and may be based entirely on unreliable hearsay. All in all, we know very little about Nathaniel Bacon. Prior to his assumption of command of the volunteers, he had shown little interest in public affairs, seldom attending meetings of the governor's Council.[16]

Bacon and the men he now commanded were angered, not only by Berkeley's failure to mount an offensive against the Indians said to be massing above the falls of the James, but also of his protective policy toward the tributary tribes living in their midst. The governor, as we have noted, did not trust those Indians and took steps to disarm them; however, he regarded the Pamunkey, Chickahominy, and other subject tribes as useful intermediaries, and claimed he needed to use them as spies to warn of impending danger from without. His critics, however, were well aware of the trade ties that bound many of the governor's associates and, by rumor, the governor himself, to the Indians he sought to protect from militia attack, and they questioned his motives. The petitioners had suggested that some of the tributary Indians had joined with the Susquehannocks, "barbarously murdered" Englishmen, and "depopulated and usurped" English settlements. There is no real evidence that was the case, but Bacon's army acted on the assumption of their guilt and waged war against them. Historian Wilcomb Washburn observes that "Bacon and his men did not kill a single enemy Indian but contented themselves with frightening away, killing, or enslaving most of the friendly neighboring Indians, and taking their beaver and land as spoils." Philip Ludwell, a prominent supporter of the governor, noted bitterly that Bacon's actions alienated almost all the tributary Indians, so now the English faced "at least 1500 enemies more."[17]

Bacon did not wait for Berkeley to grant him a commission to command the volunteers. He took to the field, marching first up the James River beyond the falls, then leading his forces into the wilderness regions in the Southwest. En route, he sent a note to the governor informing him that as "the whole Country" feared a "Generall Combination" of Indians, he acted to defend both himself and "the Countrys safety." Berkeley ordered him to desist, warning that to act without a commission was mutiny. Bacon's reply was defiant. Although professing his personal loyalty to the governor, he refused to obey, declaring that he was "going out to seeke a more agreeable destiny than you are pleased to designe me." Infuriated, Berkeley, on May 3, set out with some 300 militiamen to bring him back. However, as Berkeley's biographer notes, "Bacon beat him to the falls and got away. Saddle sore and marrow tired, Berkeley sickened. He was not just ill and irate: he looked asinine and incompetent. Bacon stood vigorous and bold, and out of reach, which enraged Berkeley all the more."[18]

Returning to Jamestown, the governor then published and gave wide circulation to a proclamation dated May 10, 1676, stripping Bacon of all his offices and declaring him a rebel. He prefaced that proclamation with a declaration that Virginia was in the midst of "daingerous and calamitous times." Not only had "the Susquehannocks & other Indian Nations . . . committed severall bloody murthers & depradations" within the colony, but there were "very probable grounds" to believe that they were in league with the "bloody & implacable heathen people" who had "perpetuated & committed many horrible murthers upon our Country men & brethren in New England." There was, Berkeley declared, evidence of a general Indian conspiracy "utterly to overthrow & ruine all his Majesties Colonys and Plantations in America." The Assembly had wisely determined to build and man new forts at "the heads of the severall rivers" that gave access to English settlements on the Virginia frontier, and thereby guarantee their safety. However, the governor continued, one member of the Council, Nathaniel Bacon, Jr., defying his orders, had joined with "divers rude dissolute and tumultuous persons" who sought to bring about "the ruin & overthrow of the Government," thereby "endangering . . . the whole Country . . . in these times wherein our bloody enimies the Indians (whom I will prosecute with all just severity) threten us with dayly asaaults and murthers." He called on Bacon's volunteers to put down their arms and submit to his authority, promising "pardon and indemnity" to all but Bacon himself and two of his close associates. Berkeley ended by expressing amazement that anyone would chose to disregard his own 34 years of sterling service to the colony and be "seduced & carried away by so young, unexperienced, rash, & inconsiderate person as said Nathaniel Bacon, Jr."[19]

While the governor's agents were distributing his proclamation against Bacon, the general and his forces continued their march against the Indians. They terrorized the Pamunkey, who frustrated their would-be attackers by fleeing into Dragon Swamp. However, Bacon and his men soon found other Indians to kill, and, like the Pamunkey, they were not hostiles. The royal commission reported that when Bacon's forces "fell upon the Indians," they "killed some . . . of our best friends," allies who "had fought against the Susquehannocks." The victims were Occoneechee, members of a small, friendly tribe living on a island in the Roanoke River near the North Carolina border. Hungry and tired, Bacon and his men had taken refuge with them in their fort. Their hosts had recently rebuffed Susquehannock efforts to enlist them in a war against the English, and now told Bacon that there were two Susquehannock–fortified encampments nearby, one five miles away and the other, 10 miles. When Bacon expressed a desire to attack the nearest group, the Occoneechee offered to do the job for him. With the help of some captives they were holding, they did just that, bringing back a number of prisoners, some of whom were immediately put to death. However, Bacon and the Occoneechee soon quarreled over Bacon's demand that he be given all the surviving captives, and all the furs and wampum found in the Susquehannock fort. The Indians protested that those spoils were theirs, as "they had got it with the hazard of their lives and they knew not how any one besides themselves could pretend any title to it." Attacking by stealth after midnight, Bacon's men besieged the fortifications, firing into the enclosure through the logs. Those Indians who lived outside the gate, they slaughtered. Although accounts vary, it appears that the Occoneechees put up an effective resistance, killing 11 of the attackers and wounding others, some mortally. In one source we read that Bacon prevailed only by when he lured the *werowance* Posseclay and several other tribal leaders to a parlay, then "surprised and killed . . . them." Another narrator, however, tells us that Bacon retreated in some disarray. Although he later boasted of his cunning in creeping up on the Occoneechee village when most of its inhabitants were asleep, Bacon provided no explanation of his decision to murder members of a tribe that had just fought against the colony's enemies. Later, one of his soldiers claimed the action was necessary because the Occoneechee had refused to provide Bacon's army with provisions and, being treacherous by nature, no doubt intended to do them harm. Some historians have echoed that claim. It is not credible.[20]

On the same day that he proclaimed Bacon a rebel, the governor had called for the election of a new House of Burgess to convene on June 5. In his proclamation he professed bewilderment over public grumbling against his old Assembly, for its "soo long continuance" (in fact, it had sat since 1660), but avowed his ever-constant intent to "take Redress of all just Grievances." To that end, he promised that he would now work with a newly elected Assembly. Its charge: to find means to provide for "the better security of the country from our Barbarous Enemies the Indians and for the better settling and quieting our domestick disorders and discontents." In an effort to deal with the anger against the privileged, whom he believed Bacon was exploiting, Berkeley gave the right to vote, previously restricted to property holders, to all freemen. He also declared that "all and every person or persons" were to "have liberty" to present their grievances to the newly elected Assembly members. Should the Assembly find him responsible for the colony's problems, "I will most gladly joine with them in a Petition to his Sacred Majesty to appoint a new Governor of Virginia and thereby to ease and discharge mee from the great care and trouble thereof in my old age."[21]

Among the grievances against Berkeley, as we have noted, was the belief that he was indifferent to the Indian menace. This was far from the case. If anything, he was excessively distrustful of the tributary tribes within the colony. On the same day Berkeley issued his proclamation for a new election, he sent a private letter to militia captain Thomas Goodrich, calling for an all-out offensive against all Indians. "I believe," he wrote,

> all the Indians our neighbours are engaged with the Susquehannocks and there-fore I desire you to spare none that has the name of an Indian. . . . God I hope will enable us to resist all of them for the present and destroy them all for the future. . . . I beseech you doe your best to destroy all of what Nations soever they are.

He intended, he advised Goodrich, "to meet with his Council . . . publiquely to declare a Warr against all Indians." He faulted Bacon, not for marching against Indians, but for staging a rebellion that divided the colony and thereby embold-ened "all the Indians" to "shew themselves our Enemies." The governor told the captain that "these poore men that have been killed [in Indian raids] will have their blood laid to Bacon's charge." Had the colony not been distracted, he argued, his plan for fortifications and patrols would have been put in place, and lives preserved.[22]

Upon convening in June, the new Assembly promptly passed a resolution ask-ing Berkeley to remain the colony's governor. In dealing with the Indian war, the governor and the burgesses saw eye to eye on most matters, but not on the role to be played by Nathaniel Bacon. The anti-Indian measures the Assembly man-dated were draconian, but stopped short of total extermination. The governor, who may have learned that some of the rumors that had led him to tell Goo-drich that all Indians were enemies were not in fact true, was in a somewhat less bloodthirsty mood. When the Assembly convened, Berkeley, in what one observer characterized as a "short abrupt speech" with a "pathetic Emphasis" deplored the murder, under pretense of a parlay, of the Susquehanna chiefs the previous year.

The governor was intent on waging a disciplined, controlled war. The declaration he asked for was less extreme than his letter to Goodrich had suggested. The Assembly, at his behest, included a preamble that expressed doubt that "all Indians are combined against us," and spoke of the need to protect the innocent. Neighboring Indians who surrendered all their arms and ammunition, provided hostages, and remained within the bounds of their own villages unless authorized to travel by English authorities were to be protected. Those who did not conform to those conditions were deemed enemies, to be killed on sight or enslaved. Berkeley was content to wage the war on those terms. Nathaniel Bacon was not.[23]

Although outlawed by Berkeley, Bacon was elected to the new House of Burgess as a representative of Henrico County. The voters, and most of the members of the newly elected Assembly, did not share the governor's view of Bacon as a rebel. Berkeley later complained that there were "but eight of the Burgesses that [were] not of his faction and at his direction." The royal commission for its part declared the enfranchisement of the unpropertied had led to the elevation of men "that had but lately crept out of the condition of servants." Although both exaggerated the radicalism of the new burgesses, the governor soon discovered that he was now in no position to disarm Bacon and his followers. The day after the Assembly convened on June 5, Bacon, with 50 followers, entered Jamestown under cover of darkness and conferred with William Drummond and Richard Lawrence, two notables sympathetic to his cause. Berkeley, learning of his presence, ordered his arrest. Bacon was apprehended on his sloop and ordered to appear before the Assembly to answer the governor's charges against him. Although supported by several hundred settlers who crowded into the capital to demand his release, Bacon, on June 9, confessed his errors to the governor and Assembly, and begged pardon on bended knee. Berkeley granted pardon, declaring three times "God forgive you, I forgive you," and with consent of Council and Assembly admitted Bacon to the House of Burgess. He also reappointed him to the governor's Council.[24]

Despite his presumed submission to the governor, Bacon had no intention of accepting the prohibition of attacks on submissive local Indians contained in the Burgess's war declaration. One of Berkeley's supporters later related that the governor had promised Bacon a military commission to raise volunteers "to Goe against the Indians" conditioned on his "Future Good behaviour." The burgesses had resolved that such commissions must "strictly . . . prohibit the falling upon or injureing in any sort any Indians, who are and continue in friendship with us." Bacon would agree to no such restriction, nor did he wish to command only a small body of volunteers. Supported by the mob that had flocked into Jamestown on news of his earlier arrest, he demanded that he be put in charge of the Indian war. On June 23, at the head of an armed force of some 600 men, he stood outside the state house in Jamestown declaiming, "God damne my Bloode, I came for a commission, and a commission I will have before I goe." His initial request to the Assembly had been denied, on grounds that only the governor could grant a commission. Bacon now confronted Berkeley, who refused his demand, and denounced Bacon as a rebel. In one account we read that the elderly governor bared his breast and shouted at the young man, "Here! Shoot me, fare god, fair Mark! Shoot!" But, sensing the weakness of his position, Berkeley then reluctantly agreed to make Bacon the general in command of all volunteers. Bacon refused his offer, demanding total military power, as "General of all forces in Virginia against the Indians." Berkeley exclaimed that he'd rather have both his hands cut off, and walked away accompanied by his Council. Gesticulating and tossing his sword from hand to hand, Bacon, accompanied by "a Detachment of Fulsileers," followed him. Berkeley stopped, turned back to Bacon and suggested they spare the colony any further upheaval and "decide this controversye by our swords." Bacon refused, exclaiming that he had come not to fight a duel with Berkeley but "for redress of the peoples grievances." What grievances? Berkeley demanded. Bacon "replyed two were already delivered, and the rest they would loudly proclaim." Berkeley then turned on his heels and went back into his apartment in the state house.[25]

As Bacon and Berkeley quarreled in the street, the members of the Assembly watched and listened from the windows of the state house. After the governor's withdrawal, Bacon and his men turned their attention to the burgesses. The would-be general shouted that if he were not given his commission immediately, he would pull down the state house and kill the lot of them. His followers, aiming their weapons at the men standing in the windows, cried, "We will have it! We will have it!" A frightened legislator waved a handkerchief from the window crying over and over again, "You shall have it! You shall have it." The Burgess, many of whom were sympathetic to Bacon, capitulated and advised Berkeley to grant the commission. Reluctantly, the governor gave in, later explaining, "I could do the king little service by dying for him." He returned to his estate at Spring Hill, where he signed Bacon's commission, affixed his signature to some others Bacon had demanded, then left it to subordinates to issue the rest. The Indian war was now in Bacon's hands. However, Berkeley never regarded those commissions, signed under duress, as legitimate. He bided his time.[26]

Because the Assembly did nothing to contest his authority prior to dissolving, Bacon's orders and requisitions were generally honored, and he dispatched scouting parties into the backcountry to seek out Indians to kill or enslave. However, before he could mount a major offensive, some of the citizens of Gloucester County, angered by the exactions of Bacon's troops that, they argued, left them vulnerable to Indian attack, challenged his right to command and petitioned Berkeley for relief. The governor, in reply, denounced Bacon's pretentions, declaring him no better than a thief. Berkeley then assumed military command himself, issuing a call for troops to protect the Gloucester settlers and others against Indian attack, but very few answered his summons. Isaac Allerton, his recruiting agent, reported that the people suspected that the governor's real intention was to fight Bacon, who deserved everyone's support, as "he was now advanceing against the common enimy, who had in a most barbarous manner murthered som hundreds of our deare Bretheren and Countrey Men." Bacon, learning of Berkeley's efforts to raise an army, turned his own around and marched to Middle Plantation (later named Williamsburg), arriving on July 29. The governor, finding himself without the means to oppose Bacon, abandoned Jamestown and, accompanied by a handful of his associates, withdrew to the Eastern Shore, where he took up residence at Arlington.[27]

Bacon, at Middle Plantation on July 30, issued "A Declaration of the People" wherein he proclaimed himself "General, by the consent of the people," and declared Berkeley and those who supported him "Traytors to ye King & Countrey." His indictment of the governor he now deposed reiterated complaints of favoritism and corruption. It stressed, in particular, his profiteering from the beaver trade monopoly and his "having in that unjust game betrayed and sold his Majesty's Country and the lives of loyall subjects, to the barbarous heathen." The proclamation ordered Berkeley and any person who supported him to surrender and submit to Bacon within four days or be deemed guilty of treason. Property owners who did not support the people's general would face confiscation of their estates.[28]

Bacon's call for Indian extermination was promulgated in another document issued around the same time. In the "Manifesto," Bacon charged that none of the Indians the governor and his associates sheltered deserved "the Benefit and Protection of the law" as all of them "have bin for these Many years enemies to the King and Country, Robbers and Thieves and Invaders of his Majesty's Right and our Interest and Estate." There were, this manifesto implied, no good Indians. Accordingly, Virginians must no longer be forbidden to attack the Pamunkey and other Indians presumably allied with the English. Bacon noted that he had been charged with intending "to ruin and extirpate all Indians." He did not deny that charge, but retorted that the governor had "unjustly" favored the colony's enemies.[29]

Determined to apprehend Berkeley, on August 1, Bacon dispatched a small flotilla to Accomac under the command of Giles Bland. That expedition, as we shall see, failed. As Bland made his way into Chesapeake Bay, Bacon led the main body of his troops against the Indians. If their objective was the punishment of the Susquehannock and their confederates, that mission also failed. Finding no hostiles, Bacon attacked the Pamunkeys in Dragon Swamp. The royal commission later noted that "it was well knowne to the whole country" that the Pamunkeys "had nere at any time betray'd or injury'd the English," but to Bacon "it matter'd not whether they bee friends or Foes so they bee Indians." Bacon robbed his victims of "3 horse loads" of goods, described by the commissioners as "Indian matts, Basketts, matchcotes, parcells of wampampaeg and Roanoke (which is their money) in Baggs, skins, Furrs, Pieces of Lynnen, Broad cloth, and divers sorts of English goods (w'ch the Queene had much value for)." A number of Pamunkey were killed outright, and 45 others enslaved. The commissioners reported that Cockacoeske "to save her Life betooke herself to flight with onely one little Indian Boy of about 10 yeares old along with her," but she then decided to return "with designe to throw herself upon the mercy of the English." However, on the trail back to her makeshift village in Dragon Swamp, Cockacoeske saw a deade Indian woman lyng in the way being one of her own nation; which struck such terror in the Queene that fearing their cruelty by that ghastly example shee went on her first intended way into wild woodes where she was lost and missing from her owne People fourteen dayes, all that time being Sustained alive onely by gnawing sometime upon the legg of a terrapin, which the little boy found in the woods when she was ready to die for want of Foode.

Only after Bacon's forces withdrew did Cockacoeske and a handful of other survivors emerge from their hiding places.[30]

The Assembly elected in June in response to the governor's summons had passed a series of laws that came to be referred to as "Bacon's Laws." The term is a misnomer. Nathaniel Bacon played little if any role in their enactment, and one of them, which barred any person not resident in Virginia for three years or more from serving in public office, if enforced, would have forced him back into private life. The laws did, however, strike at the worst abuses of the colony's oligarchy, prohibiting multiple office holding, restricting the fees charged for various public services, stripping the members of Berkeley's Council of their tax exemptions, strengthening county governments, and extending the franchise. Overall, the laws reflected both the anger of property owners outside the governor's circle and their concern over the deep disaffection of the unpropertied. The Assembly felt sufficient anxiety about the latter that it also passed a resolution calling for rigorous enforcement of England's laws against "unlawfull tumults, routs and riots." Bacon, although personally a member of the elite, had appealed to the alienated in his campaign against Berkeley. "The poverty of the Country is such," he declared in his appeal for troops, "that all the power and sway is got into the hands of the rich, who by extortious advantages, having the common people in their debt, have always curbed and oppressed them in all manner of ways." Many of Virginia's most humble residents—indentured servants, landless laborers, blacks as well as whites—rallied to his standard, and continued to fight Berkeley even after Bacon's death.[31]

Bland's naval expedition against Berkeley miscarried badly. Crossing Chesapeake Bay commanding four ships and around 300 men, he demanded a meeting with the deposed governor, who in response parlayed with Bland's second in command, Captain William Carver, at Arlington on September 1. Carver was accompanied by a guard of around 100 troops. Unbeknown to Bland and Carver, the governor had received an offer of help from Thomas Larrimore, an English captain whose ship, the merchantman *Rebecca*, had been commandeered, along with the ship *Honor & Duty*, by Bland in the James River. Larrimore had pretended support for Bacon's cause, but now promised Berkeley that if the governor would prolong the conference with Carver, he would strike the rebels. During the early hours of September 2, some 26 Berkeley loyalists led by Larrimore and Berkeley's long-time associate Philip Ludwell, boarded Bland's flagship and took both Carver and Bland prisoner. The 100 or so men who had accompanied Carver to the parlay, now cut off and surrounded, surrendered. Some swore a new oath of allegiance to the royal government; the others were imprisoned. Berkeley's forces soon captured the remainder of the Baconite naval squadron. Berkeley ordered Captain Carver hanged three days later. Bland was held in chains in the *Rebecca* for some five and a half months, then tried and executed. His defeat was the turning point in Virginia's civil war. Berkeley was now ready to mount a counter-offensive.[32]

Soon after the capture of Bland and Carver, several hundred Eastern Shore fighters enlisted or were conscripted to serve under Berkeley's banner. The governor promised them, in addition to 12 pence a day, 25 years' exemption from taxation and, in the blunt word of the royal commissioners, "plunder" from the seizure of the estates of Bacon supporters. There were also rumors that indentured servants bound to Bacon's landed supporters would receive their freedom if they joined the governor's forces. With his newly recruited army, and his augmented naval forces, Berkeley set out on September 7 to recapture Jamestown. With Bacon and his army busy terrorizing the Pamunkey in Dragon Swamp, Jamestown was lightly defended. Bacon's men, badly outnumbered, withdrew soon after Berkeley's landing. On September 7, his troops entered the city unopposed, and spent the next week looting the houses of Bacon's supporters and drinking up whatever alcohol could be found. By September 14, however, Bacon returned from the interior, resolved to retake Jamestown. During the ensuing siege, Berkeley's naval forces retained control of the James River and raided the plantations of landowners loyal to Bacon. At Jamestown, the governor ordered three public executions. On September 15, Captain William Cookson, taken prisoner on one of the raids, was hanged for treason. Another man Berkeley executed as a spy for communicating with Bacon, and a third, named Digby, was put to death for assuming the title of captain under Bacon when he was, in fact, only a servant. Historian Stephen Webb comments: "Soldier, citizen, climber, the three men executed on September 15, 1676 personified the revolutionary aspirations which excited the loyalists' social fears."[33]

A day later, Berkeley's mercenary army tried to break Bacon's siege. That effort failed miserably, one narrator writing that some 700 or 800 of them "(like scolers goeing to school) went out with hevie harts but returned home with light heeles." It was reported that Berkeley's commanders forced conscripts and servants into the front ranks, but when those reluctant warriors suffered casualties, the officers in the rear fled the field. Bacon's conduct was no less ungallant, as he used the captured wives of loyalists and Indian captives taken in the Pamunkey raid as shields for his men. The display of Indians was intended to reinforce Bacon's image as a defender of the colony from savages and Berkeley's as an Indian lover. From his lines outside Jamestown, Bacon mounted an artillery bombardment of the city and of the river. Plagued by desertions of that newly recruited army that the royal commission later characterized as comprised of the cowardly and base, the governor abandoned Jamestown on September 19. Bacon reoccupied the city and, on September 20, burned it to the ground. Berkeley reestablished his base of command on the Eastern Shore.[34]

The course of the civil war after Jamestown was put to the torch was chaotic. An armed force numbering some 1,000 men under the command of Giles Brent, formerly a rebel but now committed to the governor, threatened Bacon from the North. However, on receiving news of Bacon's reoccupation and burning of the capital, Brent's men ousted their commander and swore loyalty to Bacon. Throughout the colony, Bacon's men, out of control, plundered the estates of those who would not swear loyalty to the general, and robbed some who did. One Berkeley loyalist, Colonel Edward Hill, later testified that his house with all his business records was burned by the rebels and that he also lost all his "sheep . . . wheat, barley, oats, and Indian graine . . . brandy, Butts of wyn, and syder by pales full." Finally, "to finish theire barabarism [they] take my wife bigg with child prisoner. Beat her with my Cane, tare her childbed out of her hands, and with her ledd away my Children, where they must live on corne and water and lye on the ground, had it not been for the charity of good people." Bacon's efforts to curb such excesses proved of little effect. His movement had tapped into social antagonisms and class hatreds that reached far beyond the issues of Indian policy and personal leadership that had inspired his initial challenge to the governor.[35]

The weather in Virginia during late summer and early fall 1676 was unseasonably cold and rainy. Some blamed the storms on malevolent Indian shamans. In late October, General Bacon sickened and died. His death was attributed to "the bloody flux" and was said to have been marked also by "Lousey Disease," an infestation of lice. Berkeley, ever vindictive, later quoted with satisfaction an unnamed minister who had expressed regret "that Lice and flux should take the hangman's part." On hearing of Bacon's passing, the governor took the offensive, making particularly effective use of his advantage in naval power to attack the Baconites from the lower James River. With Joseph Ingram taking command of the rebel forces, the fighting continued for several months. As Berkeley gained the advantage, he put to death those principle rebel commanders who fell into his hands. No less greedy than vindictive, the governor and his clique also sought to confiscate the properties of those who had sworn loyalty to Bacon, even though it was well known that many had sworn that oath under severe duress.[36]

Berkeley's excesses did not win favor in London. On receiving word of the insurrection in Virginia, England's king dispatched a military expedition of 1,000 men to apprehend Bacon, and a commission of investigators to determine how and why he had gained power. Named as commissioners were Sir John Berry, Francis Moryson, and Colonel Herbert Jeffreys. Because Berkeley had earlier requested that he be relieved, his majesty designated Jeffreys his successor, declaring somewhat uncharitably that "age and infirmities" had rendered him "totally unsuitable" for the heavy task of governing Virginia. By the time the commissioners arrived, Bacon was dead and Berkeley was back in control. In a phrase often misattributed to the king, the commissioners complained that the governor, in punishing the rebels, had already hung or planned to hang "more than ever Suffre'd Death for the Horrid Murder of that late Glorious Martyr of Blessed Memory," the father of the reigning monarch. Defying the wishes of the commissioners who sought to restore popular morale, Berkeley declined at first to publish a proclamation from Charles II granting pardon to most of the participants in the rebellion, and finally complied only under duress. The commissioners were appalled that the governor and his friends, without due process of law, were trying to seize the property of those they accused of treason. Regarding the cause of the uprising, the commissioners, after considering numerous letters of complaint and interviewing some colonists, concluded that Berkeley and his clique had levied "extreme and grievous taxes" for their own selfish benefit and had, in effect, provoked rebellion. The royal government upheld most the reforms passed by the burgesses, excepting most notably the enfranchisement of the unpropertied. The commissioners warned that, without reform, "the sullen and obstinate" people of Virginia might desert the colony or, even worse, "cast off the Yoke" of British rule "and Subjugate themselves to a Foreigne Power." Berkeley, after quarrelling with Jeffreys, journeyed to England to plead his case, but died, in disgrace, soon after landing in May 1677.[37]

The instructions to the royal commission stressed the importance of restoring peace with Virginia's Indians. The commission's findings were highly critical of both Bacon and Berkeley, the former for unjust attacks on peaceful Indians, the latter for the mismanagement that provoked Bacon's rebellion. London saw no advantage and much risk in Bacon's indiscriminant program of Indian killing and enslavement. Accordingly, in May 1677, Governor Jeffreys negotiated the Treaty of Middle Plantation with the Pamunkeys, Nottoways, Waonokes, and Nansemonds. The preamble of the treaty conceded that the colony's Indian tributaries had been deprived of "land sufficient to plant upon" and had been victimized in other ways "by Violent Intrusions of divers English." Henceforth, their land holdings were to be guaranteed "in as free and firm a manner as theirs His Majesties Subjects." To prevent future conflict, the governor agreed that no Englishmen henceforth would be permitted to plant within three miles of an Indian town. Those who did so would be removed by force. Tributary Indians under this agreement were to enjoy full protection of the law. Should crimes be committed against "their persons, goods and propertyes," the offenses were to be treated "as if such hurt or injury had been done to any Englishman." The treaty outlawed Indian slavery. For Indians who bound themselves by indenture to Englishmen, the term of service was not to "serve for any longer time then English of the same ages." The tributary Indians were to serve as military allies of the English, were obligated to report on "any March of strange Indians near the English Quarters or Plantations," and were to assist in their removal if so requested. There was little that was new in this treaty. Its key provisions had been part of Berkeley's failed policy. The royal government, as historian Stephen Saunders Webb has emphasized, was now determined to govern Virginia with a firmer hand. However, in the area of Indian relations, little changed, despite the treaty's guarantees.[38]

Under the new regime, the tributary tribes for a time enjoyed a protected, if marginalized, existence. The treaty recognized both the tribal *werowances'* right "to Governe their owne people" and the special status of "the Queene of Pamunkey" as heiress of the remnants of the old Powhatan Confederation. In both numbers and land, the surviving Powhatans were only a shadow of their former selves, numbering by the century's end only around 600. Although the Treaty of Middle Plantation declared that tributary Indians were entitled to the rights of English subjects, the Indians who lived and worked within the English settlements were increasingly subjected to exploitation. The treaty's probation against Indian slavery was formally repealed in 1682, in a statute that "declared all servants who were not Christians at the time of purchase, as well as all servants sold by 'neighboring Indians or any other people'" were slaves for life. Although illegal, and consequently poorly documented, an extensive trade in Indian slaves had flourished in the colony from mid century onward, with the frontier forts serving as launching posts for raids into the interior conducted by English traders aided by Indians, most notably Pamunkey and Appamatuck. The celebrated fortune of the William Byrd family was built, in part, on the profits of the Indian slave trade. One recent study suggests that although no statistical estimate is possible, by the century's end, "on any given Virginia plantation African slaves were likely to be found working side by side with indigenous peoples" who were also held in bondage. By the century's end, Indians and blacks, free or enslaved, were increasingly lumped together in law and custom. In 1691, both intermarriage and sexual relations between whites and Indians, Christian or not, were formally outlawed. The legal definition of Indians as members of an inferior race followed early in the next century, as they were included in the Black Code of 1705, and under its provisions forbidden to hold office, testify in court cases, sue whites, or strike a white person, even in self-defense. Those legal restrictions and penalties prevented the tributary Indians (presumably guaranteed land rights and liberty under the Treaty of Middle Plantation) from "legally resisting white persons who tried to keep them in servitude or squat on their land." The promises of royal protection of Indian rights that followed the defeat of Baconites were empty promises.[39]

Conclusions

Historian Gary Nash, in his comparative study of racial interactions in Britain's North American colonies, suggests that the only reason any Indians in Virginia survived the second Anglo-Powhatan war was that the "English were too weak to carry out their genocidal urges on native peoples."[1] The evidence we have reviewed in this study lends some support to Nash's conjecture. The hopes for a harmonious biracial colonial order grounded in Native American acceptance of English rule and of the Christian faith harbored by some of England's armchair planners of the empire were not shared by many of Virginia's early white settlers. They brought deep prejudices and anxieties with them as they crossed the Atlantic. To most, the Indian was an object of fear, treacherous by nature and therefore not to trusted. Encounters with Indians during the first decade and a half, although not entirely negative, generally reinforced distrust and generated animosities on both sides. Abuse and dispossession of Indians provoked acts of resistance and retaliation that deepened racial hatreds, leading to Opechancanough's 1622 uprising. In the decade that followed that event, English survivors in Virginia and their English sponsors, with virtually no dissent, called for the elimination of their Indian neighbors. It is well documented that the suspension of the annual campaigns of Indian killing in Virginia during the mid 1620s was an expedient prompted only by a shortage of guns and ammunition, not an abandonment of the long-term determination to create an Indian-free Virginia. The decision, in 1632, to make peace with the Powhatans after a decade of war was justified by Governor Harvey on the expedient ground of the difficulty and expense of hunting down and killing the survivors. It was not a popular decision, and was cited by the governor's opponents as a reason for his removal. During the following decade, when Governor Berkeley ended the third Anglo-Powhatan war with a peace treaty, he offered the same argument. Harvey and Berkeley both shared popular feelings about Indians. Both regarded them as inherently untrustworthy, as potentially dangerous neighbors, but neither considered their total elimination a practicable policy goal.

Although the sparsely populated English colony in Virginia in 1622 did not have the means to carry out a program of extermination, by the 1640s, the survivors of the Powhatan Confederacy within the colony were so few in number and so weakened that their total elimination through killing and enslavement by the now-dominant white majority was not out of the question. Extermination might well have been the response to the second uprising led by Opechancanough. However, Governor Berkeley's Indian policy, as expressed in the treaty of 1646 and in subsequent legislative enactments, although harsh, was also protective of the defeated Indians who accepted tributary status. When the Susquehannock crisis of 1676 led to a popular movement that demanded indiscriminate war against all Indians, the governor fought a civil war rather than grant its leader the power he demanded. The royal commission that investigated Bacon's rebellion was very critical of Berkeley's overall conduct as governor, but it expressed no sympathy for Bacon's program of unrestricted Indian war. London demanded that Virginia make peace with her Indians. Under that mandate, Berkeley's successor negotiated a new treaty with the dependent tribes. Yet the documents of that period disclose little sympathy for Indians. As noted previously, several years before Bacon's uprising, Berkeley himself had recommended that frontier militia leaders wage an exterminatory war against those "Northern Indians" who were not bound to the English in a tributary relationship. His Council called for the total elimination of the Doegs and Potomacs, lest they make common cause with Indians rumored to be migrating into the region. Nothing came of that resolution, as the frontier remained relatively quiet. Later, however, during the Susquehannock crisis, Berkeley at one point suspected that even the tributaries were plotting to drive the English out of Virginia. One of his successors in the governorship described Pamunkey expressions of interest in Christianity as duplicitous, given their inherent treachery. We must ask ourselves, why, given the vehement hatred and fear of Indians so prevalent among settlers, did Virginia's policy toward Indians during the 17th century evolve into one of subordination, dispossession, and relocation on "reserves" rather than outright elimination?

Three conditions must be met before "genocidal urges" are translated into full-scale unrestrained and sustained killing. The first is ideological, requiring that members of the targeted victim group be seen inherently as not only inferior, but also degenerate, amoral, treacherous, vicious, and therefore not worthy of membership in the community. They must, in a word, be dehumanized and demonized. The second necessary condition is the belief that they constitute a sufficient threat to the ongoing security, prosperity, or integrity of the dominant group to justify expenditure of manpower and resources to achieve their elimination. The final condition is the presence of the opportunity to effect their elimination without undue risk to the exterminators. The risk that might deter outright extermination might be danger of effective resistance and retaliation, or it might be loss of vital economic services (trade and/or labor) furnished by the victim group. Those indigenous populations that are economically marginal to the new colonial order are, of course, the most vulnerable.

With regard to the first condition, belief that the target group was unworthy of inclusion in the community, English assessments of Indian character and potential prior to colonization were varied and inconsistent. Sixteenth-century English advocates of empire sometimes fantasized about noble savages eagerly awaiting the blessing of civility and Christianity, but more often saw Indians as sadistic savages. Portrayals of Native Americans as devil worshippers, witches, cannibals, and sodomites are ubiquitous in the travel narratives published by Richard Eden, Richard Hakluyt, and other promoters of the empire. Some of the early colonial planners thought that colonizers in North America would encounter both good Indians, kindly and gentle, and vicious savages, given to cannibalism and human sacrifice. They recommended that alliances be made with the good Indians, who would presumably be deeply grateful for protection not only from cannibals, but also from the cruel Spanish. However, early interactions in Virginia were not reassuring. The records left by the first English colonists reveal their suspicions about the character of the Powhatans. They were quick to assume the worst, misinterpreting rituals, such as the Black Boy ceremony, as evidence of human sacrifice, and perceiving various other Indian actions and gestures as indicative of devil worship or cannibalism. Their suspicions soon coalesced into a view of the character of Virginia's indigenous people as essentially treacherous, and of their culture as not only backward, but diabolical as well. Out of that view came a strategy for dealing with Indians that relied upon threat, coercion, and often disproportionate violence. The colonists took what they wanted, with frequent demands for foodstuffs backed up by the sword, often punished Indian thefts with death or dismemberment, and responded to opposition with mass killing. The retaliations such terrorist measures provoked reinforced the English conviction that controlled use of force, not reason—and certainly not trust—must drive their Indian policy.

It is telling that the Virginia Company during the early years of the colony warned that coexistence with Indians would be possible only after all their devil-worshipping priests had their throats cut. When their immediate elimination proved impossible, the colony's planners then placed great stock in the notion of breaking their power by educating Indian children. Throughout the 17th century, Virginia leaders repeatedly asked the Powhatans to send children to Jamestown for vocational training and religious instruction. Powhatan leaders were uncooperative and refused to give up their young. Their recalcitrance reinforced doubts about Indian capacity for reformation. This was crucial, because the English were persuaded that long-term coexistence would be impossible without a major transformation in Indian character. There could be no lasting peace with devil-worshipping savages.

One of the key assumptions of English imperialism, expressed in Thomas More's *Utopia* a century before Jamestown and later by many others, held that savages who resisted the civilizing program of the colonizers had no right to remain in control of the land and its resources. That premise was fundamental to the Virginia enterprise. One is struck, when perusing the early records of Jamestown, by the unthinking disregard of boundaries. Although few in number, the English took what they wanted, looting villages and fields, often driving Indians off the lands they coveted. Resistance to their demands triggered responses startling in their violence. One thinks, for example, of the "Queen," whose children were thrown overboard and used for target practice before she herself was accorded the mercy of death by the sword rather than by burning alive. One reads, with some incredulity, the accounts of raids that forced people already facing severe deprivation to give up their modest food supplies to provision the English, or lose life and limb. We cannot fully reconstruct the mind-set that enabled the perpetrators of such larcenies and atrocities to regard them as ordinary and justifiable transactions, but we can surmise that the victims were seen as less than worthy of decent treatment. We see evidence of the presence of what Nash correctly terms "genocidal urges" rooted in an ideology that, under the right circumstances, could easily justify extermination of recalcitrant "savages."

Those circumstances required, as we have noted, belief that the continued existence of the target group constituted a mortal threat justifying sacrifices to effect their total elimination. In the judgment of the colony's leaders, that condition was met only intermittently in colonial Virginia. For the most part, English contempt for Indians led them to believe the danger was not that grave. The colonizers generally shared Captain Smith's conviction that, if properly intimidated, Indians could be kept in check. Belief in the old formula of teaching Indians to love the English through inspiring fear, although discredited by events, was never abandoned. Because of English complacency, Opechancanough's warriors were able, on two occasions, to mount surprise attacks that killed hundreds of unprepared colonists. Although the 1622 attack was followed by a decade in which extermination was the stated official goal, the policy adopted thereafter stressed confinement of Indians to limited areas and minimization of contact. The high Indian mortality rate had tipped the demographic equation radically in favor of the English, so by the time Nathaniel Bacon called for the killing or enslavement of all Indians, there was little reason for such a program other than race hatred and greed.

From the vantage point of both Jamestown and London, a war against peaceful tributary Indians made little sense, either in terms of economic development (the surviving Indians had already lost most of their land) or military security. To the contrary, Virginia's leaders believed that there were very serious risks in undertaking a total war against Indians. A close reading of Berkeley's correspondence and proclamations before and during Bacon's rebellion indicates that he was deeply fearful of a pan-Indian uprising spreading from New England southward that would drive the English from North America. Berkeley's protection of Indians within Virginia came from his sense of weakness; he had no principled aversion to

Indian killing. Indeed, a few years earlier he had responded to certain disquieting rumors by suggesting an exterminatory war against Indian intruders on Virginia's frontiers. However, as he dealt with the Susquehannock belligerency, Berkeley was fearful of a general pan-Indian uprising, and with that in mind sought to control all military operations to avoid further provocations. A review of the policies of Virginia's governors, then, offers some confirmation of Nash's conjecture. The governors curbed the settlers' "genocidal urges" not out of humane concern for Indians, but because of their perceptions of the colony's vulnerability. Better to use the local Indians as trading partners, intelligence sources, and, on occasion, military allies than try to eliminate them altogether. Ongoing campaigns of extermination, as they saw it, would not only be prohibitively expensive, but might provoke a broadly based pan-Indian alliance that would place the colony in jeopardy.

It must be emphasized, however, that the English in Virginia had little incentive or reason to seek the inclusion of any substantial numbers of Native Americans in the colonial economy. In the Spanish colonies to the South, Indians were an essential source of labor for plantations and mines. The Spanish both exploited and protected Indians as an essential lower laboring class. In French Canada, the sparse European population was dependent on Indians as trading partners, guides, and warriors. The English colonies, by contrast, relied upon white immigration, both free and indentured, and, later on, African slaves to provide labor. Indians were very quickly marginalized. Although there were a few Indian slaves and even some free Indian workers in Virginia, they were never an important source of labor. Indeed, as we have seen, restrictive legislation, rooted in fear of their presumed savagery, discouraged their use. The Virginia colonial economy cast off its dependency on Indian trade within the first generation, and had never relied upon Indian labor.

The English occupation of Virginia had a devastating effect on the indigenous peoples of the region. Scholars generally agree that the Indian population in 1700 stood at less than 10 percent of its 1600 level. Some of this population attrition was the direct result of measures used in time of war to kill or starve the Indian population. The colony's policies in times of peace also had lethal consequences, as Indians were forced off their best lands, becoming, through deprivation and demoralization, more susceptible to infectious diseases of European origin for which they had no immunity. Although many who deny that genocide occurred in British North America point, correctly, to disease as the main cause of Indian population loss, we cannot hold the colonizers blameless, for the conditions created by colonialism greatly elevated disease mortality. Colonialism, by its attack on the land base and cultural integrity of the colonized peoples, is deadly in its effects quite apart from the avowed intentions of the occupier. If we define genocide narrowly as intentional state-sponsored physical extermination, Virginia's official Indian policies were genocidal only during the decade following Opechancanough's uprising. However, that definition, although frequently implicitly or explicitly invoked by historians of colonial America, is not only inadequate, but also contrary to the intentions of the original framers of the concept. Genocide is better understood as an escalating series of discriminatory and violent actions, grounded in the belief that the victim population is unworthy of inclusion in the community and therefore not entitled to protection. Those genocidal acts sometimes, but not always, culminate in state-supported systematic killing. The Virginia colony's Indian policies generally, although not always, fell short of official programs of outright extermination. However, they were lethal in effect, and there can be no doubt that the English bear a heavy responsibility for the massive dying off of Virginia's native population during the 17th century. English acts of genocide ranged from deliberate and systematic destruction of Indian villages and cornfields, and indiscriminate killing of Indian men, women, and children during the worst years, to a perennial and callous failure to enforce the colony's own laws against robbing, enslaving, or killing Indians during the more peaceful years. The roots of the recurrent genocidal violence against Native American peoples in 17th-century Virginia are to be found not only in the economic demands and aspirations of the colonizers, but also in a mind-set that denied the right of people labeled "savage" to their own way of life and sometimes even to life itself should they fail to conform to the occupiers' expectations. This is a sad, painful, and disgraceful aspect of our history. To deny that genocide occurred in this colony is to ignore the evidence and to minimize the tragedy.

Notes

INTRODUCTION

1. Elazur Barkan, "The Genocides of Indigenous Peoples," in Robert Gellately and Ben Kiernan, eds., *The Specter of Genocide: Mass Murder in Historical Perspective* (New York: Cambridge University Press, 2003), 131. On the absence of studies of genocide in the Americas, see also Mark Levene, "Nation-States, Empires, and the Problem of Historicizing Genocide: A Response to Wolfgang Reinhard and Anthony Pagden," *Journal of Genocide Research,* 9(2007), 131. The two preeminent radical works on this topic are Ward Churchill, *A Little Matter of Genocide: Holocaust and Denial in the Americas 1492 to the Present* (San Francisco: City Lights Books, 1997), and David E. Stannard, *American Holocaust* (New York: Oxford University Press, 1992). As to the quip quoted earlier, a Google search revealed several reports of its use during after-dinner speeches. A very accessible example is "Albany Society Reunion," *The New York Times,* January 13, 1899, 2.

2. James Axtell, *Beyond 1492: Encounters in Colonial America* (New York: Oxford University Press, 1992), 261–262.

3. Paul B. Bartrop, "The Powhatans of Virginia and the English Invasion of America," in Colin Tanz, ed., *Genocide Perspectives* (Sydney: Center for Comparative Genocide Studies, Macquarie University, 1997), I: 92. There are a few exceptions. To cite an example of particular relevance to this study, Gary B. Nash, a mainstream historian and a distinguished one, in *Red, White and Black,* a seminal comparative study of race relations in colonial North America first published in 1974, characterized the attitudes of the early English settlers at Jamestown as "genocidal," and suggested that had they been stronger, the colonists would have exterminated all of Virginia's Indians, friendly or otherwise. Gary B. Nash, *Red, White and Black: The Peoples of Early America,* 4th edition (Upper Saddle River, NJ: Prentice-Hall, 2000), 73.

4. Ben Kiernan, *Blood and Soil: A World History of Genocide and Extermination from Sparta to Dafur* (New Haven: Yale University Press, 2007), 9–20; Frank Chalk, "Redefining

Genocide," in George J. Andreopolous, ed., *Genocide: Conceptual and Historical Dimensions* (Philadelphia: University of Pennsylvania Press, 1994), 52.

5. A. Dirk Moses, "Conceptual Blockages and Definitional Dilemmas in the 'Racial Century': Genocides of Indigenous Peoples and the Holocaust," in A. Dirk Moses and Dan Stone, eds., *Colonialism and Genocide* (London: Routledge, 2007), 164–165. For an overview of genocidal practices in the New World, see Alfred A. Cave, "Genocide in the Americas," in Dan Stone, ed. *The Historiography of Genocide* (London: Palgrave MacMillan, 2008), 273–295. The Brazilian delegate's statement is in Leo Kuper, "Theoretical Issues Relating to Genocide: Uses and Abuses," in George Andreopolous, ed., *Genocide: Conceptual and Historical Dimensions* (Philadelphia: University of Pennsylvania Press, 1994), 33.

6. Norbert Finzsch, "'It Is Scarcely Possible to Conceive That Human Beings Could Be So Hideous and Loathsome': Discourses of Genocide in Eighteenth- and Nineteenth-Century American and Australia," in Moses and Stone, eds., *Colonialism and Genocide*, 7. It should be noted that not all scholars regard the original intentions of the colonizers of the Americas as non-genocidal. Radical writers often do not accept this premise. Ward Churchill's declaration that the colonizers anticipated "the behavior and the logic that have come to be associated with Hitler's SS" and understood "war only in the sense of the annihilation of the racial enemy" offers an extreme statement of the contention that racial extermination was a cardinal objective of the colonial enterprise from the outset. David E. Stannard, although less extreme in his rhetoric, is persuaded that the colonizers believed that God not only permitted, but directed, "the mass destruction of the native peoples." Churchill is quoted in M. Annette Jaimes, "Sand Creek: The Morning After," in Jaimes, ed., *The State of Native America: Genocide, Colonization and Resistance* (Boston: South End Press, 1992), 3. See David E. Stannard, *American Holocaust* (New York: Oxford, 1992), 219.

7. Tony Barta, "Relations of Genocide: Land and Lives in the Colonization of Australia," in Isidor. Walliman and Michael N. Dokowski, eds., *Genocide in the Modern Age: Etiology and Case Studies of Mass Death* (Syracuse, NY: Syracuse University Press, 2000), 239. See also Alison Palmer, *Colonial Genocide* (Adelaide: Crawford House, 2000).

8. Herschel is quoted in Alan S. Rosenbaum, ed., *Is the Holocaust Unique? Perspectives on Comparative Genocide* (Boulder, CO: Westview Press, 2001), 211.

9. Moses, "Conceptual Blockages," 171; Chalk, "Redefining Genocide," 52; Edmund Morgan, *American Slavery, American Freedom: The Ordeal of Colonial Virginia* (New York: Norton, 1975), 70. Morgan's work, although primarily concerned with the origins of slavery, contains many valuable insights on Indian–white relations. Among the other scholarly works of relevance to this topic, several deserve special mention. Helen Rountree's various works on the Powhatan Indians cited later in this study are invaluable. Frederic W. Gleach's *Powhatan's World and Colonial Virginia: A Conflict of Cultures* (Lincoln: University of Nebraska Press, 1997) offers a very perceptive assessment of the early years. It is unfortunate that John Frederick Fausz's doctoral dissertation on "The Powhatan Uprising of 1622" (College of William and Mary, 1977) has not been published in book form. His numerous articles, published primarily in *The Virginia Magazine of History and Biography,* are well worth examining. There are two seminal studies of Bacon's Rebellion: Wilcomb E. Washburn's *The Governor and the Rebel* (Chapel Hill: University of North Carolina Press, 1957) and the relevant chapters in Stephen Saunders Webb's *1776: The End of American Independence* (New York: Alfred A. Knopf, 1984). Michael Leroy Oberg's *Dominion and Civility: English Imperialism and Native Americans, 1585–1685* (Ithaca, NY: Cornell University Press, 1999) places events in Virginia in a larger imperial context.

CHAPTER 1

1. In Richard Eden's 1555 translation, More declares "the way to heaven out of all places is of like length and distance." See David Beers Quinn, ed., *The Voyages and Colonising Enterprises of Sir Humphrey Gilbert* (Nendein, Liechtenstein: Kraus Reprints, 1967), 89n. On "savages," see Thomas More, *Utopia,* trans. Paul Turner (Baltimore, MD: Penguin Books, 1965), 69–70. For a detailed discussion of More's conception of America, see Alfred A. Cave, "Thomas More and the New World," *Albion* 23(1991), 209–230.

2. Edward Surtz and Jack. H. Hexter, *The Complete Works of St. Thomas More,* 14 vols. (New Haven, CT: Yale University Press, 1965) IV: 137, 207–209. Sholomo Avierni, "War and Slavery in More's Utopia," *International Review of Social History* 7(1962), 263–289.

3. Nicholas P. Canny, *The Elizabethan Conquest of Ireland: A Pattern Established 1565–76* (London: The Harvester Press, 1976), 101, 122–126; Edmund S. Morgan, *American Slavery, American Freedom* (New York: Norton, 2003 [1975]), 26n. For a thorough and persuasive discussion of the agrarian issue, see Ben Kiernan, *Blood and Soil: A World History of Genocide and Extermination from Sparta to Darfur* (New Haven, CT: Yale University Press, 2007), 169–214. Keirnan regards agrarianism as one of the principle ideological justifications of genocide throughout history.

4. David Quinn, ed., *The Voyages and Colonising Enterprises of Sir Humphrey Gilbert* [1955] (Nendein, Liechtenstein: Kraus Reprint, 1970) 17, 118–128 [originally published by the Hakluyt Society in 1970]. Canny, *The Elizabethan Conquest of Ireland,* 122–126.

5. Kiernan, *Blood and Soil,* 196, 204, 608; Edmund Spencer, *A View of the Present State of Ireland* [1596 or 1597], quoted in Kiernan, *Blood and Soil,* 209.

6. Anghierra, Pietro Martire, *The Decades of the Newe World or West India,* trans. Richard Eden (London, [sn], 1555). Quotations in the text are taken from Edward Arber, ed., *The First Three English Books on America, 1511–1555* (New York: Kraus Reprint, [1885] 1971), 69–78, 89–94. Oviedo is translated and reprinted in Arber, ed., *The First Three English Books on America,* 215–241; Fráncisco López de Gómara, *The Pleasant Historie of the Conquest of the Weast Indie, Now Called New Spayne,* trans. T. Anno (London: Henry Bynneman, 1578). On the satanic theme, see Jorge Canizares-Esguerra, *Puritan Conquisadores: Iberianizing the Atlantic, 1500–1700* (Stanford: Stanford University Press, 2006). On homosexuality, see Richard C. Trexler, *Sex and Conquest: Gendered Violence, Political Order and the European Conquest of the Americas* (Ithaca, NY: Cornell University Press, 1995). The quotation is in Jonathan Goldberg, *Sodometries: Renaissance Texts, Modern Sensibilities* (Stanford: Stanford University Press, 1992), 203.

7. Bartolome de las Casas, *The Spanish Colonie, or Brief Chronicle of the Acts and gestes of the Spaniardes in the West Indies* (London: Dawson, 1583), A!–Alv. George Abbot, *A Briefe Description of the Whole World* (London: J. Judson for John Brow, 1605), R.2.v. The first edition appeared in 1599, the last in 1664, 31 years after Abbot's death. Walter Raleigh, *Works of Sir Walter Raleigh,* 8 vols. (Oxford: Oxford University Press, 1829), IV: 693–694. Karen Ordahl Kupperman argues that positive images of Native American cultures were more widespread and influential than usually believed, and that scholars have generally provided simplistic overgeneralizations. See her *Settling with the Indians: The Meeting of English and Indian Cultures in North America* (London: J. M. Dent, 1980) and *English & Indians: Facing Off in Early America* (Ithaca, NY: Cornell University Press, 2000). Her point, although somewhat overstated in my point of view, is well taken.

8. Quinn, ed., *The Voyages and Colonising Enterprises of Sir Humphrey Gilbert,* I:161. Quotation in J. H. Eliot, *Empires of the Atlantic World* (New Haven, CT: Yale, 2006), 53.

9. The quotations and other materials from the reports of the Frobisher voyages are taken from Vilhjalmur Stefansson, ed., *The Three Voyages of Martin Frobisher,* 2 vols. (London: The Argonaut Press, 1938), I: 4, 7, 57; II: 17. These texts may also be found in Richard Hakluyt, *The Principle Navigations, Voyages Traffiques and Discoveries of the English Nation,* 10 vols. (Glasgow: J. MacLehose and Sons, 1904), VII: 219–227, 280–282, 292–314, 335–338; VIII: 291–234.

10. Stefansson, ed., *The Three Voyages of Martin Frobisher,* I: 68.

11. Ibid., I: 166.

12. Ibid., I: 58, 68–70; II: 17.

13. Samuel Eliot Morison, *The European Discovery of America: The Northern Voyages* AD *500–1600* (New York: Oxford University Press, 1971), 526.

14. Stefansson, ed., *The Three Voyages of Martin Frobisher,* I: 68–70, 124, 128,

15. David B. Quinn, ed., *The Voyages and Colonizing Activities of Sir Humphrey Gilbert,* 2 vols. (London, The Hakluyt Society, 1938), I: 182–185; II: 287.

16. Ibid., II: 452.

17. Ibid., II: 453.

18. Ibid., II: 450–460.

19. Ibid., I: 185.

20. David Beers Quinn, ed., *The Roanoke Voyages, 1584–1590,* 2 vols. (London: The Hakluyt Society, 1955, I: 82–89.

21. Quoted in David Beers Quinn, *Set Fair for Roanoke* (Chapel Hill: University of North Carolina Press, 1985), 50.

22. Richard Hakluyt, *A Discourse Concerning Western Planting* (Cambridge, MA: J. Wilson, 1877).

23. David B. Quinn, ed., *The Roanoke Voyages, 1584–1590,* 2 vols. (London: The Hakluyt Society, 1955), I: 138.

24. Barlowe's report is reprinted in Quinn, *The Roanoke Voyages, 1584–1590* I: 92–166.

25. Quinn, *The Roanoke Voyages, 1584–1590,* I: 81, 91–117.

26. For a narrative history of the Roanoke ventures, Quinn, *Set Fair for Roanoke*, cited earlier, is the most thorough. For a provocative reassessment, see Michael Leroy Oberg, *The Head in Edward Nugent's Hand: Roanoke's Forgotten Indians* (Philadelphia: University of Pennsylvania Press, 2008). Still of use is Karen Ordahl Kupperman's, *Roanoke: The Abandoned Colony* (Lanham, MD: Rowman & Littlefield, 1984). There are many popular accounts. David N. Durant's *Raleigh's Lost Colony* (London: Weidenfeld and Nicholson, 1981) is eminently readable.

27. The text of Hariot's report is found in Quinn, ed., *The Roanoke Voyages, 1584–1590,* I: 317–387. For reproductions of White's superb work, see Paul Hulton, *America 1585: The Complete Drawings of John White* (Chapel Hill, University of North Carolina Press, 1984).

28. Quinn, ed., *The Roanoke Voyages, 1584–1590* I: 317–387.

29. Ibid.

30. Quinn, ed., *The Roanoke Voyages, 1584–1590* I: 191, 255–293. Samuel Eliot Morison, *The European Discovery of America: The Northern Voyages* (New York: Oxford University Press, 1971), 644, 647–648.

31. Quinn, ed., *The Roanoke Voyages, 1584–1590* I: 259–288; Quinn, *Set Fair for Roanoke,* 217–219. See also Oberg, *The Head in Edward Nugent's Hand.*

32. Kupperman, *Roanoke,* 11, 67.

33. Quinn, ed., *The Roanoke Voyages,* I: 204, 266.

34. Quinn, *Set Fair for Roanoke*, 341–412.

35. Helen Rountree is skeptical of the Smith account, pointing out that it is not found in any of Smith's early writings, but only in a later secondhand report published in an anti-Indian polemic. That report is in Samuel Purchas, *Hakluytus Posthumus, or Purchas His Pilgrims*, 4 vols. (Glasgow, James MaLehose, 1905–1907), IV: 1728, 1813. However, there is evidence that other early Jamestown settlers did believe Powhatan was responsible. See Helen Rountree, *Pocahontas' People: The Powhatan Indians of Virginia Through Four Centuries* (Norman: University of Oklahoma Press, 1990), 21–22.

36. A contemporary account of the abandonment of the colony is contained in William Strachey, *The Historie of Travelle into Virginia Britania* [1614] (London: Hakluyt Society, 1953). An excellent collection of primary documents can be found in Henry O. Thayer, ed., *The Sagadahoc Colony* (New York: B. Blom, 1971).

37. James P. Baxter, *Sir Ferdinando Gorges and His Province of Maine*, 3 vols. (Boston: The Prince Society 1890), III: 149, 154–159; Ferdinando Gorges, "Brief Narration of the Original Undertakings and of the Advancement of Plantations into the Parts of America," *Maine Historical Society Collections*, 1st ser., 2(1847), 17–18. For an analysis of all the documentary evidence on this issue, including some materials not available to Thayer, see Alfred A. Cave, "Why Was the Sagadahoc Colony Abandoned? A Reconsideration of the Evidence," *New England Quarterly*, 68(1995), 625–640.

CHAPTER 2

1. Fronde is quoted in George Brunner Parks, *Richard Hakluyt and the English Voyages* (New York: The American Geographical Society, 1928), 187. The Virginia Company instructions are reprinted in James L. Barbour, ed., *The Jamestown Voyages Under the First Charter 1606–1609*, 2 vols. (Cambridge: The Hakluyt Society, 1969), I: 49–54.

2. Barbour, ed., *The Jamestown Voyages*, I: 43–44; Robert Johnson, *Nova Britannia*, reprinted in David Beers Quinn, ed., *New American World: A Documentary History of North America to 1612*, 5 vols. (New York: Arno Press, [1609] 1979), V: 240.

3. Edward Wright Haile, ed., *Jamestown Narratives: Eyewitness Accounts of the Virginia Colony* (Champlain, VA: Roundhouse, 1998), 123–124. Although the report is unsigned, stylistic similarities to the Gosnold voyage account lead most authorities to attribute this report to Archer.

4. George Percy, "Observations Gathered out of a Discourse of the Southern Colony in Virginia by the English, 1606," in Haile, ed., *Jamestown Narratives*, 86–87.

5. Ibid., 90.

6. Ibid., 91–92.

7. Ibid., 92–93. Helen Rountree believes the *werowance* did suspect the visitor of the earlier attack. See Helen Rountree, *Pocahontas' People: The Powhatan Indians of Virginia through Four Centuries* (Norman: University of Oklahoma Press, 1990), 30.

8. Percy, "Observations," 93.

9. Rountree, *Pocahontas' People*, 30.

10. Percy, "Observations," 94–95.

11. Philip L. Barbour, ed., *The Complete Works of Captain John Smith*, 3 vols. (Chapel Hill: University of North Carolina Press, 1986), II: 139; William Kelso, *Jamestown: The Buried Truth* (Charlottesville: The University of Virginia Press, 2006).

12. Barbour, ed., *The Jamestown Voyages,* I: 95–98; J. Frederick Fausz, "An Abundance of Blood Shed on Both Sides: England's First Indian War, 1609–1614," *Virginia Magazine of History and Biography,* 98(1990), 9.

13. Barbour, ed., *The Complete Works of Captain John Smith,* I: 53, II: 126; William Strachey, *The History of Travelle into Virginia Britania* [1612] (London: The Hakluyt Society, 1849), 49.

14. Helen Rountree, *Pocahontas, Powhatan, Opechancanough: Three Indian Lives Changed by Jamestown* (Charlottesville: University of Virginia Press, 2005), 27–28; Barbour, ed., *The Complete Works of Captain John Smith,* I: 175; Martin D. Gallivan, *James River Chiefdoms: The Rise of Social Inequality in the Chesapeake* (Lincoln: University of Nebraska Press, 2003), 163. For earlier developments in the region, see also Stephen R. Potter, *Commoners, Tribute, and Chiefs: The Development of Algonquian Culture in the Potomac Valley* (Charlottersville and London: University Press of Virginia, 1993).

15. Strachey, *The History of Travelle into Virginia Britania,* 41; Rountree, *Pocahontas' People,* 140; James Mooney, *The Siouan Tribes of the East: Bureau of American Ethnology Bulletin 22* (Washington, DC: Government Printing Office, 1894), 18–37.

16. Barbour, ed., *The Complete Works of Captain John Smith,* II: 27; Strachey, *The History of Travelle into Virginia Britania,* 51–52.

17. Helen Rountree, ed., *Powhatan Foreign Relations* (Charlottesville: University of Virginia Press, 1993), 10–11. See also Frederick Gleach, *Powhatan's World and Colonial Virginia* (Lincoln: University of Nebraska Press, 1997), 29.

18. Strachey, *The History of Travelle into Virginia Britania,* 51–53; Barbour, ed., *The Complete Works of Captain John Smith,* I: 174; Helen Rountree, *The Powhatan Indians of Virginia: Their Traditional Culture* (Norman: University of Oklahoma Press, 1988), 109–112. Archaeological evidence does indicate that food storage areas in the region during the late Woodland period were increasingly centralized and removed from individual family areas, and that inequities in dwelling sizes also increased—both of which provide evidence of growing inequality and political consolidation. See Gallivan, *James River Chiefdoms,* 171–176.

19. Rountree, *Pocahontas, Powhatan, Opechancanough,* 31–32; Barbour, ed., *The Complete Works of Captain John Smith,* I: 169–174.

20. Margaret Holmes Williamson, *Powhatans Lords of Life and Death: Command and Consent in Seventeenth Century Virginia* (Lincoln: University of Nebraska Press, 2003), 59ff; Rountree, *The Powhatan Indians of Virginia,* 141; Samuel Argall, "Letter to Hawkes, June 1613," in Edward Wright Haile, ed., *Jamestown Narratives: Eyewitness Accounts of the Virginia Colony* (Champlain, VA: Roundhouse, 1998), 753.

21. All the available documents are reprinted in Spanish and in English translation in Clifford M. Lewis and Albert J. Loomie, eds., *The Spanish Jesuit Mission in Virginia, 1570–1577* (Chapel Hill: University of North Carolina Press, 1952). On the ill-founded claim that Opechancanough was Don Luis, see Helen Rountree, *Pocahontas' People,* 15–20.

22. Lewis and Loomie, eds., *The Spanish Jesuit Mission in Virginia,* 89.

23. Ibid., 109, 110, 119, 133, 134.

24. Seth Mallios, "The Apotheosis of Ajacan's Jesuit Missionaries," *Ethnohistory,* 34 (2007), 223–244.

25. Lewis and Loomie, eds., *The Spanish Jesuit Mission in Virginia,* 134; Rountree, *Pocahontas' People,* 24.

26. Strachey, *The History of Travelle into Virginia Britania*, 101; Fausz, "An Abundance of Blood Shed on Both Sides," 13.

27. Barbour, ed., *The Jamestown Voyages*, I: 144–145.

28. Strachey, *The History of Travelle into Virginia Britania*, 50–51, 102.

29. Barbour, ed., *The Jamestown Voyages*, I: 145; Barbour, ed., *The Complete Works of Captain John Smith*, I: 210.

30. Barbour, ed., *The Jamestown Voyages*, I: 145.

31. Ibid., I: 91; Gallivan, *James River Chiefdoms*, 164.

32. Stephen R. Potter "Early English Effects on Virginia Algonquian Exchange and Tribute in the Tidewater Potomac," in Peter H. Wood et al., eds., *Powhatan's Mantle* (Lincoln: University of Nebraska Press, 1989), 151.

33. Barbour, ed., *The Complete Works of Captain John Smith*, I: 160.

34. George Percy, "A True Relation of the proceedings and occurences of moment that have hap'ned in Virginis.." in Haile, *Jamestown Narratives*," 504

35. Barbour, ed., *The Complete Works of Captain John Smith*, I: 169.

36. Barbour, ed., *Jamestown Voyages*, I: 147–150.

37. Barbour, ed., *The Complete Works of Captain John Smith*, I: 171–172.

38. Samuel Purchas, Haklyutus Posthumus, or *Purchas His Pilgrims*, 20 vols. (Glasgow,: James Maclehose and sons, 1905–1907) 19: 953; Williamson, *Powhatan Lords of Life and Death*, 201, 209..

39. Rountree, *The Powhatan Indians of Virginia*, 82.

40. Robert Beverley, *The History and Present State of Virginia* (Chapel Hill: University of North Carolina Press, [1705] 1947), 202, 205–209.

41. Beverley, *The History and Present State of Virginia*, 198; Williamson, *Powhatan Lords of Life and Death*, 176; Rountree, *The Powhatan Indians of Virginia*, 136; quotation from Ruth Benedict, in Elisabeth Tooker, ed., *Native North American Spirituality of the Eastern Woodlands* (New York: Paulist Press, 1979), 17.

42. Strachey, *The History of Travelle into Virginia Britania*, 88–89.

43. Susan Meyer Kingsbury, *Records of the Virginia Company of London*, 4 vols. (Washington, DC: U.S. Government Printing Office, 1906–1935), III: 14; Robert Gray, *A Good Speed to Virginia* (New York: Scholars' Facsimiles, [1609] 1937), B1–C3; William Symonds, *Virginia: A Sermon Preached at White Chappell in the Presence of Many Honourable and Worshipful, the Adventurers and Planters for Virginia* (London: I. Windet, 1609), A1–A3.

44. [Robert Johnson], *The New Life of Virginia* (London: William Welby, 1617), 18–19. For a detailed analysis of these writings, see Alfred A. Cave, "Canaanites in a Promised Land: The American Indian and the Providential Theory of Empire," *American Indian Quarterly*, 12(1988), 277–297.

45. Alexander Whitaker, *Good Newes from Virginia* (London: William Welby, 1613), 24–26; Barbour, ed., *The Complete Works of Captain John Smith*, I: 159, 169.

46. Strachey, *The History of Travelle into Virginia Britania*, 46–47, 91–93. See Colin Kidd, *The Forging of Races: Race and Scripture in the Protestant World, 1600–2000* (Cambridge: Cambridge University Press, 2006), for numerous other examples of the use of the Ham curse theme in justification of enslavement and dispossession of nonwhite peoples.

47. Williamson, *Powhatan Lords of Life and Death*, 202, 204, 235; Barbour, ed., *The Complete Works of Captain John Smith*, I: 16.

48. Strachey, *The History of Travelle into Virginia Britania*. 101.

CHAPTER 3

1. The primary source for Smith's biography is his *The True Travels:, Adventures and Observations of Captain John Smith in Europe, Asia, Africa and America from Anno Domini 1593 to 1629*, first published in London in 1630 and available in Philip L. Barbour, ed., *The Complete Works of Captain John Smith*, 3 vols. (Chapel Hill: University of North Carolina Press, 1986), III: 135–251. There are numerous biographies of Smith, some excellent, but Philip Barbour's *The Three Worlds of Captain John Smith* (Boston: Houghton Mifflin, 1964) remains indispensable.

2. Barbour, ed., *The Complete Works of Captain John Smith*, III: 154–156. The actual text of the *Meditations of Marcus Aurelius* had not yet been translated into English. Smith probably used a spurious version, marked by misogyny, written by a Spanish priest, Don Anthony de Guevara, and available under the title *The Diall of Princes*. See Dorothy and Thomas Hooker, *Captain John Smith, Jamestown and the Birth of the American Dream* (Hoboken, NJ: Wiley, 2006), 19–20.

3. Barbour, ed., *The Complete Works of Captain John Smith*, III: 157–162.

4. Ibid., III: 166–179.

5. Ibid., III: 173–174.

6. Ibid., III: 186–187, 200–209.

7. Lewis L. Kropf, "Captain John Smith of Virginia," *Notes and Queries*, 7th ser., 9(1890), 1–2, 41–43, 102–104, 161–162, 223–224, 281–282. Laura Polanyi Striker offers a meticulous assessment of the numerous errors in Kropf's reading of the sources in "The Hungarian Historian, Lewis L. Kropf, on Captain John Smith's *True Travels*: A Reappraisal," *Virginia Magazine of History and Biography*, 66(1958), 22–43, and in "Captain John Smith's Hungary and Transylvania," in Bradford Smith, ed., *Captain John Smith: His Life and Legend* (Philadelphia: Lippincott, 1953), 311–342. See also Laura Polanyi Striker and Bradford Smith, "The Rehabilitation of Captain John Smith," *Journal of Southern History*, 28(1962), 474–481.

8. Barbour, *The Three Worlds of Captain John Smith*, 83–84.

9. Ibid., 112–113.

10. Barbour, ed., *The Complete Works of Capt. John Smith*, I: 206–207.

11. Ibid., I: 31, 206.

12. Ibid., I: 41, II: 181.

13. Ibid., III: 144–145. An earlier account of this expedition offers far less detail, omitting in particular the description of the "Idoll" (see I: 35–37).

14. Ibid., I: 81–82.

15. Ibid., I: 93.

16. This letter is reprinted, with a matching page facsimile, in Barbour, ed., *The Complete Works of Captain John Smith*, I: 26–108. For this encounter, see I: 45.

17. Ibid., I: 45–46.

18. Ibid., I: 59, II: 149–150; Frederick Gleach, *Powhatan's World and Colonial Virginia* (Lincoln: University of Nebraska Press, 1997), 111.

19. Barbour, ed., *The Complete Works of Captain John Smith*, I: 49.

20. Ibid., I: 53.

21. Ibid., I: 53–57.

22. Ibid., II: 151. For the earlier versions, see Ibid., I:53; 213–214.

23. Ibid., I: 213.

24. The most prominent recent critic of the Smith story of rescue by Pocahontas is Helen Rountree. She finds the sequence of events described by Smith improbable, and points out that death by braining was "normally meted out to disobedient subjects, not captured foreigners," and has nowhere been described as part of an adoption ceremony. "Smith's account," she concludes, "simply does not ring true." Helen Rountree, *Pocahontas' People: The Powhatan Indians of Virginia through Four Centuries* (Norman: University of Oklahoma Press, 1990), 38–39. Adams's account, later revised, first appeared in "Captain John Smith," *North American Review*, 104(1867), 1–30. For a thorough and judicious review of all the evidence, see J. A. Leo Lemay, *Did Pocahontas Save Captain John Smith?* (Athens: University of Georgia Press, 1992). Lemay demonstrates, from quotation from his correspondence, that Adams was driven by anti-Southern prejudice, and knew very well that there were reasons to accept Smith's account. Lemay's reading of the article suggests that Adams, determined to undermine the prestige of Virginia, used evidence very selectively, using, at certain junctures, arguments lacking in logic and consistency. The letter to Queen Anne was published by Smith in 1624. The original has never been found. Lemay argues that its contents were no doubt discussed at court, and as no one challenged the story, accepted as true. See Lemay, *Did Pocahontas Save Captain John Smith?*, 14–40.

25. For the case in support of this interpretation, see Gleach, *Powhatan's World and Colonial Virginia,* 116–121. For Smith's encounter with Pocahontas see Barbour, ed., *The Complete Works of Captain John Smith,* II: 261.

26. Barbour, ed., *The Complete Works of Captain John Smith,* II: 152, 261.

27. Ibid., II: 224–231; Helen Rountree, *Pocahontas, Powhatan, Opechancanough: Three Indian Lives Changed by Jamestown* (Charlottesville: University of Virginia Press, 2005), 110–111.

28. Barbour, ed., *The Complete Works of Captain John Smith,* II: 152. Rountree (*Pocahontas, Powhatan, Opechancanough,* 82) doubts that Pocahontas, a girl of 11 at the time, played much of a role in this.

29. Edward Wright Haile, ed., *Jamestown Narratives: Eyewitness Accounts of the Virginia Colony* (Champlain, VA: Roundhouse, 1998), 196. Barbour, ed., *The Complete Works of Captain John Smith,* II: 152. Smith makes no mention of his pending execution in his 1608 account, only that his enemies used the occasion to try to remove him from the Council. Wingfield's testimony indicates that the true story was suppressed in 1608, probably not to put the Virginia enterprise in too bad a light. Barbour, ed., *The Complete Works of Captain John Smith,* I: 61.

30. Barbour, ed., *The Complete Works of Captain John Smith,* II: 157–158.

31. Ibid., I: 216–219.

32. Ibid., I: 61–63, II: 155–156.

33. Ibid., I: 61–67, II: 155–156.

34. Ibid., I: 69, II: 154–156; Rountree, *Pocahontas, Powhatan, Opechancanough,* 99.

35. Barbour, ed., *The Complete Works of Captain John Smith,* II: 154, 156.

36. Ibid., I: 75–77. Francis Perkins, "Letter from Jamestown to a Friend, 28 March 1608," in Haile, ed., *Jamestown Narratives,* 134. Perkins' letter, in Spanish translation, was found in the Spanish royal archives. The original has been lost. Nothing is known about the circumstances, but the content does not suggest that the letter was the work of a spy.

37. Barbour, ed., *The Complete Works of Captain John Smith,* II: 180–192; Susan Meyer Kingsbury, *Records of the Virginia Company of London,* 4 vols. (Washington, DC: U.S. Government Printing Office, 1906–1935), III: 14.

38. Barbour, ed., *The Complete Works of Captain John Smith*, II: 180–181.

39. Ibid., II: 180–183. Robert Beverley, writing in 1705, described the Powhatans' customary hospitality to a visitor of note as including at bedtime

a Brace of young Beautiful Virgins . . . chosen, to wait upon him that night, for his particular refreshment. These Damsels are to undress this happy Gentleman, and as soon as he is in Bed, they gently lay themselves down by him, one on one side of him, and the other on the other. They esteem it a breach of Hospitality not to submit to every thing he desires of them. . . . And the young Women are so far from suffering in their Reputation for this Civility, that they are envied for it by all the other Girls, as having the greatest Honour done them in the World.

Robert Beverley, *The History and Present State of Virginia* (Chapel Hill: University of North Carolina Press, [1705] 1947), 189.

40. Barbour, ed., *The Complete Works of Captain John Smith*, II: 183–184.

41. Ibid., I: 238, II: 187–190. The original of Smith's letter to the Company has not survived. We know it only from the version published in his 1624 history. Some authorities suspect it is an authentic.

42. Ibid., II: 186–191.

43. Ibid., II: 189–194.

44. Ibid.; Rountree, *Pocahontas, Powhatan, Opechancanough*, 119.

45. Barbour, ed., *The Complete Works of Captain John Smith*, II: 195.

46. Ibid., II: 196.

47. Ibid., II: 196–197.

48. Ibid., II: 195–199.

49. Ibid., II: 199–200; Barbour, *The Three Worlds of Captain John Smith*, 251.

50. Barbour, ed., *The Complete Works of Captain John Smith*, II: 200–202.

51. Ibid.

52. Rountree, *Pocahontas, Powhatan, Opechancanough*, 15.

53. Barbour, ed., *The Complete Works of Captain John Smith*, I: 259–262, II: 209–211.

54. Ibid., I: 223–233, II: 223.

55. Ibid., I: 258–262.

56. Ibid., II: 221–223; George Percy, *A True Relation of the Proceedings and Occurrences of Moment which Have Hap'ned in Virginia from the Time Sir Thomas Gates Was Sshipwarcl'd upon the Bermudes, Anno 1609, Until My Departure out of the Country, which Was in Anno Domini 1612*, in Haile, ed., *Jamestown Narratives*, 503–504; Rountree, *Pocahontas, Powhatan and Opechancanough*, 138.

57. Barbour, ed., *The Complete Works of Captain John Smith*, II: 221–223; J. Frederick Fausz, "An Abundance of Blood Shed on Both Sides: England's First Indian War, 1609–1614," *Virginia Magazine of History and Biography*, 98(1990), 22. Henry Spelman, a troubled teenager placed with Tanx-Powhatan to learn the language, claimed he had been sold to the Indians in exchange for the village. He was probably mistaken. Spelman's "Relation of Virginia" is reprinted, with modernized spelling, in Haile, ed., *Jamestown Narratives*, 481–495. Casualty figures are from Fausz, "An Abundance of Blood Shed on Both Sides," 5. Other quotations are from Rountree, *Pocahontas, Powhatan and Opechancanough*, 139; and Daniel Richter, "Tsenacoommacah and the Atlantic World," in Peter C. Mancall, ed., *The Atlantic World and Virginia* (Chapel Hill: University of North Carolina Press, 2007), 58.

58. Percy, *A True Relation*, 501–504; Benjamin Woolley, *Savage Kingdom: The True Story of Jamestqn, 1607, and the Settlement of America* (New York: Harper Collins, 2007), 230.

59. Strachey, "A True Repertory,"in Haile, ed., *Jamestown Narratives*, 441; Henry Spelman, "Relation of Virginia," in Haile, ed., *Jamestown Narratives*, 485; Fausz, "An Abundance of Blood Shed on Both Sides," 5.

60. Strachey, "A True Repertory," 441–442.

CHAPTER 4

1. Captain Butler, "The Unmasked Face of Our Colony in Virginia as It Was in the Winter of the Year 1622," quoted in Francis Jennings, *The Invasion of America: Indians, Colonialism and the Cant of Conquest* (New York: Norton, 1976), 79. A systematic census of all emigrants to Virginia from 1607 to 1624 confirmed an 80 percent attrition of population, but found it impossible to distinguish between those who died in Virginia and those who returned to England. The latter were, however, clearly a small minority. John Camden Hotten, *The Original Lists of Persons of Quality . . . and Others Who Went West from Great Britain to the American Plantations, 1600–1700* (New York: G. A. Baker, 1931), 201–265.

2. William Strachey, *For the Colony in Virginia Britannia: Lawes Divine, Morall and Martiall* (Charlottesville: University Press of Virginia, 1969), 20; George Percy, "A True Relation," in Edward W. Haile, ed., *Jamestown Narratives: Eyewitness Accounts of the Virginia Colony, Champlain Virginia: Roundhouse, 1998)*, 518; James Horn, *A Land as God Made It* (New York: Basic Books, 2005), 311; Nicholas Canny, "The Permissive Frontier: The Problem of Social Control in English Settlements in Ireland and Virginia, 1550–1650," in Andrews, Canny, and Hair, eds., *The Westward Enterprise: English Activities in Ireland, the Atlantic and America 1480–1650* (Detroit, MI: Wayne State University Press, 1979), 31–32.

3. Percy, "A True Relation," 505, 507; William Strachey, "A True Repertory of the Wrack and Redemption of Sir Thomas Gates, Knight, upon and from the Islands of the Bermuda; His Coming to Virginia, and the Estate of That Colony Then, and after under the Government of Lord La Warre, July 15, 1610," reprinted in Edward Wright Haile, ed., *Jamestown Narratives: Eyewitness Accounts of the Virginia Colony* (Champlain, VA: Roundhouse, 1998), 440.

4. Strachey, "A True Repertory," 419.

5. Percy, "A True Relation," 504–505.

6. J. Frederick Fausz, "An Abundance of Blood Shed on Both Sides: England's First Indian War, 1609–1614," *Virginia Magazine of History and Biography*, 98(1990), 25; [Anon.]"True Declaration of the Estate of the Colony,"[1610] reprinted in Peter Force, *Tracts and Other Papers* (Gloucester, MA: Peter Smith, [1963], 3: no. 1, 15–16; Percy, "A True Relation," 505, 508, 518; Strachey, "A True Repertory," 439.

7. Susan Meyer Kingsbury, *Records of the Virginia Company of London*, 4 vols. (Washington, DC: U.S. Government Printing Office, 1906–1935), III: 12–24.

8. Ibid.

9. Percy, "A True Relation," 516–518; Strachey, "A True Repertory," 427.

10. Percy, "A True Relation," 516–518; "Thomas West, Lord Delaware, to Salisbury, rec'd September 10, 1610" in Haile, ed., *Jamestown Narratives*, 465–467. "Jamestown Fiasco," is a chapter title in Edmund Morgan's, *American Slavery, American Freedom: The Ordeal of Colonial Virginia* (New York, 1975), 71–91.

11. Strachey, "A True Repertory," 429; William Crashaw, *A Sermon Preached in London before the Right Honorable the Lord Lavvare, Lord Gouvernour and Captain Generall of Virginia, and Others of His Maiesties Counsell for that Kingdome* (London: William Welby, 1610).

12. Strachey, "A True Repertory," 429.

13. Ibid., 434. Thomas West, Lord de la Warre, "Letter to the Virginia Company of London," in Haile, ed., *Jamestown Narratives*, 459, 461, 463–464; George Somers, "Letter to Salisbury, 15 June 1610," in Haile, ed., *Jamestown Narratives*, 456.

14. Strachey, "A True Repertory," 432–443; Fausz, "An Abundance of Blood Shed on Both Sides," 28–32; Kingsbury, ed., *Records of the Virginia Company of London*, III: 24–29; Edward Arber, ed., *Travels and Works of Captain John Smith 2 vols.* (Edinburgh: J. Grant, 1910), II: 927–928.

15. Percy, "A True Relation," 508; Strachey, "A True Repertory," 430, 435; Fausz, "An Abundance of Blood Shed on Both Sides," 32.

16. Strachey, "A True Repertory," 436–437.

17. Ibid., 437.

18. Percy, "A True Relation," 508–511.

19. Fausz, "An Abundance of Blood Shed on Both Sides," 34.

20. Strachey, "A True Repertory," 442.

21. On the propaganda campaign mounted by the Company, see Louis B. Wright, *Religion and Empire: The Alliance between Piety and Commerce in English Expansion, 1558–1625* (New York, 1965), 85–104; John Parker, "Religion and the Virginia Colony 1609–1610," in Andrews, Canny, and Hair, eds., *The Westward Enterprise*, 245–270.

22. Barbour, ed., *Complete Works of Captain John Smith*, I: 226,266, 267; II: 215–216; Percy, "A True Relation," 511–512; Strachey, *Histories of Travaille into Virginia Britannia* (London: The Hakluyt Society, 56.

23. Thomas West, Lord Delaware, "A Short Relation Made by the Lord De-La Warre to the Lords and Members of the Council of Virginia," in Haile, ed., *Jamestown Narratives*, 527–532.

24. Percy, "A True Relation," 513–514; Thomas Dale, "Letter to the Council of Virginia, 25 May, 1611," in Haile, ed., *Jamestown Narratives*, 524.

25. Percy, "A True Relation," 513–515. Hakluyt is quoted in Fausz, "An Abundance of Blood Shed on Both Sides," 37–38.

26. Percy, "A True Relation," 513–515; Dale, "Letter," in Haile, ed., *Jamestown Narratives*, 523; Ralph Hamor, "A True Discourse of the Present Estate of Virginia," in Haile, ed., *Jamestown Narratives*, 795–856; Philip L. Barbour, ed., *The Complete Works of Captain John Smith*, 3 vols. (Chapel Hill: University of North Carolina Press, 1986), II; 239; Morgan, *American Slavery, American Freedom*, 80.

27. Percy, "A True Relation," 515; Fausz, "An Abundance of Blood Shed on Both Sides," 40–41.

28. Thomas Dale, "Letter to Salisbury, 17 August 1611," in Haile, ed., *Jamestown Narratives*, 552–558.

29. Percy, "A True Relation," 514–515.

30. Reverend Alexander Whitaker, "Letter to the Reverend William Crashaw, 9 August 1611," in Haile, ed., *Jamestown Narratives*, 548–551; Percy, "A True Relation," 517.

31. Benjamin Woolley, *Savage Kingdom: The True Story of Jamestown, 1607, and the Settlement of America* (New York: HarperCollins, 2007), 308; Thomas Dale, "Letter from Henrico, 10 June 1613," in Haile, ed., *Jamestown Narratives*, 777–779; Hamor, "A True Discourse of the Present Estate of Virginia" 824–825; Fausz, "An Abundance of Blood Shed on Both Sides," 36.

32. Dale, "Letter from Henrico," 777–779; Horn, *A Land As God Made It*, 207.

33. Dale, "Letter to Salisbury," 556–557. The Spanish ambassador is quoted in Horn, *A Land As God Made It*, 211.

34. [Robert Johnson], *The New Life of Virginia* (London: William Welby, 1612), 18–21.

35. Thomas Dale to C.M., n.d., in Haile, ed., *Jamestown Narratives*, 841; Dale, "Letter from Henrico," in Haile, ed., *Jamestown Narratives* 777.

36. Alexander Whitaker, "Good Newes from Virginia," in Haile, ed., *Jamestown Narratives*, 730–731.

37. Dale, "Letter to the Council of Virginia," in Haile, ed., *Jamestown Narratives*, 524.

38. Samuel Argall, "Letter to Hawkes, June, 1613," in Haile, ed., *Jamestown Narratives*, 752–754.

39. Ibid., 754–755.

40. Hamor, "A True Discourse of the Present Estate of Virginia," in Haile, ed., *Jamestown Narratives*, 802–804; Argall, "Letter to Hawkes," in Haile, ed., *Jamestown Narratives*, 755–756.

41. Hamor, "A True Discourse of the Present Estate of Virginia," in Haile, ed., *Jamestown Narratives*, 802–806.

42. Ibid., 806–807.

43. Ibid., 807–809; Dale, "Letter to Mr. D. M.," in Haile, ed., *Jamestown Narratives*, 843–845.

44. Dale, "Letter to Mr. D. M.," in Hailie, ed., *Jamestown Narratives*, 845; Strachey, *Historie of Travaille into Virginia Britannia*, 54.

45. Dale, "Letter to Mr. D. M.," in Haile, ed., *Jamestown Narratives*, 845.

46. Strachey, *Historie of Travaille into Virginia Britannia*, 54.

47. Dale, "Letter to Mr. D. M.," in Haile, ed., *Jamestown Narratives*, 844–845; Hamor, "A True Discourse of the Present Estate of Virginia," in Haile, ed., *Jamestown Narratives*, 848.

48. Dale, "Letter to Mr. D. M.," in Haile, ed., *Jamestown Narratives*, 844–845; Hamor, "A True Discourse of the Present Estate of Virginia," in Haile, ed., *Jamestown Narratives*, 848; David D. Smits, "'Abominable Mixture' Toward the Repudiation of Anglo-Indian Intermarriage in Seventeenth-Century Virginia," *Virginia Magazine of History and Biography*, 95(1987), 157–192; Judith Reynolds, "Marriage between the English and the Indians in Seventeenth Century Virginia," *Quarterly Bulletin of the Archaeological Society of Virginia*, XVII(1962), 19–25.

49. "Letter of John Rolfe," in Lyman Tyler Gardiner, ed., *Narratives of Early Virginia, 1606–1625* (New York: Scribner, 1907), 240–241.

50. Hamor, "A True Discourse of the Present Estate of Virginia," in Haile, ed., *Jamestown Narratives*, 809; Arber, ed., *Travels and Works of Captain John Smith*, II: 527, 529, 573.

51. Robert Beverley, *The History and Present State of Virginia* (Chapel Hill: University of North Carolina Press, 1947), 38–39.

52. Hamor, "A True Discourse of the Present Estate of Virginia," in Haile, ed., *Jamestown Narratives*, 830–837.

CHAPTER 5

1. Susan Meyer Kingsbury, *Records of the Virginia Company of London*, 4 vols. (Washington, DC: U.S. Government Printing Office, 1906–1935), III: 31; Helen Rountree, *Pocahontas, Powhatan, Opechancanough: Three Indian Lives Changed by Jamestown* (Charlottesville:

University of Virginia Press, 2005), 176–186; Robert Beverley, *The History and Present State of Virginia* (Chapel Hill: University of North Carolina Press, 1947), 43–44.

2. William Crashaw, "Epistle Dedicatory," in Whitaker, *Good Newes from Virginia, (London: William Welby, 1613),* C2r; John Frederick Fausz, "The Powhatan Uprising of 1622: A Historical Study of Ethnocentrism and Cultural Conflict" (PhD diss., The College of William and Mary, 1977), 286–305; Robert C. Johnson, "The Lotteries of the Virginia Company," *Virginia Magazine of History and Biography,* LXXXIV(1966), 262–274.

3. Governor Yeardley to Sir Edwin Sandys, January 30, 1621/22, Kingsbury, ed., *Records of the Virginia Company of London,* I: 446, 588; Fausz, "The Powhatan Uprising of 1622," 335–339.

4. Philip L. Barbour, ed., *The Complete Works of Captain John Smith,* 3 vols. (Chapel Hill: University of North Carolina Press, 1986), II: 262–266; Kingsbury, ed., *Records of the Virginia Company of London,* I: 566, II: 36, III: 278–280, 298–300; Phillip A. Bruce, *Economic History of Virginia in the Seventeenth Century* (New York: MacMillan, 1895); Charles E. Hatch, Jr., *The First Seventeen Years: Virginia, 1607–1624* (Charlottesville: University of Virginia Press, 1957), 17–18; Rountree, *Pocahontas, Powhatan, Opechancanough,* 194–195; Fausz, "The Powhatan Uprising of 1622," 306–307.

5. Kingsbury, ed., *Records of the Virginia Company of London,* IV: 277.

6. Ibid., III: 92; Michael Leroy Oberg, *Dominion and Civility: English Imperialism and Native America 1585–1685* (Ithaca, NY: Cornell University Press, 1999), 73; Rountree, *Pocahontas, Powhatan, Opechancanough,* 192.

7. Kingsbury, ed., *Records of the Virginia Company of London,* III: 592.

8. Barbour, ed., *The Complete Works of Captain John Smith,* II: 265; Rountree, *Pocahontas, Powhatan, Opechancanough,* 189; Samuel Purchas, *Purchas His Pilgrimes* (London: William Welby, 1619), 956–957; Kingsbury, ed., *Records of the Virginia Company of London,* III: 73–74. On the relationship between Opechancanough and Itoyatin, see Frederick Gleach, *Powhatan's World and Colonial Virginia* (Lincoln: University of Nebraska Press, 1997), 146.

9. Purchas, *Purchas His Pilgrimes,* 956; Barbour, ed., *The Complete Works of Captain John Smith,* II: 256–257; Kingsbury, ed., *Records of the Virginia Company of London,* IV: 117–118; Beverley, *History and Present State of Virginia,* 45; Rountree, *Pocahontas, Powhatan, Opechancanough,* 196–197.

10. Kingsbury, ed., *Records of the Virginia Company of London,* I: 220, 310, III: 92, 220, 275–276; Rountree, *Pocahontas, Powhatan, Opechancanough,* 197.

11. Kingsbury, ed., *Records of the Virginia Company of London,* III: 93; The Ancient Planters, "A Brief Declaration of the Plantation of Virginia during the First Twelve Years," Edward Wright Haile, ed., *Jamestown Narratives: Eyewitness Accounts of the Virginia Colony* (Champlain, VA: Roundhouse, 1998), 905, 908.

12. Kingsbury, ed., *Records of the Virginia Company of London,* III: 93, 228.

13. Ibid., III: 80, 93, 128–129, 147, 164–166; IV, 11.

14. Ibid., III: 161, 163–165, 171–172.

15. Ibid., III:161, 163–165, 174–175, 242–245, 253, 307–312.

16. Ibid., I: 351, 266, II: 94, III: 244, 347; Rountree, *Pocahontas, Powhatan, Opechancanough,* 199–200; Fausz, "The Powhatan Uprising of 1622," 328–329.

17. Kingsbury, ed., *Records of the Virginia Company of London,* I: 269, 447; III: 102, 305, 487.

18. Fausz, "The Powhatan Uprising of 1622," 331–335.

19. Kingsbury, ed., *Records of the Virginia Company of London,* III: 447, 452.

20. Barbour, ed., *The Complete Works of Captain John Smith*, II: 285–286.

21. Fausz, "The Powhatan Uprising of 1622," 335–339; Kingsbury, ed., *Records of the Virginia Company of London*, III: 446; Purchas, Haklyutus Posthumus, or *Purchas His Pilgrims, 20 vols. (Glasgow: James Maclehose and Sons, 1905–1907)* 19: 153.

22. Kingsbury, *Records of the Virginia Company of London*, III: 584.

23. Fausz, "The Powhatan Uprising of 1622," 343; Kingsbury, eds., *Records of the Virginia Company of London*, III: 584.

24. Fausz, "The Powhatan Uprising of 1622," 347–348.

25. Kingsbury, ed., *Records of the Virginia Company of London*, III: 583–584, IV: 10; Fausz, "The Powhatan Uprising of 1622," 350.

26. Patrick Copland, *Virginia's God be Thanked: A Sermon of Thanksgiving for the Hapie Success of the Affayres of Virginia the Last Year* (London: W, Sheffefard and John Bellanie: 1622), 9–10, 25–26; Kingsbury, ed., *Records of the Virginia Company of London*, I: 447.

27. Purchas, Haklyutus Posthumus, 19:231–232; Benjamin Woolley, *Savage Kingdom: The True Story of Jamestown, 1607, and the Settlement of America* (New York: HarperCollins, 2007), 335–336.

28. Barbour, ed., *The Complete Works of Captain John Smith*, II: 293; Fausz, "The Powhatan Uprising of 1622," 353–357. Rountree believes that Nemattanew's death occurred the previous fall during Yeardley's governorship, pointing to a passage in a report from the Council in Virginia wherein Opechancanough was said to have expressed indifference to Yeardley about Nemattanew's death. However, the passage is somewhat ambiguous and may have referred to a prospective event. As Fausz points out, the March date is accepted in all other sources, including the Company's official report prepared by Waterhouse. See Helen Rountree, *Pocahontas' People: The Powhatan Indians of Virginia through Four Centuries* (Norman: University of Oklahoma Press, 1990), 302, n. 45; Fausz, "The Powhatan Uprising of 1622," 356, n. 7. The Council document in question is in Kingsbury, ed., *Records of the Virginia Company of London*, IV: 11.

29. Kingsbury, ed., *Records of the Virginia Company of London*, III: 541–579.

CHAPTER 6

1. Robert C. Johnson, ed., "Some Correspondence of the Reverend Joseph Mead," *Virginia Magazine of History and Biography*, LXXI(1963), 408–409. Rolfe had died of natural causes earlier in the month.

2. Susan Meyer Kingsbury, *Records of the Virginia Company of London*, 4 vols. (Washington, DC: U.S. Government Printing Office, 1906–1935), III: 611–615.

3. Waterhouse's account, published as *A Declaration of the State of the Colony and Affaires in Virginia and Relation of the Barbarous Massacre*, is reprinted in Kingsbury, ed., *Records of the Virginia Company of London*, III: 541–579. Some authorities believe Chanco and the young Indian who warned Pace were two different people. See Helen Rountree, *Pocahontas' People: The Powhatan Indians of Virginia through Four Centuries* (Norman: University of Oklahoma Press, 1990), 73. The Company's records do suggest that more than one Indian may have warned of the attack, but the reference is too vague to confirm the identity of the others, because it speaks only of "those Indians whom God used as instruments." See Kingsbury, ed., *Records of the Virginia Company of London*, III: 673.

4. Kingsbury, ed., *Records of the Virginia Company of London*, III: 550–579. The dead are enumerated in pages 565–571. For a detailed and meticulous analysis of those casualty

claims by each specific area, see John Frederick Fausz, "The Powhatan Uprising of 1622: A Historical Study of Ethnocentrism and Cultural Conflict" (PhD diss., The College of William and Mary, 1977), 367–403. Smith is quoted in Fausz, "The Powhatan Uprising of 1622," 401.

5. Kingsbury, ed., *Records of the Virginia Company of London*, III: 666–672.

6. Ibid., II: 397.

7. Ibid., III: 557–564.

8. Ibid.

9. Christopher Brooke, *A Poem on the Late Massacre in Virginia* (London, 1622). Anti-Indian hate literature is analyzed in Fausz, "The Powhatan Uprising of 1622," 427–445.

10. Kingsbury, ed., *Records of the Virginia Company of London*, III: 683; Wyatt to unknown correspondent, 1623 or 1624, in "Letters of Sir Francis Wyatt, Governor of Virginia, 1621–1626," *William and Mary Quarterly*, 2nd ser., 6(1926), 118.

11. Kingsbury, ed., *Records of the Virginia Company of London*, III: 704–706.

12. Purchas's treatise "Virginia Verger" is in Samuel Purchas, *Hakluytus Posthumus, or Purchas His Pilgrims* (Glasgow: James MacLehose, 1907–1909) 19: 218–297.

13. Kingsbury, ed., *Records of the Virginia Company of London*, III: 614, IV: 58–60, 525, 541; William S. Powell, "Aftermath of the Massacre: The First Indian War, 1622–1632," *Virginia Magazine of History and Biography*, 66(1958), 48–49.

14. Kingsbury, ed., *Records of the Virginia Company of London*, III: 654–655; H. R. McIlwaine, ed., *Minutes of the Council and General Court of Virginia, 1622–1632, 1670–1676* (Richmond: Virginia State Library, 1924), 29–30; Helen Rountree, *Pocahontas' People*, 75–76; Fausz, "The Powhatan Uprising of 1622," 460–461.

15. Philip L. Barbour, ed., *The Complete Works of Captain John Smith*, 3 vols. (Chapel Hill: University of North Carolina Press, 1986), II: 309–317.

16. Kingsbury, ed., *Records of the Virginia Company of London*, III: 314, IV: 9; McIlwaine, *Minutes of the Council and General Court of Virginia*, 48–50; Rountree, *Pocahontas' People*, 75–76; Fausz, "The Powhatan Uprising of 1622," 460–461.

17. McIlwaine, ed., *Minutes of the Council and General Court of Virginia*, 14, 48–50, 85; Edmund Morgan, *American Slavery, American Freedom: The Ordeal of Colonial Virginia* (New York: Norton 1975), 124.

18. Kingsbury, ed., *Records of the Virginia Company of London*, IV: 10, 508.

19. Ibid., IV: 10, 524–527.

20. Ibid., II: 483, IV: 37–38, 98–99, 190.

21. Lionel C. Sackville, "Lord Sackville's Papers Respecting Virginia, 1613–1631," *American Historical Review*, XXVII(1922), 507; Fausz, "The Powhatan Uprising of 1622," 497–499. For the controversy over Potts's role in the poisoning, see Fausz, "The Powhatan Uprising of 1622," 498. On his character, see Morgan, *American Slavery, American Freedom*, 122. Complaints about his mistreatment of servants as well as his stealing of livestock are scattered throughout the Virginia court records.

22. Kingsbury, ed., *Records of the Virginia Company of London*, II: 478, 482, 486, IV: 102, 167, 190, 250–251, 405; Fausz, "The Powhatan Uprising of 1622," 507.

23. Kingsbury, ed., *Records of the Virginia Company of London*, IV: 448, 470; William Waller Hening, ed., *Statutes at Large; Being a Collection of All the Laws of Virginia from the First Session of the Legislature in the Year 1619*, 13 vols. (New York: R&W&G, Bartow, 1823), I: 126–128.

24. Kingsbury, ed., *Records of the Virginia Company of London*, IV: 507–508.

25. McIlwaine, ed., *Minutes of the Council and General Court of Virginia*, 101–107.

26. Kingsbury, ed., *Records of the Virginia Company of London*, IV: 569; McIlwaine, ed., *Minutes of the Council and General Court of Virginia*, 101–107, 147, 151, 172, 481; Rountree, *Powhatan's People*, 79–81; William L. Shea, *The Virginia Militia in the Seventeenth Century* (Baton Rouge: Louisiana State University Press, 1983), 45.

27. McIlwaine, ed., *Minutes of the Council and General Court of Virginia*, 184–185, 198, 484; Hening, ed., *Statutes at Large*, I: 176; Rountree, *Powhatan's People*, 79–81; Shea, *The Virginia Militia in the Seventeenth Century*, 47.

28. McIlwaine, ed., *Minutes of the Council and General Court of Virginia*, 111, 116; Kingsbury, ed., *Records of the Virginia Company of London*, III: 673, IV: 58–60.

29. McIlwaine, ed., *Minutes of the Council and General Court of Virginia*, 184–185; Hening, ed., *Statutes at Large*, I: 153,177, 202; Wesley Frank Craven, "Indian Policy in Early Virginia," *William and Mary Quarterly*, 3rd. ser., I(1944), 73–74.

30. Hening, ed., *Statutes at Large*, I: 167, 173–176, 192–193, 198, 219; Michael Leroy Oberg, *Dominion and Civility: English Imperialism and Native America 1585–1685* (Ithaca, NY: Cornell University Press, 1999), 177; Shea, *The Virginia Militia in the Seventeenth Century*, 53; Rountree, *Pocahontas's People*, 81.

31. Hening, ed., *Statutes at Large*, I: 224; "The Aspinwell Papers," *Massachusetts Historical Society Collections*, 4th ser., 9(1871), 131–145; J. Miles Thornton III, "The Thrusting Out of Governor Harvey: A Seventeenth Century Rebellion," *Virginia Magazine of History and Biography*, 76(1968), 11–26; Oberg, *Dominion and Civility*, 177–179.

CHAPTER 7

1. Susan Meyer Kingsbury, *Records of the Virginia Company of London*, 4 vols. (Washington, DC: U.S. Government Printing Office, 1906–1935), IV: 569; Helen Rountree, *Pocahontas's People: The Powhatan Indians of Virginia through Four Centuries* (Norman: University of Oklahoma Press, 1990), 79.

2. Rountree, *Pocahontas's People*, 82–83. The text of the 1639 legislative order has not survived, but has been inferred from other sources. See Rountree, *Pocahontas's People*, 308, n. 186.

3. H. R McIlwaine, ed., *Minutes of the Council and General Court of Virginia, 1622–1632, 1670–1676* (Virginia State Library, 1924) 478, 483; Rountree, *Pocahontas's People*, 83.

4. William Waller Hening, ed., *Statutes at Large; Being a Collection of All the Laws of Virginia from the First Session of the Legislature in the Year 1619*, 13 vols. (New York: R&W&G, Bartow, 1823), I: 290, 285–286. [William Berkeley], "A Perfect Description of Virginia," in Peter Force, ed., *Tracts and Other Papers Relating to the Origin Settlement and Progress of the Colonies in North America from the Discovery of the Country to the Year 1776* (Gloucester, MA: Peter Smith, 1963), vol. II, book 8: 20; William L. Shea, *The Virginia Militia in the Seventeenth Century* (Baton Rouge: Louisiana State University Press, 1983), 59.

5. McIlwaine, ed., *Minutes of the Council and General Court of Virginia*, 501–502; Warren M. Billings, ed., *The Papers of Sir William Berkeley* (Richmond: The Library of Virginia, 2007), 60–66, Shea, *The Virginia Militia in the Seventeenth Century*, 62–64. The definitive biography is Warren M. Billings, *Sir William Berkeley and the Forging of Virginia* (Baton Rouge: Louisiana State University Press, 2004).

6. Hening, ed., *Statutes at Large*, I: 292–293; Shea, *The Virginia Militia in the Seventeenth Century*, 65, 70.

7. Hening, ed., *Statutes at Large,* I: 315–319; Robert Beverley, *The History and Present State of Virginia* (Chapel Hill: University of North Carolina Press, 1947), 60–62; Shea, *The Virginia Militia in the Seventeenth Century,* 66–68.

8. Hening, ed., *Statutes at Large,* I: 318, 323–324; Billings, ed., *The Papers of Sir William Berkeley,* 70–73.

9. Hening, ed., *Statutes at Large,* I: 323–329; Berkeley, "A Perfect Description of Virginia," 13; Rountree, *Pocahontas' People,* 87–88; Martha M. McCartney, "Cockacoeske, Queen of the Pamunkey: Diplomat and Suzeraine," in Peter Wood et al., ed., *Powhatan's Mantle* (Lincoln: University of Nebraska, 1989), 173.

10. Hening, ed., *Statutes at Large,* I: 353, 393–396.

11. Warren H. Billings, ed., "Some Acts Not in Hening's *Statutes:* The Acts of Assembly, April 1652, November 1652, and July 1653," *Virginia Magazine of History and Biography,* LXXXIII(1975), 68, 72; Michael Leroy Oberg, *Dominion and Civility: English Imperialism and Native America 1585–1685* (Ithaca, NY: Cornell University Press, 1999), 183–184; Rountree, *Pocahontas' People,* 91–92; W. Stitt Robinson, "Tributary Indians in Colonial Virginia," *Virginia Magazine of History and Biography,* 67(1959), 57.

12. Kingsbury, ed., *Records of the Virginia Company of London,* III: 18–19; Robinson, "Tributary Indians in Colonial Virginia," 49–64.

13. McCartney, "Cockacoeske, Queen of the Pamunkey," 173–175.

14. Hening, ed., *Statutes at Large,* I: 402–403, 422, 436; Shea, *The Virginia Militia in the Seventeenth Century,* 79–80.

15. Hening, ed., *Statutes at Large,* I: 393–396, 410, 455, 456, 481–482; Billings, ed., "Some Acts not in Hening's *Statutes,"* 63–65; J. Douglas Deal, *Race and Class in Colonial Virginia: Indians, Englishmen, and Africans on the Eastern Shore During the Seventeenth Century* (New York: Garland, 1993), 49–51; Susie M. Ames, *Studies of the Virginia Eastern Shore in the Seventeenth Century* (New York: Russell & Russell, 1973), 73–74; Rountree, *Pocahontas's People,* 91–92, 136–140.

16. Hening, ed., *Statutes at Large,* I: 393–396, 410, 455, 456, 481–482; Billings, ed., "Some Acts not in Hening's *Statutes,"* 63–65; Oberg, *Dominion and Civility,* 183; Rountree, *Pocahontas's People,* 136–137; W. Stitt Robinson, Jr., "Indian Education and Missions in Colonial Virginia," *Journal of Southern History,* 18(1952), 152–168. The Andros quotation is Robinson, "Indian Education and Missions in Colonial Virginia," 161.

17. Hening, ed., *Statutes at Large,* III: 138–141, 155–156.

18. Billings, *Sir William Berkeley and the Forging of Virginia,* 75.

19. Billings, ed., *The Papers of Sir William Berkeley,* 325; Hening, ed., *Statutes at Large,* II: 12–14.

20. Deal, *Race and Class in Colonial Virginia,* 3, 8–9; Oberg, *Dominion and Civility,* 184; Christian F. Feest, "Nanticoke and Neighboring Tribes," in Bruce Trigger, *Handbook of North American Indians: Northeast* (Washington, DC: Smithsonian Institution, 1978), 240–252; C. A. Weslager, "Indians of the Eastern Shore of Maryland and Virginia," in Charles B. Clark, ed., *The Eastern Shore of Maryland and Virginia* (New York: Lewis Historical Publishing, 1950), I: 35–69.

21. Deal, *Race and Class in Colonial Virginia,* 8–9.

22. Hening, ed., *Statutes at Large,* II: 13–14; McIlwaine, ed., *Minutes of the Council and General Court of Virginia,* 353, 359, 518; Billings, ed., *The Papers of Sir William Berkeley,* 133; Deal, *Race and Class in Colonial Virginia,* 9–22.

23. Billings, ed., *The Papers of Sir William Berkeley,* 90; Deal, *Race and Class in Colonial Virginia,* 25–40.

24. Billings, ed., *The Papers of Sir William Berkeley*, 380; Deal, *Race and Class in Colonial Virginia*, 39.

25. Hening, ed., *Statutes at Large*, I: 322, 385–390, II: 150–151, 193–194; Billings, ed., *The Papers of Sir William Berkeley*, 209; Oberg, *Dominion and Civility*, 186; Rountree, *Pocahontas' People*, 118.

26. Hening, ed., *Statutes at Large*, II: 193–194; Gregory Waselkov, "Relations between Settlers and Indians," in Walter Briscoe Norris, ed., *Westmoreland County* (Montrose, VA: Westmoreland County Board of Supervisors, 1983), 21; Edmund Morgan, *American Slavery, American Freedom: The Ordeal of Colonial Virginia* (New York; Norton, 1975), 250; Billings, *Sir William Berkeley and the Forging of Virginia*, 200.

27. Billings, ed., *The Papers of Sir William Berkeley*, 284; Billings, *Sir William Berkeley and the Forging of Colonial Virginia*, 200–202 (Ludwell quote is on page 201).

CHAPTER 8

1. [Thomas Mathew], "The Beginning, Progress and Conclusion of Bacon's Rebellion, 1675–1676," in Charles Mclean Andrews, ed., *Narratives of the Insurrections, 1675–1690* (New York: Scribner, [1705] 1915), 15–16.

2. "A True Narrative of the Late Rebellion in Virginia, by the Royal Commissioners, 1677," in Andrews, ed., *Narratives of the Insurrections*, 105–106.

3. [Mathew], "The Beginning, Progress and Conclusion of Bacon's Rebellion," in Andrews, ed., *Narratives of the Insurrections*, 17.

4. W.H. Brown, ed., *Archives of Maryland* (Baltimore: Maryland Historical Society, 1883) II: 428–429, III: 116–117, 375–378, 420–421, 428, 471–472, 549–550; Michael Leroy Oberg, *Dominion and Civility: English Imperialism and Native America 1585–1685* (Ithaca, NY: Cornell University Press, 1999), 195–198; Barry C. Kent, *Susquehanna's Indians* (Harrisburg: Commonwealth of Pennsylvania, Pennsylvania Historical and Museum Commission, 1984), 38–39; Francis Jennings, "Glory, Death and Transfiguration: The Susquehannock Indians in the Seventeenth Century," *Proceedings of the American Philosophical Society*, 112(1968), 25–26; Elizabeth Tooker, "The Demise of the Susquehannock: A Seventeenth Century Mystery," *Pennsylvania Archaeologist*, 54(1984), 1–10.

5. [Mathew], "The Beginning, Progress and Conclusion of Bacon's Rebellion," in Andrews, ed., *Narratives of the Insurrections*, 17, "A True Narrative of the Late Rebellion in Virginia, by the Royal Commissioners, 1677," in Andrews, ed., *Narratives of the Insurrections* 105–106; Warren M. Billings, *Sir William Berkeley and the Forging of Virginia* (Baton Rouge: Louisiana State University Press, 2004), 238; Warren M. Billings, ed., *The Papers of Sir William Berkeley* (Richmond: The Library of Virginia, 2007), 485–486; Wilcomb E. Washburn, *The Governor and the Rebel* (New York: Norton, 1972), 21–22.

6. Brown, ed., *Archives of Maryland*, II: 475–487, 501–504, V: 134; [Mathew], "The Beginning, Progress and Conclusion of Bacon's Rebellion," in Andrews, ed., *Narratives of the Insurrections*, 23; [Richard Lee], "History of Bacon and Ingram's Rebellion, 1676," in Andrews, *Narratives of the Insurrections*, 47–48; Washburn, *The Governor and the Rebel*, 23–24; Oberg, *Dominion and Civility*, 199–200.

7. [Mathew], "The Beginning, Progress and Conclusion of Bacon's Rebellion," in Andrews, ed., *Narratives of the Insurrections*, 19–20; [Richard Lee], "History of Bacon and Ingram's Rebellion, 1676," in Andrews, *Narratives of the Insurrections*, 48–49; Washburn, *The Governor and the Rebel*, 24–25; Oberg, *Dominion and Civility*, 200–201; Billings, *Sir William Berkeley and the Forging of Virginia*, 229. The exact number of settlers killed by Indians

in these incidents is not known. Although contemporary sources claimed several hundred, Washburn has argued that the actual total was much lower. He relies on reports of specific killings (a total of 33). The surviving sources do not permit us to resolve this issue, but do indicate that the English at the time believed the number was high.

8. Billings, ed., *The Papers of Sir William Berkeley*, 498–499; Wilcomb E. Washburn, "Governor Berkeley and King Philip's War," *William and Mary Quarterly*, 30(1957), 363–377.

9. [Mathew], "The Beginning, Progress and Conclusion of Bacon's Rebellion," in Andrews, ed., *Narratives of the Insurrections*, 25–27.

10. William Waller Hening, ed., *Statutes at Large; Being a Collection of All the Laws of Virginia from the First Session of the Legislature in the Year 1619*, 13 vols. (New York: R&W&G, Bartow, 1823), II: 326–339; Washburn, *The Governor and the Rebel*, 28–30.

11. [Mathew], "The Beginning, Progress and Conclusion of Bacon's Rebellion," in Andrews, ed., *Narratives of the Insurrections*, 20; Washburn, *The Governor and the Rebel*, 28–30.

12. Stephen Saunders Webb, *1676: The End of American Independence* (New York: Alfred K. Knopf, 1984), 13–21; Billings, ed., *The Papers of Sir William Berkeley*, 536–538; Edmund Morgan, *American Slavery, American Freedom: The Ordeal of Colonial Virginia* (New York: Norton,] 1975), 227; Richard L. Morton, *Colonial Virginia* (Chapel Hill: University of North Carolina Press, 1960), 219–220.

13. Billings, ed., *The Papers of Sir William Berkeley*, 536–538; Michael L. Oberg, ed., *Samuel Wiseman's Book of Record: The Official Account of Bacon's Rebellion in Virginia, 1676–1677* (Lanham, MD: Lexington Books, 2005), 145; Morgan, *American Slavery, American Freedom*, 227; Richard L. Morton, *Colonial Virginia*, 219–220. Washburn (*The Governor and the Rebel*, 28) maintains that Berkeley was not personally profiting from the Indian trade at this time; however, he had long been closely associated with those who were.

14. Oberg, ed., *Samuel Wiseman's Book of Record*, 145; Washburn, *The Governor and the Rebel*, 28, 32–35; Thomas Jefferson Wertenbaker, *Torchbearer of the Revolution: The Story of Bacon's Rebellion and Its Leader* (Cranbury, NJ: Scholar's Bookshelf, [1940] 2005), 89.

15. Oberg, ed., *Samuel Wiseman's Book of Record*, 146–148.

16. Oberg, ed., *Samuel Wiseman's Book of Record*, 146; [Richard Lee], "History of Bacon and Ingram's Rebellion, 1676," in Andrews, *Narratives of the Insurrections*, 97; Webb, *1676*, 27; Washburn, *The Governor and the Rebel*, 17–18, 35–36.

17. Washburn, *The Governor and the Rebel*, 38.

18. Billings, ed., *The Papers of Sir William Berkeley*, 516–517; Billings, *Sir William Berkeley and the Forging of Virginia*, 235–236.

19. Billings, ed., *The Papers of Sir William Berkeley*, 517–519.

20. [Mathew], "The Beginning, Progress and Conclusion of Bacon's Rebellion," in Andrews, ed., *Narratives of the Insurrections*, 21; Oberg, ed., *Samuel Wiseman's Book of Record*, 147; William Sherwood, "Virginia's Deplored Condition," in *Massachusetts Historical Society Collections* (Boston: The Massachusetts Historical Society) 4th ser., (1871) IX: 167–168. For a thorough and judicious assessment of the evidence relating to the attack on the Occoneechee, see Washburn, *The Governor and the Rebel*, 42–46.

21. Billings, ed., *The Papers of Sir William Berkeley*, 520–521.

22. Ibid., 521.

23. [Mathew], "The Beginning, Progress and Conclusion of Bacon's Rebellion," in Andrews, ed., *Narratives of the Insurrections*, 22–23; Hening, ed., *Statutes at Large*, II: 341–343.

24. Billings, ed., *The Papers of Sir William Berkeley,* 570; "Commissioners' Narrative," in Andrews, ed., *Narratives of the Insurrections,* 113, Hening, ed., *Statutes at Large,* II: 543–544; [Mathew], "The Beginning, Progress and Conclusion of Bacon's Rebellion," in Andrews, ed., *Narratives of the Insurrections,* 23, H. R McIlwaine, ed., *Minutes of the Council and General Court of Virginia, 1622–1632, 1670–1676* (Richmond: Virginia State Library, 1924), 516.

25. Thomas Ludwell to Henry Coventry, quoted in Washburn, *The Governor and the Rebel,* 52–53; McIlwaine, ed., *Minutes of the Council and General Court of Virginia,* 65.

26. [Mathew], "The Beginning, Progress and Conclusion of Bacon's Rebellion," in Andrews, ed., *Narratives of the Insurrections,* 29, "Commissioners' Narrative," in Andrews, ed., *Narratives of the Insurrections,* 117; Billings, ed., *The Papers of Sir William Berkeley,* 568–573.

27. "Commissioners' Narrative," in Andrews, *Narratives of the Insurrections,* 120–121; Billings, ed., *The Papers of Sir William Berkeley,* 570–571; Washburn, *The Governor and the Rebel,* 69–70.

28. The "Declaration" may be found in *Massachusetts Historical Collections,* 4th ser., IX: 184–187.

29. The text of the Manifesto is in *Virginia Magazine,* I(1893), 55–58.

30. "Commissioners' Narrative," in Andrews, ed., *Narratives of the Insurrections,* 123–127.

31. Hening, ed., *Statutes at Large,* II: 341–365. The Bacon quotation is in Wesley Frank Craven, *The Southern Colonies in the Seventeenth Century, 1607–1689* (Baton Rouge: Louisiana State University Press, 1949), 377.

32. [Mathew], "The Beginning, Progress and Conclusion of Bacon's Rebellion," in Andrews, ed., *Narratives of the Insurrections,* 36–37; [Richard Lee], "History of Bacon and Ingram's Rebellion, 1676," in Andrews, *Narratives of the Insurrections,* 64–65; Billings, ed., *The Papers of Sir William Berkeley,* 571; Webb, *1676:* 53–57, 151; Washburn, *The Governor and the Rebel,* 77–78.

33. Webb, *1676,* 62.

34. [Richard Lee], "History of Bacon and Ingram's Rebellion, 1676," in Andrews, *Narratives of the Insurrections,* 70; "Commissioners' Narrative," in Andrews, ed., *Narratives and the Insurrections,* 135; Webb, *1676,* 62–64.

35. Hill is quoted in Washburn, *The Governor and the Rebel,* 84–85.

36. Billings, ed., *The Papers of Sir William Berkeley,* 573; Washburn, *The Governor and the Rebel,* 85.

37. See the relevant documents in Oberg, ed., *Samuel Wiseman's Book of Record,* 56–133. The quotations are from a letter of Commissioners John Beery and Francis Moryson to Thomas Watkins dated February 10, 1677, on pages 66–67 above. For an excellent, and balanced, account of Berkeley's relations with the commissioners, see Billings, *Sir William Berkeley and the Forging of Virginia,* 248–266.

38. Webb, *1676,* 132–165. The treaty text is in Oberg, ed., *Samuel Wiseman's Book of Record,* 134–141.

39. Hening, ed., *Statutes at Large,* II: 490–492, III: 251, 298, 452–453; Paul Kelton, *Epidemics and Enslavement: Biological Catastrophe in the Native Southeast 1491–1715* (Lincoln: University of Nebraska Press, 2007), 124; Helen Rountree, *Pocahontas' People: The Powhatan Indians of Virginia through Four Centuries* (Norman: University of Oklahoma Press, 1990), 137–143.

CONCLUSIONS

1. Gary B. Nash, *Red, White and Black,* 4th edition (Upper Saddle River, NJ: Prentice-Hall, 2000), 74.

Index

Lightning Source UK Ltd.
Milton Keynes UK
UKHW012352250721
387578UK00011B/302